A HISTORY

—— *of* ——

JONATHAN
ALDER

A HISTORY

of

JONATHAN ALDER

His Captivity and Life with the Indians

BY HENRY CLAY ALDER

Transcribed and with a foreword by Doyle H. Davison

Compiled, annotated, edited, and with an introduction by Larry L. Nelson

THE UNIVERSITY OF AKRON PRESS

All inquiries and permissions requests should be addressed to the pub-
lisher, The University of Akron Press, Akron, OH 44325-1703
Manufactured in the United States of America
First edition 2002
05 04 03 02 5 4 3 2 1

Library of Congress Cataloging-in-Publication Data

Alder, Henry Clay, 19th cent.
A history of Jonathan Alder : his captivity and life with the Indians /
by Henry Clay Alder ; transcribed and with a foreword by Doyle H.
Davison ; compiled, annotated, edited, and with an introduction by
Larry L. Nelson. — 1st ed.
p. cm. — (Series on Ohio history and culture)
"The version within these pages is the Doyle Davison transcript
of the Henry Clay manuscript held by the Ohio Historical
Society . . . "—Introd.
Includes bibliographical references (p.) and index.
ISBN 1-884836-80-1 (hardcover : alk. paper)
1. Alder, Jonathan, b. 1773. 2. Indian captivities—Ohio.
3. Shawnee Indians—Social life and customs.
4. Mingo Indians—Social life and customs.
5. Frontier and pioneer life—Ohio.
I. Davison, Doyle H.
II. Nelson, Larry L. (Larry Lee), 1950– .
III. Title. IV. Series.
E99.S35 A45 2002
974.004′973—dc21

2001006416

Manufactured in the United States of America
The paper used in this publication meets the minimum requirements of
American National Standard for Information Sciences—Permanence of
Paper for Printed Library Materials, ANSI z39.48—1984.

Contents

Foreword

Out of the dim past comes the romantic story of Jonathan Alder, so engrossing, so improbable as viewed from our twentieth-century standpoint, that we may be prone to feel that the narrator has drawn upon his imagination in dealing with the life of this remarkable man, or that possibly, he has selected him as a romantic figure around which to build a colorful story of the pioneer days of Madison County. But in refutation of any such theory, and disclaiming any desire to add unearned luster to the memory of Jonathan Alder, the writer points to the old "round log" cabin on Big Darby in which he dwelt with his Indian wife, and the hewed log cabin adjoining it to which he took a charming bride in the person of Mary Blont, still standing at this late date, one hundred and twenty-four years afterwards, as mute evidence of the truth. Add to these the old moss-covered slab in the Foster Cemetery lying broken on the ground, having been replaced in the year 1916 by a fine granite stone with suitable inscription by the children of Henry Clay Alder as a tribute to their father.

In 1927, the old log cabin was torn down and moved to the Alder Chapel Churchyard by all the great-grandchildren of Jonathan Alder, as it was his wish that the old cabin be preserved, and here it is hoped it will stand for another one hundred years.

In 1928, a flagpole and flag was placed by the cabin, the gift of a great-grandson, James W. Alder of Chicago.

In 1922, a chapter was formed by the women of Madison County and named the Jonathan Alder Chapter, Daughters of 1812, which has met once a month ever since. Each year on September 17th, his birthday, this chapter, with relatives and friends from the surrounding country, meet at his last resting place and cover his grave with a blanket of flowers.

In addition to these visible relics of the past, there is Jonathan Alder's own story of his life as told to his son Henry nearly one hundred years ago, and written down by the latter. This story, which covered over one hundred pages of manuscript, was loaned to Henry Howe in the preparation of *Howe's Historical Sketches,* but it afterwards was lost for a long time. Howe did not print it in its entirety but took only the main facts and, therefore, much was lost.

The following manuscript, a copy of which is the one that was lost for more than eighty years, was accidentally found by a grandson, Henry Betts, with the aid of Henry Alder, a great-grandson—so we herewith present it to you.

Doyle H. Davison
(1935)

Acknowledgments

Many people assisted me as I prepared Alder's narrative, and it gives me great pleasure to acknowledge their hard work on my behalf. Louise Jones, Durea Kemp, and Tom Starbuck at the Ohio Historical Society's Library/Archives Division responded promptly to numerous requests for reference materials and administrative help as I prepared the manuscript for publication. Amy Johnson assisted with the manuscript's early copyediting. Randy Buchman of Defiance College, Mike Pratt at Heidelberg College, Chris Duckworth at *Timeline Magazine*, Don Rettig at Toledo Metro Parks, and Adam Sakel, my colleague at Fort Meigs State Memorial, all read and commented on early drafts of the book. Will Currie and his staff at the Firelands College library were very responsive to my requests for interlibrary loan materials, as were the OhioLINK staff at Bowling Green State University's Jerome Library. Al Gutchess gave me the opportunity to refine my thinking about Alder by allowing me to discuss my work at his annual Eastern Woodland Indian conference. Gretchen Green, the director of the Madison County (Ohio) Historical Society, Catherine Alder of Fort Worth Texas, Bill and Rita Alder of Newport, Oregon, and Dorothy Walley of Waterville, Ohio, assisted me with Alder's genealogy and in tracking down the still elusive Henry Clay Alder manuscript. To all of them go my sincerest thanks.

Larry L. Nelson

Introduction

On a brilliant spring morning in May 1782, nine-year-old Jonathan Alder and his older brother David set out to find a mare that had wandered from their isolated cabin in southwest Virginia and into the rugged mountains and dense forests of the surrounding countryside. Later in the day, the boys found their horse, but as they struggled to lead the reluctant animal home, they were attacked by a party of Indians from Ohio. David was killed and Jonathan taken prisoner. His captors brought Alder back to Ohio, where he was adopted by a Mingo warrior and his Shawnee wife. Here he spent the next thirteen years. During that time, Alder lived fully as an Indian. He learned their language and observed their customs. He hunted, traded, and fought at their side. In 1795, after the death of his adoptive parents, Alder left the Indians and eventually settled in Pleasant Valley, near present-day Plain City in central Ohio. At the urging of an acquaintance, he traveled to Virginia in 1805, where he had the extraordinary good fortune to find his mother and remaining siblings still living in the neighborhood where he had been captured as a youth. After his reunion, he married a woman from Virginia, returned to Pleasant Valley, and became something of a local celebrity as a result of his childhood adventures. In the late 1830s or early 1840s, probably at the insistence of his family and friends, Alder composed his memoirs, in which he recounted his life with the Ohio Indians and his experiences as one of the area's earliest pioneers.

Captivity narratives from the Ohio frontier have excited the imaginations of readers from the colonial era to the present day. The best of these narratives evoke a sense of high adventure and romance that, to many, define the frontier era. Within their pages, one en-counters thrilling tales of border warfare, Indian raids, hairbreadth escapes, and daring rescues. They depict episodes of the most heart-wrenching tragedy and abject cruelty as well as those of remarkable courage and endurance. Moreover, they provide what at times is an unparalleled view into the world of the Ohio Country Indian na-tions.

The Alder captivity narrative is particularly important because Alder continued his tale to include his experiences long after he left the Indians. The account chronicles Alder's life from his captivity in the late eighteenth century to the early 1830s. The narrative, there-fore, provides a unique perspective on the Old Northwest, its trans-formation from wilderness to statehood, and the evolving relation-ship between Ohio's Indians and whites from the Revolutionary War era to a time when many of the state's native peoples had been re-moved.

Alder's captivity narrative is one of the most extensive personal accounts to survive from Ohio's frontier and early settlement eras. His reminiscence spans half a century, beginning with his capture in 1782, when Ohio had no permanent European settlement and was still the exclusive domain of the Ohio Indian nations, to 1832, when the state was emerging as an industrial power and canals and the Na-tional Road (which passed only a few miles from Alder's Pleasant Valley home) linked Ohioans and Ohio products to the East and markets throughout the world. Alder's recollection provides an ex-ceptional look at early Ohio. His portrait of his captors is revealing, complex, and sympathetic. The latter part of his narrative, in which he relates his experiences in Pleasant Valley, is an extraordinarily rich account of the tribulations of pioneer society and the continuing ten-sions that existed among the region's early European settlers and be-tween whites and the area's native residents long after the Indian wars era had ended.

Alder was fortunate in that he encountered many of the persons and took part or knew about many of the events that have become touchstones in Ohio's frontier history. He knew Simon Girty and held him in high esteem. Later, he became a close friend of Simon Kenton, and Alder's extended interview with the famed frontiersman near the end of his narrative constitutes an important addition to the literature dealing with pioneer era Ohio. Alder comments on the burning of Colonel Crawford, on Benjamin Logan's 1786 raid against the Mad River Indian settlements, and on the death of Chief Leather Lips. He participated in the Battle of Fort Recovery and describes in detail the Battle of Fallen Timbers. His recollections are among the few extant accounts of these actions told from a Native American perspective. Further, during his time with the Ohio Indians, Alder came into contact with other captives. He tells their stories as well, nested within his reminiscences like Russian dolls.

The Alder family was part of an increasingly insistent migration that flowed into Virginia's Shenandoah Valley beginning at the conclusion of the French and Indian War. Two great tides formed this migration. Palatinate Germans came to the region in large numbers, traveling in families and settling at first between Winchester and Staunton and then gradually pushing westward into present-day Smyth, Bland, Washington, and Wythe Counties. A second wave of migration originated in north Britain, northern Ireland, and Scotland. Like the Palatinates, these north Britain borderers came in families. Unlike their German neighbors, many of these immigrants were poor and some nearly destitute. Most moved quickly to the southwesternmost end of the Shenandoah Valley, where they settled among the region's rugged backcountry highlands. The Alder family belonged to this second wave of migration. Jonathan Alder's father, Bartholomew, was born in Long Sutton, Lincolnshire County, England, in February 1734. He came to America sometime before 1766, the year that he married Jonathan's mother, Hanna Worthington, in Gloucester, New Jersey. The Alders stayed in Gloucester until 1775, when they migrated to western Virginia.[1]

The Germans living in the valley were wiser and more honest than their neighbors, claimed J. Hector St. John de Crevecoeur, who traveled through the region in the late eighteenth century. "They launch forth," he noted, "and by dint of sobriety, rigid parsimony, and the most persevering industry, they commonly succeed." Likewise, he believed that the Scots were "frugal" and "industrious." The Irish, though, did "not prosper so well; they love to drink and to quarrel." "They are litigious," he said, and when they had an opportunity, they abandoned their farms to hunt game for a living, "which is the ruin of everything." But Philip Vickers Fithian, a Presbyterian missionary who came to the area the same year as the Alders, claimed that the backcountry Irish were among the most generous people that he had ever encountered. The very air of Virginia, he claimed, seemed to "inspire all the Inhabitants with hospitality."

Every thing they possess is as free to a stranger as the *Water* or the *Air*. Living, to be sure, is not amongst these frugal Irish so fantastical and costly as with native Virginians. But they have in very great abundance the leading supports to human Subsistence. And by these, and their healthy Situation among the Mountains and pure waters, through God's Blessing, they raise a Brood of Youth, young men and young women, for size, activity, and Complection, such as I have seen in no Place before.[2]

The Alders undoubtedly reached their new home by traveling along the Great Wagon Road. The Great Wagon Road had been built upon an ancient path stretching nearly eight hundred miles from New York to Georgia, used by the northern Iroquois to make war on their enemies in the Carolinas. Virginia acquired use of the trail in 1744. By the third quarter of the century, the path had become the principal thoroughfare to the colony's backcountry settlements. Originating in Philadelphia, the route moved westward to Lancaster, York, and Gettysburg, Pennsylvania, before veering to the southwest via Hagerstown, Maryland, and then through Winchester and Staunton, Virginia, to Roanoke. At Roanoke, the road divided into two parts. One leg continued to the south, through the Moravian settlements at Wachovia on the North Carolina Piedmont, and beyond to the road's terminus at Augusta, South Carolina. The second leg from Roanoke carried travelers nearly due west to the road's western limit at Fort Chiswell (near present-day Max Meadows, Virginia), only a few miles from the Alder homestead. In 1775, the year that the Alder family moved to the area, Daniel Boone extended the reach of the Great Wagon Road by blazing a trail from the vicinity of Fort Chiswell westward through the Cumberland Gap and into Kentucky. This path, when widened to accommodate wagons in 1796, would become the Wilderness Road.[3]

Those who migrated into the region did so at great peril. Throughout the late eighteenth century, the region was a favorite target for Indian raiding parties that originated west of the mountains. "All of the People in these back Settlements are very taleful of the Indian Wars," remembered Philip Fithian. "Deeply have they suffered from Savage Cruelty." Those whom he met spoke almost obsessively about their encounters with the Indians. "Their stories are moving," he claimed, "and force the attention. They fill me with melancholy Meditations." At one cabin he met a widow "thirteen years with the Indians. . . . She gave me a long & moving Narration of their Usage of her." At another, he spoke with a woman whose husband had been killed at the Battle of Point Pleasant. Since his death, she had told her family many times that it was her "wish and steady Purpose, to die with unabated Lamentation." "The Tumult of Mind with which she was constantly exercised brought upon her repeatedly violent convulsions," said Fithian. "Those however now are moderated into casual Hystericks." At another time he spoke with Colonel John Dickinson, "an able, long-experienced Soldier in the Indian Service." Dickinson was riddled with wounds and spent the afternoon showing Fithian scars in his hands, back, and legs and telling the traveler the story behind each one. "Now he is in Health," remarked Fithian. "I view this Gentleman with great Veneration." "It is not a Wonder that these Inhabitants are filled with high Indignation against those savage Heathen."[4]

Among these Indians were many from north of the Ohio River. Native Americans had lived for nearly thirteen thousand years in the area that would eventually become Ohio. Prehistoric Paleo-Indians had entered the region at the end of the Wisconsin Ice Age and had hunted big game in the shadow of the glaciers that then covered much of the area. As the climate warmed nearly eight thousand years ago, these early people were replaced by others who, over time, invented the bow and arrow, learned to farm, created majestic earthworks of amazing scale and sophistication, fashioned jewelry and other objects of astounding beauty, and carved enigmatic petroglyphs whose meanings remain a mystery to this day.[5]

In 1500, the start of the historic era, many different Indian cultures occupied the region that would become Ohio. Most lived in small hamlets or villages, but others lived in larger communities, and some lived in large fortified towns occupied by several hundred individuals. Nearly all were farmers who added to their diet by fishing, gathering wild plants, and hunting game such as deer, bear, and raccoon. Archaeological evidence suggests that European trade goods began to find their way into the region as early as 1550, over one hundred years before the first European explorers entered the area. Many historians suspect that European diseases also entered the region during the 1500s.

Among the first Europeans to write about the Indians living in what is now Ohio were Jesuit missionaries living in Canada in the early and mid-1600s. Early Jesuit writings and French maps from the era speak of several Indian nations living in the region, including the Assistaeronons, Ontarraronons, and Squenquioronons. By the middle of the 1600s, many of these tribes were involved in the fur trade, trading pelts taken in the Great Lakes region for trade goods manufactured in Europe. By the 1640s, beaver had been trapped nearly to extinction in the Northeast. In 1649, the Onondagas, members of the Iroquois Confederacy, a powerful league of five tribes living in upstate New York, attempted to acquire more productive lands for trapping by declaring war on the tribes living to their west. The Onondagas began the war in March 1649 by attacking and defeating their western neighbors the Hurons. Continuing the offensive, the Onondaga and their Iroquois allies vanquished the Tobacco Nation in December 1649 and the Neutral Nation in 1651. In 1654 an Iroquois army numbering between 1,200 and 2,000 warriors invaded present-day northwestern Pennsylvania along the southern shore of Lake Erie, the home of the Eries, or Cat Nation. The assault was swift and brutal. The Eries, unprepared for an attack of this magnitude, attempted to defend themselves in a crude stockade made of tree trunks, but were eventually overpowered. With the Eries defeated, the Iroquois continued to push westward. Eventually, the Onondagas either destroyed all of the other Indian nations living in their path or forced them to flee. The Iroquois wanted territory in the area only for hunting and did not settle the area after their conquest. Therefore, by the mid-1660s, what is presently Ohio was uninhabited and entered only occasionally by roving hunting bands and war parties.[6]

Indians began to move back into what is now Ohio in the early 1700s. Among the first to resettle within the area were the Wyandots. Wyandots were remnants of the Hurons who were dispersed at the beginning of the Beaver Wars. They had originally lived in what is today southern Ontario, but had scattered as far away as the region near present-day southern Wisconsin, in the face of Iroquois aggression. Later, they had moved near the French trading centers at Michilimackinac and, after its founding in 1701, Detroit. Friction with the French caused some of the Detroit Wyandots to leave for present-day Ohio in the 1730s. One group under the leadership of Orontony (Nicholas) established a settlement and trading post along Sandusky Bay in 1739. Later, other groups migrated to the Cuyahoga and Muskingum River valleys.[7]

Like the Wyandots, the Ottawas were pushed into what is now present-day Wisconsin by the Iroquois and eventually resettled near Detroit after 1701. The nation slowly moved into the Ohio country beginning in the 1750s, establishing homes on the lower Maumee River and along Maumee Bay.[8]

The Miami Indians also entered present-day Ohio at about the same time. The Miamis migrated into the state during the 1740s from the Wabash and Maumee River valleys in eastern Indiana. By 1747, they had established settlements along the Great and Little Miami River valleys in what is now southwestern Ohio and had opened trade with the British at Pickawillany, a trading post near present-day Piqua.[9]

The Shawnee Indians also returned to the region in the 1730s and 1740s. Iroquois violence had greatly fragmented the Shawnee nation, and the Beaver Wars had pushed the remnants of the tribe into what is now southern Illinois, Kentucky, and perhaps as far south as Georgia and Alabama. During the early 1700s, many Shawnees migrated back to eastern Pennsylvania and Maryland. European settlement in the area drove the tribe westward, and by the 1730s and early 1740s, the Shawnees had established settlements along the Ohio River and the lower Scioto valley.[10]

Mingos entered the region in the mid-1740s, settling near the Cuyahoga River valley. Mingos were members of the Iroquois Confederacy who had voluntarily left their traditional lands in New York and moved to the Ohio country. Most Ohio Mingos were either Senecas or Caughnawagas (French Catholic Mohawks), but many Cayugas, Onondagas, Oneidas, and Tuscaroras also lived within the region.[11]

Lastly, many Delawares, or Lenni Lenapes, also entered present-day Ohio with the Shawnee from Pennsylvania. Originally from the Delaware River Valley, the nation also moved west in response to European settlement along the East Coast. The Delaware entered the area following the Seven Years (French and Indian) War. Many moved into the region from western Pennsylvania with Moravian missionaries who established mission towns along the Tuscarawas and Muskingum River valleys in the 1770s.[12]

Although the Ohio Indians were from two distinct linguistic groups, the Iroquoian and the Algonquian, they shared the same broad Eastern Woodland culture. All were part of a "tribe" or nation that linked its members to one another through shared language, social customs, and religious beliefs. These nations, like the nations of Europe, were politically sovereign and acted independently and in their own self-interest. Each tribe occupied a territory whose boundaries were recognized and respected by other nations within the region. Within each nation's territory, its members lived in bands of varying sizes which, like the nation they were part of, were also independent and autonomous. The bands lived in semipermanent villages located near a source of firewood, water, and land suitable for farming. They were hunters and agriculturalists who cultivated corn, beans, and squash and also, as the historic era progressed, an ever-widening variety of crops from both Europe and Africa. Some tended orchards, and a few watched over livestock. Women looked after their children and their fields; the men hunted, traded, conducted diplomacy, and made war on their enemies. Both men and women actively took part in the governance of their village.

Indian men plucked the hair from their bodies except for a scalp lock grown in the crown of their head. Many also slit their ear lobes and distended the fleshy protuberances so that they brushed the tops of their shoulders. Men decorated themselves with tattoos, and both men and women adorned themselves with paint. But by the time of Alder's captivity, the influence of European culture could be seen in every Indian village in Ohio. Men and women alike wore clothes made from European fabrics; cooked in iron kettles and tin pots manufactured in Europe; slept wrapped in European blankets; decorated themselves with beads, silver, and jewelry fashioned in Europe; hunted with European firearms; ate from European china; and used European tools to clear their fields and cultivate their crops. Many lived in log cabins, and some professed Christianity. Contact with Europeans had undoubtedly increased the material comforts of native society. But it had also brought liquor and with it, drunkenness and a particularly vicious, self-destructive sort of violence unseen in times of sobriety that threatened to undermine the stability of Indian society. Trade with the whites was also slowly eroding the traditional sense of self-sufficiency that undergirded native material and political life.[13]

The cycle of the seasons regulated life among the Ohio Indians. In the winter, each village would disperse into small hunting camps made up of only a family or two. These small groups would subsist until spring, living on stockpiled food reserves and what game they could harvest from the forest. In the spring, the village would reassemble to clear fields, plant crops, and rebuild their homes. In late fall, the cycle would repeat again.

Eastern Woodland people embraced a core set of religious beliefs that were sophisticated and complex. Indians inhabited a world filled with spirits. Most Indians believed in a powerful "Great Spirit," or Manitou, who had created the world, but they also recognized a host of other lesser entities. Some were personal protectors, while others were associated with a particular animal species or place. Some were good and some were evil. Some would intercede only for men, others only for women. Seers, shamans, prophetesses, and arcane rites could open the path between this world and into the spiritual realm. Indians punctuated the annual cycle with a series of rituals and celebrations held throughout the year that gave thanks to the Manitou, acknowledged the spirit world, honored ancestors, comforted the grieving, healed the sick, permitted communication with the animal kingdom, and explained the deepest mysteries of the cosmos.[14]

Although spiritual in focus, these celebrations were also occasions for athletic contests, dancing, and other forms of community entertainment. Indians were fond of games, and men and women both gambled. Men engaged in footraces and played lacrosse. Members of both sexes sometimes played in a rough-and-tumble form of football, men against the women. Feasts and dances could be social or religious in character and could be used to cement diplomatic alliances, prepare for war, invoke the spirit world, honor guests, or for simple social diversion.[15]

When Alder was captured in 1782, Indians in Ohio had been at war for over a generation with Europeans who were pushing their way slowly across the Appalachian Mountains. Violent conflict between Europeans and Ohio's native peoples raged intermittently throughout the region from about 1750 to the conclusion of the War of 1812. Indians and Europeans went to war for many of the same reasons: to advance or protect their nation's diplomatic and economic interests, to punish their enemies, to seek revenge, to acquire honor and esteem, to obtain plunder, and to defend their homes. But many Indian raiding parties also set out with the explicit goal of taking captives. European armies frequently took Indian captives, and Indians, like Europeans, desired captives to be held for ransom, to be exchanged for family or friends, and as sources of information about their foes. Those captured by the Indians faced an uncertain future. It was not uncommon for captives to be executed or abused as they were led back to their captors' homes. And tales that spoke of torture so hideous as to defy description, while undoubtedly exaggerated, were based enough on fact to elicit very real concern. But motives other than military expediency or a desire for retribution also guided Indian actions. Indians also sought captives to adopt into their nation.[16]

Violence and disease had depleted native populations considerably by the mid–eighteenth century. Indians attempted to compensate for these losses by replacing the deceased with newcomers, particularly adolescents and young adults. Native peoples were extraordinarily successful in acculturating captives into their new circumstances. Like Alder, many fortunate captives found themselves placed in the homes of genuinely loving Indian families. In 1755, eighteen-year-old James Smith was taken prisoner in western Pennsylvania and brought back to Ohio, where he was adopted by the Caughnawagas. At his adoption ceremony, Smith was told that his new Indian family was "now under the same obligations to love, support, and defend you that we are to love and to defend one another." Smith at first doubted the truth of what he had been told, but later recollected that "from that day I never knew them to make any distinction between me and themselves in any respect whatever." When Henry Bouquet entered the Ohio Country in 1764 to retrieve captives taken during the French and Indian War, he observed that the Indians were "cruel and unmerciful by habit and long example." "Yet whenever they come to give way to the native dictates of humanity, they exercise virtues which Christians need not blush to imitate. No child is otherwise treated by the persons adopting it than the children of their own body. The perpetual slavery of those captivated in war is a notion which even their barbarity has not yet suggested to them. Every captive whom their affection, their caprice, or whatever else, leads them to save, is soon incorporated with them, and fares alike with themselves."[17]

The affection that Indians felt for their adopted family was clearly reciprocated by many captives. Although most captivity narratives were written by those who later escaped, were rescued, or who voluntarily elected to return to their original homes, the literature of the period is filled with episodes in which captives, when given the opportunity, refused to leave their adoptive families or, if forced to do so, did so only after vigorous protest and the demonstration of genuine grief and sorrow. When Henry Bouquet gathered his returned captives in 1764, he noted that "among the children who had been carried off young and had long lived with the Indians, it is not to be expected that any marks of joy would appear on being restored to their parents or relatives."

Having been accustomed to look upon the Indians as the only connections they had, having been tenderly treated by them, and speaking their language, it is no wonder that they considered their new state [i.e. their return to the English] in the light of a captivity and parted from the savages with tears.

But it must not be denied that there were even some grown persons who showed an unwillingness to return. The Shawnee were obliged to bind several of their prisoners and force them along to the camp; and some women who had been delivered up afterwards found means to escape and run back to the Indian towns. Some who could not make their escape clung to their savage acquaintance at parting and continued many days in bitter lamentations, even refusing sustenance.[18]

The Treaty of Paris, signed in September 1783, ended the Revolutionary War, but not the decades-long conflict along the Ohio Valley. In the agreement, Great Britain ceded the land north and west of the Ohio River to the United States, which then claimed the region "by right of conquest." But Indians living within the region were outraged by the treaty. England had not consulted its native allies as it had negotiated the pact, did not inform them of the agreement's terms before it was ratified, nor did it own the territory that it had given to the new American republic. Further, most of the Indians living in Ohio had allied themselves with the British during the war and had fought ably during the contest. They knew they had not lost the war and they certainly had not given up possession of their homes. In the years following, the Ohio nations continued the fight and waged a protracted, determined resistance against white expansion into the region.[19]

In response, the United States attempted to negotiate with the warring nations. But Kentucky, impatient with the pace of diplomacy and angered at the ferociousness of the attacks directed in large measure against its citizens, launched a series of raids conducted by backwoods irregulars against Indian settlements in Ohio (including one against the town in which Alder was living in 1786). Indians responded by abandoning much of southern and eastern Ohio and relocating along the Maumee River all the way from its headwaters at present-day Fort Wayne, Indiana, to Lake Erie's western basin. Here, shielded on the south by the Great Black Swamp and near a source of ammunition, supplies, and provisions at British-controlled Detroit, they renewed their incursions into Kentucky. These raids, in turn, prompted further retaliation from south of the Ohio River. By 1790, the cycle of violence was inextricably entrenched, and negotiation had proven fruitless. The United States, therefore, declared war on the Ohio nations. Indians under the leadership of Blue Jacket, Little Turtle, Egushaway, and Buckongahelas soundly defeated two American expeditions in 1790 and 1791. But disease, dislocation, and political, economic, and cultural disruption, all the inevitable consequences of a lifetime of warfare, had taken their toll. Indians could neither sustain the means nor the will to continue the conflict. Anthony Wayne's victory over the confederated Indian nations at Fallen Timbers in 1794 and the subsequent Treaty of Greenville in the following year ended the conflict and imposed a fifteen-year period of peace along the Ohio frontier. The Ohio nations were drawn into war once again in 1812 under the leadership of Tecumseh and his brother, the charismatic mystic, Tenskwatawa, The Prophet. But the results were the same. When Tecumseh was killed at the Battle of the Thames in 1813, the Indian resistance collapsed. The Treaty of Ghent, signed in 1814, marked the end of the War of 1812 and the conclusion of the Indian wars in Ohio. From that time forward, the Ohio nations were a defeated and subjugated people.[20]

The years following the Indian wars era were difficult ones for the Ohio Indian nations as they struggled to adjust to their new status and to form new relationships with Euro-Americans who now were rushing into the state. Some sought accommodation with the federal government and their new American neighbors, while others looked for new homes beyond the Mississippi River. Alder's life during this period also reflects a great deal of cultural and emotional ambiguity. While he lived with the Indians, his adoptive father woke him one winter night to tell him that he had had a dream in which a white bear had attacked and then eaten Alder. Believing the dream to be an omen, his father directed Alder to bathe in the river that flowed by their camp in order to remove himself from danger. Alder did so, and his father was satisfied that his son was no longer in peril. But eventually, Alder's father's worst fears were realized. Nothing within his power could stop the white bear from devouring his son. After 1795, Alder left the Indians and began a slow return to white society.

Following the Treaty of Greenville, Alder moved to Darby Creek in central Ohio, apart from the Indians with whom he had grown up. Central Ohio was clearly an area that would be open to white settlement, and Alder's decision to live there reflected, perhaps, a growing psychological as well as physical distance from his Indian community. His marriage to an Indian woman during this time also ended in failure, in part because she grew "cross and peevish" whenever white people came to their home. Alder's increasing contact with white settlers as they came to Darby Creek allowed him the opportunity to build friendships and to provide useful services for his new neighbors. Slowly, and at times awkwardly, Alder forged a new identity as a Euro-American. When he was first adopted by the Indians, the ceremony concluded when he was dressed in a new suit of Indian clothes. In 1804, as he prepared to travel back to Virginia to contact his original family, Alder went to Franklinton (present-day Columbus) and purchased enough cloth to make three suits so that he could be "dressed up in the order of the whites" during his journey. "I dropped the Indian costume that I had been accustomed to for the last twenty years entirely," he observed, and from that time forward, it is clear that he no longer thought of himself as an Indian.

Indians living on Ohio's reservations, though, could not accomplish the transformation that Alder had performed successfully. Even those Indians who had accepted reservation life, adopted European-style agriculture, converted to Christianity, and assisted the United States during the War of 1812 were eventually forced to cede their Ohio homes.[21] Indians began voluntarily to leave the state soon after the 1795 Treaty of Greenville, some going to Canada and others traveling to Spanish-controlled territory west of the Mississippi River. What had begun informally as an Indian initiative in the late eighteenth century became an official policy of the United States government following the War of 1812. After the conflict, the Indians who remained in Ohio lived on numerous reservations scattered throughout the state's northern tier and northwest corner. Beginning in 1817, state and federal authorities worked energetically to remove the Ohio nations from their homes. Government officials entered into a series of agreements with the state's tribes that extinguished their title to lands in Ohio in exchange for farming implements, annuities, and land in the trans-Mississippi West. After the tribes with whom Alder had lived migrated westward in 1832, only small remnants of the Ottawas along the Maumee River and a large population of Wyandots at Upper Sandusky remained within the state. The Ottawas emigrated in 1837 and 1839, the Wyandots in 1843.[22]

When Alder left the Indians in 1795 and settled in Pleasant Valley, he was one of only a few whites who were living permanently in the state. In 1800, Ohio had barely 42,000 European residents within its boundaries, nearly all of whom were living in settlements that stretched along the Ohio River or probed tentatively northward along the Miami, Scioto, and Muskingum River valleys. Beech or mixed oak forests covered much of the state with the exception of small pockets of prairie grasslands, bottomland forests, oak savannas, bogs, or swamps. Wildlife abounded within the region. Travelers often encountered raccoons, ducks, geese, and white-tailed deer as well as such long-extirpated species as the mountain lion, bobcat, bison,

Canadian lynx, and American elk. Passenger pigeons flocked together in nearly incomprehensible numbers. "The air is darkened by their flight," reported the Moravian missionary David Zeisberger in 1777. The noise they made while gathered together, he claimed, was such "that it is difficult for people near them to hear or understand each other."[23]

Settlers who came to Ohio generally did so by drifting down the Ohio River to their destinations in flatboats acquired in Pittsburgh. These awkward, stern-sweep craft were about fifteen feet wide, anywhere from forty to one hundred feet in length, and could carry from twenty to seventy tons of cargo. Some were "large and roomy, and have comfortable and separate apartments fitted up with chairs, beds, tables, and stoves," claimed Timothy Flint, a longtime observer of immigrants making their way to the western country. "It is not an uncommon spectacle to see a large family, old and young, servants, cattle, hogs, sheep, fowls, and animals of all kinds . . . all embarked and floating down on the same bottom."[24]

But once away from river towns and waterways, travel overland could be extremely difficult. Few roads existed, and those were barely worthy of the name. Zane's Trace, in actuality little more than a blazed path, opened in 1797. The route formed a graceful arc as it traversed southern Ohio from Wheeling, West Virginia, to Limestone (Maysville), Kentucky, by way of Zanesville and Chillicothe. In addition, a second route formed by Anthony Wayne as he battled the northwestern tribes connected Fort Washington in present-day Cincinnati with the Maumee River by traveling nearly due north up the Miami River valley. It too was little more than an overgrown, unimproved track marked by downed trees and rapidly fading wagon ruts. Beyond these, travelers had few options other than the Indian trails that penetrated the state's interior.[25]

Alder noted that it was only a short time after the 1795 Treaty of Greenville until "white people began to make their appearance amongst us." Wayne's victory had demolished the last great barrier to settlement in Ohio. By 1810, the state's population tallied nearly 231,000 souls. In 1820, over 581,000 citizens called the Buckeye

State home. The next decade saw Ohio's population grow by an astonishing 61.3 percent, nearly twice as fast as the nation as a whole. In 1830, at about the time that Alder concluded his narrative, Ohio could boast that its nearly 938,000 residents made it the fourth most populous state in the Union, bested only by Virginia, Pennsylvania, and New York.[26]

Immigrants settled nearly every corner of the state. New Englanders made their way to the Western Reserve along Lake Erie's shore, southerners from Virginia and Kentucky made new homes in southern Ohio, and migrants from the Middle Atlantic states, particularly Pennsylvania, moved eastward across the central portion of the state. By 1850, about the time that Jonathan Alder died, "Ohio Fever" had run its course and the state began losing more migrants than it gained. But the rush into Ohio had brought enormous change in its wake. Travel was infinitely easier and more convenient than it had been in the state's early years. Steamboats traveled both the Ohio and the Muskingum Rivers as well as the length of Lake Erie. The National Road proceeded nearly due east and west through the center of the state, linking Wheeling, West Virginia, Columbus, and Springfield. Travelers using the route in the 1830s and 1840s enjoyed one of the finest roads in America. In addition, turnpikes and other roadways provided access to much of the remainder of the state. Miles of canals connected Ohio's major metropolises with one another, Lake Erie, and the Ohio River. Passengers, produce, industrial products, raw materials, and finished goods found their way to Ohio consumers and distant markets alike. Further, by the early 1850s, steam-powered rail lines served nearly all of Ohio's largest cities, and a network of rail tracks wove its way across the state in a broad corridor extending from Cincinnati in the southwest to Cleveland in the northeast. Ohio was still rural and still agricultural, but industry and commerce were contributing to urban growth and the state's emergence as one of the most economically vigorous regions in the Union.[27]

Population and prosperity brought about other changes as well. Ohioans were no longer the rough and unsophisticated pioneers of bygone years. By midcentury, colleges and universities dotted the state's landscape. Painters, sculptors, poets, and essayists found employment in Cincinnati and other metropolitan areas. And writers like Caleb Atwater, Henry Howe, and Jacob Burnett were setting about to document the history of Ohio's frontier era, an age that they understood had already been gone for nearly a generation.[28]

Jonathan Alder had lived through an extraordinary period in Ohio's history. He had known Ohio's native peoples intimately and witnessed their ultimate defeat and removal, and he had been able to watch as an increasing population, agriculture, and industry brought about economic growth, prosperity, and cultural attainment to those who then settled the area. He had observed the transformation of Ohio from an undeveloped wilderness to a vibrant and energetic state, eager to take its place as an economic and political leader of national consequence.

Historians labor under the knowledge that their understandings of the past will always be incomplete. First-person accounts and other types of documentation provide the lens through which we can examine historic activities. But these accounts, no matter how honestly or conscientiously created, also contain filters that subtly shape or distort our view.

The Soveraignty and Goodness of God, published in 1682 and describing the experiences of Mary Rowlandson after her capture during King Philip's War in 1676, was the first book-length Indian captivity narrative to find its way into print. Since then, these accounts have remained an enduring and popular American literary genre. These memoirs, like other types of historical documentation, were molded, in part, by the cultural currents and societal needs of the communities in which they were first written. Historians recognize that captivity narratives have passed through several distinctive stylistic and thematic phases. Early works created in New England during the late seventeenth and early eighteenth centuries, for example, were shaped strongly by Puritan theology. These narratives understood that Indian captivity was an affliction sent by God, that it was a just consequence stemming from the sins of individual captives or the community from which they had been taken, and that the experience proved that unwavering faith in the face of tribulation could bring about deliverance and salvation.[29]

By the mid–eighteenth century, Puritan theology had lost much of its previous influence. As a result, other themes also began to shape captivity narratives. At the onset of the long series of colonial wars that began in the 1750s and continued throughout the War of 1812, captivity accounts took on a propaganda-like quality that served national aims. They depicted Indians along with their French and British allies in lurid detail as they perpetrated unspeakable violence against defenseless frontier inhabitants.

By the mid–nineteenth century, when the Alder narrative was created, Ohioans were some thirty years removed from the Indian wars era. And when the Alder account was substantially edited and republished in the 1880s, Indians had been removed from the state for nearly two generations. Ohioans could allow themselves to see Indians as humans rather than bloodthirsty savages. The Alder narrative is sentimentalized, and native peoples are depicted in rich, often effusive emotional terms. "The Indians would generally collect at our camp in the evenings to talk over their hunting expeditions," claimed Alder. "I would sit up to listen to their stories and frequently fall asleep just where I was sitting. After they left, Mary [Alder's adoptive sister] would fix my bed, and with Col. Lewis [his adoptive brother-in-law] would carefully take me up and carry me to it. On these occasions, they would often say—supposing me to be asleep— 'Poor fellow! We have sat up too late for him and he has fallen asleep on the cold ground,' and then how softly would they lay me down and cover me up. Oh! Never have I, nor can I, express the affection I had for these two persons."

In addition to the evolving stylistic framework common to all captivity narratives, the Alder account in particular presents other problems. For example, the narrative, like many other captivity accounts, was created many years after the events that it purports to describe. Therefore, its reliability as an accurate witness to those events perhaps may be diminished.

Other difficulties are unique to this narrative. Henry Howe, Ohio's first great popular historian, used the Alder narrative, which he described as containing about one hundred handwritten pages and comprising a sketch of Alder's life while with the Indians, "together with a relation of many of their customs, and incidents that came under his observation," in his *Historical Collections of Ohio,* first published in 1847. Although the Howe account makes some direct quotes from the original manuscript, it is mostly paraphrased and heavily abridged. Shortly thereafter, the original manuscript prepared by Jonathan Alder was lost.[30]

Alder died in January 1849. Soon after his death, his son, Henry Clay Alder, recreated his father's narrative from memory. This manuscript, also containing about one hundred pages, disappeared in the 1850s. In 1882, Dr. George W. Hill, a physician and antiquarian with an interest in Ohio's historic and prehistoric Indians, published a serialized account entitled "The Shawnees and the Capture of Jonathan Alder from the Alder Manuscript" in the Ashland, Ohio, *Press.* Although Hill did not say where his documentation came from, the account, which appeared in weekly installments from January 26 through April 6, was far more complete than that which had in appeared in Howe's *Historical Collections.* Nonetheless, this version also showed the signs of heavy editing. Much of the narrative is presented in the third person and that which purports to be Alder's own words is written with the florid vocabulary and high emotionalism consistent with the Victorian literary taste of the late nineteenth century.

Far more worrisome, Hill seemed to be as interested in telling his readers about the central Ohio Shawnees as he was in relating Alder's tale. As a consequence, Hill's account is interspersed with a variety of ethnographical and historical information about the tribe that clearly was not derived from the Alder narrative. Further, Hill stops his account following the Treaty of Greenville in 1795, even though the original narrative continues until 1832. In 1965, Orley E. Brown, Jonathan Alder's great-grandson, surmising that Hill had come into possession of the original manuscript created by Jonathan Alder and loaned to Henry Howe, republished the Hill account minus its historical and ethnographical interpolations. But despite Brown's assertion concerning the account's origins, many of the direct quotes found in the Howe account do not appear in the Hill version. Hill, therefore, must have derived his narrative from some other source.[31]

In 1883, W. H. Beers prepared a history of Madison County, Ohio, in which he included a fifth version of the Alder narrative. Beers claimed to have used the account written by Henry Clay Alder as his main source. He also consulted the Howe account and augmented both versions by obtaining additional facts from Alder's descendants and "old settlers who knew him well." Although much more extensive than the Howe account, this version is also somewhat abridged and paraphrased.[32]

In the 1930s, one of Jonathan Alder's grandsons, Henry Betts, and a great-grandson, Henry Alder, rediscovered Henry Clay Alder's manuscript. In 1935, Doyle Davison, another descendent, made a typewritten copy of the document, added a brief forward, and deposited the transcript with the Ohio Historical Society in Columbus, Ohio. After examining these various versions, I believe that George Hill, like Beers, used the Henry Clay Alder manuscript to create his account and, like Beers, also interviewed living Alder relatives and friends to supplement the story.[33]

The present location of the manuscript created by Henry Clay Alder is unknown. Indeed, after checking the inventories of likely historical societies, libraries, and archives; searching with appropriate computer-based search engines; and making inquiries on both genealogical and historical Internet lists, I can't even say with certainty that it still exists. A story currently circulating through the Alder family claims that many years ago, during the course of a family feud, a disaffected descendent placed the document in a trunk, where it eventually disintegrated. If the manuscript does exist, it is likely in a private collection or housed in a small library or historical society whose collection inventories are not yet on-line.

After I submitted my manuscript to the University of Akron Press, I was asked bluntly by one member of the editorial staff how, given the absence of the Henry Clay Alder manuscript, I knew that the entire narrative as presented in the Davison transcript was not a fabrication. I think that we know in several ways. One is its close resemblance and obvious relation to the version published by Henry Howe in 1847. Secondly, the versions produced by Hill and Beers both appear to be based upon a document consistent with the one purportedly transcribed by Davison. Thirdly, the Hill and Beers accounts are more elaborate than the version found in the Davison transcript, indicating that they were derived from the Henry Clay Alder manuscript, not it from them. More importantly, when both Hill and Beers edited the account in the 1880s, they both consulted Jonathan Alder's family and friends, people who collectively, I believe, would have objected strenuously to the publication of a wildly fictitious account of Alder's life. That type of negative comment does not exist, originating either before or after these later versions were published. I believe that the people who cooperated with Hill and Beers understood that the account that these later editors used when they prepared their own versions of Alder's life, namely the Henry Clay Alder manuscript, was in fact a substantially accurate portrayal of Alder's life. Furthermore, I believe that the Davison transcript is a faithful reflection of the original manuscript.

The real problem, it seems, is determining what sort of document the tale's various contributors thought they were creating. Some of this account was certainly created by Jonathan Alder himself. His early voice remains strong throughout the various versions. But some of the story undoubtedly originated also with Henry Clay Alder. Still other material was added by Alder's late–nineteenth century redactors and more still by kith and kin long after Jonathan had died. The problem of authorship is, therefore, complex. But the question of attribution goes to the heart of the Alder account. The Alder narrative was, in part, an attempt to provide an accurate historical account of the events in Jonathan Alder's life. But that account was also shaped in large measure by Jonathan's personal memories and then by those of his son. Later, the account was shaped once more by the designs and the agendas of the narrative's various editors and by the combined recollection of the informants used by Beers and Hill as they created their own versions of the story. Therefore, this narrative, like all history, is an amalgam of objective description, personal reminiscence, and collective memory.[34]

The version within these pages is the Doyle Davison transcript of the Henry Clay Alder manuscript held by the Ohio Historical Society, including the foreword added by Davison in 1935. The Ohio Historical Society document suffers from infrequent misspellings, some typographical errors, and a few obvious omissions. Further, it is occasionally repetitive. The narrative is not a strict chronological retelling of Alder's story, but rather a series of anecdotes told at times in a rather haphazard fashion. Indeed, the Henry Clay Alder, Hill, and Beers accounts all have the feel of oral history rather than written documentation. I have retained the original format of the narrative and have edited the account as lightly as possible so as to preserve the feel and charm of the original manuscript. Where the Howe, Hill, or Beers accounts add to or materially differ from this version, I have inserted these details in italics and noted the source.[35]

Although the Alder narrative presented here cannot strictly be considered a primary source, that is, an account created by someone who has firsthand knowledge of the events that are being described, it nonetheless provides a useful window into Alder's life and times. The account recreated by Henry Clay Alder is the story that Jonathan Alder told publicly about his experiences with the Indians. As we read through it today, we get a sense that the reminiscence is romanticized, and that the tragedy connected with his capture and the hardships associated with his life with Indians have been glossed over, perhaps because in Alder's memory, they were emotionally overshadowed and eventually replaced by the genuine love and affection that he developed for his adoptive parents.

The Hill and Beers versions of Alder's narrative, derived from the recollections of Alder's family and closest associates, represent the story that Alder was willing to tell only privately. Within these accounts, a more emotionally deep and complex Jonathan Alder reveals himself. For example, Alder claims that when he was sixteen years old, "the Indians made up a party to go over into Kentucky in the spring to steal some horse from the whites. They coaxed me to go along, flattering me and by saying that I could get a horse. I had never owned a horse and thought that I would like to have one, and would also like the trip." In the later versions of this incident, we learn that this expedition took place following a series of raids from Kentucky against the village in which Alder and his family had been living. When Beers retold this tale, he stated that in the spring of 1790 Alder went with a party of Indians into Kentucky to steal horses "in retaliation for the destruction of our town and property." In the Hill version, Alder adds "I had never owned a horse but was very desirous of doing so, and did not reflect upon the mode proposed to obtain them. To me, nothing seemed wrong so far as the whites were concerned. We had suffered so much at their hands that all seemed to be fair. I was assured the whites would steal our horses, or anything we had, if they had a chance to do so. They had several times taken or destroyed all we had, whereby we were almost reduced to a state of starvation. Hence, I felt somewhat like retaliating if I should have the opportunity." The subsequent accounts, therefore, supply an emotional dimension that adds depth to the historical context and enhances our understanding of Alder and his actions.

The Jonathan Alder that emerges from his narrative was honest, caring, and genuinely concerned that both his Indian and white neighbors resolve their differences fairly and honorably. Beers describes Alder as "a little over six feet in height, and straight as an arrow," and adds that "his hair and eyebrows were black as coal, his complexion dark and swarthy, his face large and well-formed, denoting strength of character and firmness of purpose; his eyes were bright and piercing, while his whole appearance, gait, and actions were characteristic of the Indians. Old settlers who knew him tell us that Jonathan Alder was as honest as the sun and his whole life, while living in this county, was characterized by the most rigid uprightness and straight-forward dealings toward his fellow men."

At his death, Alder was buried in the Foster Chapel Cemetery. The cemetery is located on West Jefferson–Plain City Road, a short distance north of exit 85 on Interstate 70, just west of Columbus. His log home, originally built about a mile north of Foster Chapel on Lucas Road, was moved to a plot adjacent to the cemetery in 1927 and remained there until 1986. It is now located at the Madison County Historical Society on State Route 142, London, Ohio.

A HISTORY

—— *of* ——

JONATHAN
ALDER

A HISTORY OF THE LIFE and captivity by the Indians of Jonathan Alder, who was born the son of Bartholomew and Hanna Alder on September 17, 1775, in the state of Maryland, not far from Philadelphia (*in New Jersey, about eight miles from Philadelphia, September 17, 1773*. Howe, Beers).[36] When I was two years old, my family removed from there to Wythe County in Virginia. About four years afterwards, my father died, leaving a wife and five children. John, he was only a half-brother (my father had been married before then) and was the oldest. My brother David, and myself, and Mark, and Paul constituted the rest of the family. My father had bought a piece of land and had made some improvements before he died, and had some horses and cattle and other stock. ([His father] *purchased a small tract of land, erected a plain log cabin and began to make improvements. . . . He was possessed of several head of horses, cattle and swine, which fed upon the wild grass, herbage, and nuts of the forest and frequently strayed along the mountain valleys.* Hill) We lived near a lead mine. I can still recollect going to the mine and watching the miners dig out the ore. There was also a pure stream of water close by. I used to go there with my brother John to see him swim.

Another incident that I can still recollect is that the Negroes used to pass our house on Saturday evenings going to see their wives and would return Sunday evenings. I recollect several instances in the fall of the year when they would bring pumpkins with them and would get my mother to bake them for them to eat on their way home. There were a great many other things that I could also remember, all of which I related to my mother when I returned home after an absence of twenty-four years. A great many of these things she had entirely forgotten, but after her mind was a little refreshed, she could recollect and tell me of some that I had forgotten.

It was now in the month of May 1781 (*March 1782;* Howe, Beers) when the leaves were all out and the woods were very thick.[37] One pleasant and sunshiny morning, everything looked gay and beautiful and my mother called to my brother David and myself and told us that we must go and hunt a mare and colt that had been missing for several days. My brother did not eat but little breakfast and when the meal was over, he seemed to be very much downcast. All the necessary arrangements were made and we started, but little did we think what our sad fate was to be or who would tell the story.

We struck out into the woods and after wandering around for some time and not finding the horses, we came to a little brook that was full of willows. David gave me his knife and told me to cut some of them around the bank and he would make a basket when we went home, and while I was busy, he would look for the horses. Then he started off and left me. Now I had cut but a few of the willows till a fright came over me, and I went off and sat down on a log until David called to me and I answered. He told me to come to where he was, so we called back and forth several times before I got to him. When I got there, he had found the mare and colt, but the colt was down and could not get up. It had eaten the plant called "stagger wood"[38] that grew in that country. He told me to take the colt by the tail and he would take hold by the neck and see if we could raise it, so we lifted several times, but it was so stupid that it would not try to help itself. We stood and looked at it for some time not knowing what to do and he told me to take hold and we would try it once more, and if it did not help itself, we would go and leave it.

We got ready and just as I was in the act of stooping down he hallooed out, "Run, there is Indians!"[39] David was about sixteen years old and very quick on foot and he darted off like an arrow with two Indians after him (there were five Indians in all, and one white who had been taken prisoner years before).[40] The word "Indian" frightened me so that I was completely paralyzed. I could not move, and by the time I looked around (for they came up behind me), one Indian was right up to me and held out his hand and I took hold of it.[41] I have no language to tell you how I felt. Above all creatures in the world, the Indian was dreaded the most, and here I stood whilst one had me tightly gripped by the hand and the next thing may be the scalping knife and the tomahawk.

You may try to imagine my feelings in this perilous condition with my brother out of sight and two Indians after him. You can read

A History of Jonathan Alder

the history but you cannot realize it. But I had not long to wait until I saw my brother coming back, one Indian leading him and another holding the handle of a long spear that he had thrown into his body. When he came close to me I asked him if he was hurt and he said he was. (*These were the last words that passed between us.* Howe, Beers) By this time, one Indian stepped up and grasped him tightly around the body while another took hold of the spear and jerked it out. (*I observed some flesh on the end of it, which looked white, which I supposed came from his entrails.* Howe, Beers) They then started off in rather a hurry and we had not gone far till I saw my brother turn pale and begin to stagger. I tried several times to look back, but the Indian would give me a jerk by the hand and so I was prevented from seeing him any more. We didn't go far till they halted on a high piece of ground. We had been there but a few minutes when I saw the Indian that was left with my brother coming with his scalp in his hand, frequently giving it a shake to shake off the blood. Then I knew he was dead and whether they would kill me right there or carry me off, one or the other must be my fate.

After they had talked awhile together, then this white man began to ask me questions. He inquired how many there was in the family. I told him there was but two little brothers and my mother; my father was dead and my brother John was then a grown man and was not living at home. He then asked me where I lived and I pointed off down towards a mill where there was a fort kept.[42] He shook his head and told me I lied. Said he, "We have been there two days trying to catch Negroes and there is a heap of people there, and I know you do not live there. But if you will show us where you live, we will take your mother and the other children off with us into a fine country and will take good care of you, and you can live easy and need never to have work."

I knew that my brothers were both small and that while the Indians might take my mother with me, they would undoubtedly kill the boys for fun. I still insisted that I lived down at the mill and while we yet talked, a rooster crowed not more than half a mile off. Says he, "There is where you live." I told him it was not, but immediately all the Indians started in that direction. They had not been gone but a little bit until a man commenced chopping on a tree. "Now," thinks I, "soon I will hear a gun," and I then begged of that man to let me go, but he told me no. We had not talked long until, sure enough, the gun went off. In about half an hour, here they came with Mrs. Martin and one child about two years old (*aged four or five years;* Howe). The white man then asked me if that was my mother. I told him it was not, but told him it was Mrs. Martin. She told me that they had killed her husband and her second babe. Mr. Martin was shot down at the tree where he was chopping and the babe they killed in the house.

Now Mrs. Martin was a close neighbor and we were well acquainted, and here we was, both prisoners in the hands of the Indians. I could yet see the blood of my brother on the hands of the Indian and his scalp hanging in his belt whilst Mrs. Martin could look and see the blood of her husband and of her infant upon their hands and their scalps hanging in their belts. How do you suppose we felt?

The Indians had a little talk among themselves and then we all started off in a considerable hurry as fast as the woman and myself was able to go. My back was now turned upon home and my fate was sealed. Every step was like a dagger to my heart. They tied a buffalo tug[43] around our waists while an Indian held the other end and compelled us to follow.

We marched in regular Indian style, one right behind another in order to make as few trails as possible.[44] The Indian that had captured the small child had to carry it, and in this condition, we hurried off from about ten o'clock in the morning until after dark. Long before night, two of the Indians stopped awhile back on the trail to watch and see if there was anybody in pursuit of them. The rest went down into a deep ravine and then followed it for a considerable distance. There, among the cliffs and rocks, they pitched their camp for the night with very little preparation. The weather was not cold and they built no fires. They had some dried venison, so we ate all we wanted, but that was little with the prisoners.

They then spread their blankets and ordered us to lie down after tying buffalo tugs around our waists, leaving each end long. After giving the small child to its mother, two of the Indians also lay down, one on each side, and tied the ends of the tug around their bodies. They gave us rope enough so that we could turn ourselves if we wished, and they also had blankets to cover us. In this condition we passed the first night of our captivity with but little sleep.

We now began to despair that Providence would ever intervene for our release. We traveled as before, in single file with two of the Indians a short distance in our rear to guard against any surprise attack. Thus we traveled over hills, rocks, brooks, and vales, across mountain slopes and through forests, a rough and rugged route, one that no set of men could have pursued successfully on horseback. At about noon, the Indians made a halt and laid off their burdens. We all ate lunch and rested but a short time, and then took up our line of march again as usual until night set in. We stopped a way up in a dark ravine and in the mouth of a cave kindled a little fire, ate our supper, rested, and chatted a little. The white man would try to give us great encouragement in regard to our future prospects, but we gave him very little credit for his flatteries. The blankets was again spread and we was made fast with the ropes as before, and we laid down to sleep after putting out all the fire.

We awoke early in the morning and felt somewhat refreshed. We ate our breakfast and all things being ready, we moved off as before. The Indian that laid claim to Mrs. Martin's child had carried it the last two days and at night he seemed to be very tired. This morning, after we started, he soon fell behind. We traveled on until noon and halted for a short time, ate a bit, and moved on again. Nothing particular transpired through the day except that the Indian with the child had not been seen since he fell behind in the morning. I saw that Mrs. Martin was somewhat uneasy. About sundown they halted for the night and, in the course of half an hour or so, the Indian came up without the child. As soon as Mrs. Martin saw him without her child she noticed the scalp hanging in his belt. She commenced screaming and hallooing and crying, "My child! My child! My child!" (*Finding the child of Mrs. Martin burdensome, they soon killed and scalped it. The last member of her family was now destroyed, and she screamed in agony of grief.* Howe, Beers) The Indian stepped up to her and bade her hush, but she paid no attention to him whatever, but still screamed and hallooed. He then drew his butcher knife from its scabbard and caught her by the hair and slapped the edge of his knife against her forehead and hallooed out, "Sculp! Sculp!" She paid no attention to him, but held perfectly still as though she was willing that the man might scalp or kill her and kept screaming and crying. If she had not belonged to another Indian, perhaps he would have killed her. I was very much scared, for I expected to see the woman killed. They were then standing under a beech tree, and he let go of her hair and reached up and cut off a limb and trimmed it up and commenced whipping her. She still screamed and hallooed, "My child! My child," but he whipped her until she had to hush. (*But indifferent to life, she continued her screams, when they procured some switches and whipped her until she was silent.* Howe, Beers) I saw we was entirely at their mercy. They could kill us any moment they chose.

Mrs. Martin and myself ate but little that night. We suffered our grief as best we could and shed a great many tears. That night, mother and my brothers and home was my great theme of thought until I was overcome with sleep and dropped away and forgot myself till I awoke in the morning.

We was up early in the morning and, after the usual routine, we set out again on our journey. By this time I began to feel very sore and wore down and it was getting very wearisome to me to travel. We halted at noon to rest and eat a bite. We all sat down on a large flat rock and was there perhaps for an hour. When the word was given to rise, I felt so sore and stiff that I didn't rise immediately. It was a clear sunshiny day and I noticed on the rock right in front of me the shadow of a tomahawk and a man's arm. My captor was standing right south of me and when I saw the shadow, I turned my face and looked up and saw the Indian let down his arm with the tomahawk drawn. I rose up and the Indian commenced feeling my head, and he and I started on after the others. ([Alder] *turned and there stood an Indian, ready for the fatal blow. Upon this, he let down his arm and commenced feeling of his head. He afterward told Alder it had been his intention to have killed*

A History of Jonathan Alder

him; but as he turned, he looked so smiling and pleasant that he could not strike, and on feeling of his head and noticing that his hair was very black, the thought struck him that if he could only get him to his tribe, he would make a good Indian; but that all that saved his life was the color of his hair. Howe, Beers) (*When he felt my head he noticed that my hair was very black and thought I would make a good Indian if he could get me to his tribe. It was from this cause he spared my life and which induced the Indians to treat me with less severity.* Hill) We traveled on that evening until night without anything particular transpiring. The Indians now began to kill some wild game and we had plenty of fresh meat to eat, but no salt or bread. It seemed a very strange way of living, but hunger will make a very poor diet palatable.

On the fourth day after our capture, we were getting a considerable distance from our home. Mrs. Martin and I would frequently talk among ourselves about our prospects of getting away, but no opportunity whatever offered itself. This night we were very sad and tired. I couldn't forget the shadow of the arm and the drawn tomahawk on the rock. I knew that if the Indians tired of us, they would tomahawk us when they pleased. But the white man would frequently talk with us and assure us that we should be taken through safe and alive to a fine country where we could live easy and without work and with a great deal of fine sport in taking wild game.

This night I noticed that there was a great deal of talk amongst the Indians, and what this all meant had a tendency to give us trouble. Afterwards, we watched every move and motion they made, notwithstanding the promises of the white man. We did not feel safe but, overcome with fatigue, we dropped away to sleep and were not conscious of anything that night. We awoke early in the morning. After eating a bite, the Indians packed their blankets and shifted their course more to the northwest and seemed to travel a little slower. Nothing particular took place this day except that they camped a little earlier. With plenty of fresh meat well roasted for supper, we feasted sumptuously and retired for the night. This was our fifth day of travel. We felt a little easier that night and dropped away to sleep quickly and slept very sound. We woke early as usual and, after the necessary preparations, struck out on about the same course, traveling on until night without making any halt and without a bite to eat. This evening, we feasted sumptuously on fresh meat in abundance such as venison and turkey well roasted. The Indians seemed to be more cheerful than usual and sat up until a later hour than common. (*They told jokes, laughed, and talked as if there were no longer danger of pursuit. Hill*) This night I was not so sleepy as common and was a little more excited than the night before. I got to thinking about my mother, brothers, and home, and didn't go to sleep until a late hour. I shed a good many tears but finally dropped away to sleep and have no recollection of my dreams.

The next morning (this was our seventh day), the Indians seemed to be very lively. They ate an early breakfast and we was on the move by sun up. They traveled faster than usual but were very kind to me and were very attentive to give me all the assistance they could. (*They traveled faster than before but were kind to the prisoners. Their manner was less harsh toward Mrs. Martin. Still, she seemed despondent and in very low spirits. She was the same pitiable, heartbroken creature, and seemed to do as she was told, mechanically but without murmuring, though her eyes were frequently filled with tears. Howe*) They killed some game and packed it along. It was very surprising to me to see how much a clever Indian could pack on his back and still make headway while traveling. Soon, we struck the headwaters of the Big Sandy River.[45] The river is not very large here, but it was large enough that we needed to build canoes in order to travel down it. As soon as they struck the river, the Indians made a halt. We ate a bite, and then they all went to work peeling the bark from hickory trees and then using the bark to make canoes. They worked on three canoes throughout the afternoon and had them all completed and launched before nightfall. The Indians rowed them into the stream and then informed us that we would travel a long distance by water in these canoes. To keep everything safe, they thought it best not to camp there that night, as they had spent half a day in one place (even though they were making good time, they still always kept a watch back on their trail until night). Everything being ready, they put all of their possessions into the canoes and we all went aboard and sailed down the river. We traveled in this way for several miles with great ease and splendor and at dusk halted upon the opposite side of the river and camped for the night. Nothing worthy of note took place this evening. We ate our meal as usual and retired to sleep with the same rope about our bodies as in the start. I dreamed of home, saw my mother and my brothers, but alas, when I awoke, it was all a dream. (*Alas! When I awoke it was all a dream, and I was nothing but a poor little boy in the hands of the merciless savage.* Hill)

This was the eighth morning and here I lose all account of the time. I am not able to tell how long or how many days we was going down the river. We sailed along so easy, and the scenery was so great and so changeable, that I lost all count of days. When night would come, they would haul the canoes up on some island where they were in every way safe from attack and camp for the night. Then they would build fires and roast ducks and other game that they had taken along the river without keeping up the usual watch as before.

This mode of travel gave us great relief, for we was in every way comfortable. We could lie down in the boats and sleep if we chose, but when night came, we was glad to get on shore and to walk around and stretch our limbs. And so in this way we passed down the river, rather lost in wonder and surprise, whilst the river was getting larger and larger every day, with large bottoms on one side, and high cliffs of rocks on the other. We saw great swarms of ducks and the Indians would shoot one now and then. All of this went to fill up my mind and occasioned me to think less about home than I would otherwise. And so the time passed away, and at last the great Ohio River came into sight. (*I thought it was the grandest sight I ever beheld.* Hill) Here at this point the mouth of the Big Sandy is wide and deep.[46] The Indians kept their canoes to the upper side of the river until they struck the current of the Ohio, and then they paddled for life until they struck the north bank. The river was running swift and was considerably up, but the Indians were not at all alarmed and we all landed safe. They unloaded the canoes and cut them full of holes, and then set them adrift so as to prevent us, if we should escape, from using them to cross the river.

We crossed the Ohio about the middle of the afternoon and that evening one of the Indians went out and killed a deer. We went up to higher ground and selected a spot conveniently near to water and wood. It was always the Indians' custom to burn dry wood (something that was generally easy to find) and also to camp near water. Next, they built a wigwam,[47] or what was called an Indian camp, and peeled bark and covered it and made it tolerably comfortable to what we had been accustomed to before. And so we moved in and took full possession of the new quarters here, and they granted us full liberty. We was no more tied with the rope at night and could lie down and rise up at our leisure, but the Indians still kept a little watch over us for fear that we might be foolish enough to try to escape and give them the trouble of hunting after us. Mrs. Martin and I would stand upon the bluff and look toward Virginia, but that was all we could do, for a long road and a dense forest stood in our way and a river intervened between us and home.

The white man now became very friendly. He talked with us a great deal and tried every way to make himself sociable. But everything he did failed. My home, my mother, and my brothers were continually in my mind. Furthermore, I was entirely too young to reason with any kind of logic how to make an escape. Therefore, although I could plan and think, I could take no action whatsoever. Finally, I gave myself over to grief and anguish.

After the Indians had crossed the Ohio, they were perfectly at ease and at home. There was no dread on their mind at all of being pursued or attacked by the whites. Consequently, they made themselves perfectly easy and went to hunting. About the second or third day, they killed a large buffalo. The animal was killed some distance from our camp and so I only saw the meat and hide as they carried it in. They went to work and built a large fire of dry wood and let it burn down to a bed of coals. Then they stuck up forks around it, and laid poles that were four or five inches apart across and over the fire about four feet above the ground. When the fire was done smoking, they cut the meat into broad slices about an inch thick and spread them on these poles, and then turned it frequently until the meat was

thoroughly cooked and dried. When the meat was done, they removed it from the fire and hung it up in a dry place, and another fire
was built and another batch roasted as before, and so on until the
whole back quarters was cooked in this way. After they had gone
through this operation, they built another fire as before, but not so
hot, and dried their meat all over again. Afterwards, it was thoroughly cooked and dried. In this condition it would keep for any reason-
able length of time by occasionally airing it a little in the sun, and this
they called jerk. Jerk is ready to eat and very handy, especially on a
march. An Indian with very little trouble can pack enough of it on his
back to last two weeks when he is on the trail. And if you stew it in a
little vessel with bear's oil, it is delicious eating. (*After they crossed the
Ohio, they killed a bear and remained four days to dry the meat for packing and to
fry out the oil, which last they put in the intestines, having first turned and
cleaned them.* Howe)

We remained here about two weeks while Mrs. Martin and myself rested and recuperated. At the end of two weeks, the Indians began to prepare to march further into Ohio. When everything was
ready, they divided the jerk equally amongst themselves. Once they
shouldered their packs, we moved on, leaving our wigwam, never to
see it again. We made short marches every day, traveling in a northerly direction and crossing several small streams. We struck a creek and
crossed it to the big Scioto River, and then followed the Scioto for a
considerable distance, eventually crossing it and striking across to the
salt licks where Chillicothe is now located.[48] During our journey, the
Indians put no burden whatsoever on me or the woman. Indeed,
they showed us great kindness every way they could along the entire
route. At the licks, we found squaws and children boiling the water
and making salt. We had spent about a week in getting from the
Ohio River to here, and we stayed at the licks for about another two
weeks.

When we left the salt licks, we went up to the Pickaway Plains
and halted there for a while.[49] The Indians killed many deer and
would generally stay long enough to dry their skins and then pack
them for sale. The Indians always had a ready market for their skins,

for French and English traders were scattered among the Indians to buy all of their furs. When we left the Pickaway Plains, we passed up between Big Darby and the North Fork of Paint Creek, sometimes on one, and sometimes on the other.[50] The Indians now traveled very slowly, hunting between the two streams and camping as long as they were successful at one place and moving on if they were not. Soon, the whole summer had passed. There were fine springs on Oak Run and on Paint Creek, and also on Big Darby near old Hampton, which were always main camping places for the hunter and stopping places for the traveler.

The main Indian trail from the salt licks near Chillicothe to Upper Sandusky passes up the Scioto River to the mouth of Big Darby Creek, and then follows that creek up to its headwaters, and then on to Upper Sandusky. When we traveled, we followed this trace. We was nearly all summer getting through Pickaway, Madison, Union, and Champagne Counties, but was longer in Madison than any of the others. The Big Darby Plain was alive with deer, elk, buffalo, and bear. While hunting and roaming on Darby Plain, the Indians still kept a close watch over Mrs. Martin and myself. They would never all leave the camp at once and there would always be one or two to stay with us to keep watch and to skin the deer and dry the meat. They had not as yet put any duties whatsoever upon us. They done all the cooking and the drudgery.

We again took up our line of march and followed up Big Darby, camping a little above Pleasant Valley. We stayed here several weeks hunting and feasting on the fat of the land, which consisted of venison and deer meat without bread. When we left, we followed up Big Darby, taking the Indian trace and passing on without any more long stops. (*They camped for a time near the present location of Plain City; thence followed the Indian trace, which started from the salt lick near Chillicothe; thence up the Scioto to the mouth of Big Darby; thence up that stream to the headwaters of the Scioto, and on to Upper Sandusky.* Beers)

One evening when we were upon the headwaters of the Scioto River, they camped for the night a little before sundown. They now ventured to call on me to do some little duties and the white man

A History of Jonathan Alder

told me to take the brass kettle and go to the branch and fetch some water. This branch was directly back on the trail over which we had just come. Ever since we had left the Darby Plains and had been marching northerly, I had been more uneasy and dreaded every stop. So when I got to the branch, I dropped the kettle and ran up a hill about one hundred yards from the stream and crawled into a hollow tree. I was now about two hundred yards from the Indians and I could see their camp from where I was hidden. I watched to see what they would do and thought that if they made no stir, I would slip out and take the back-track and try to make my escape. This was the first time I had made any attempt of the kind, but I had not been there more than two minutes until I saw them all jump up and run out. The white man looked right towards me and hallooed a couple of times. I thought that he had seen me so I crawled out, picked up the kettle, and carried up the water back to camp.

When I got back, the white man began to question me to know what had kept me so. I told him "nothing," but he knew better. He told me that I was going to run off. "Now," said he, "that will never do—it is a long road from here to where we got you, and all the way is through the woods, and you would starve to death for something to eat. And you know there is a large river to cross that you would have no way of crossing. Besides, the bears or wolves would catch you and eat you up, so don't ever try that, for you will certainly perish. But be content and be a good boy, and we shall soon be through. You needn't fear, you will be used well."

He had a long discourse to me that evening and said a great many flattering things. We ate our suppers and went to bed, but I didn't go to sleep for a long time even though, like many other nights, I was weary and tired. Instead, I lay and shed tears very freely. Eventually I dropped away to sleep and was unconscious of anything until I awoke the next morning. I was refreshed and I fully determined not to make another attempt to escape. I resigned myself to my fate, let that be what it would. I hoped for the better, but I assure you, there was nothing very promising about my situation.

(*In the year 1780, a party of whites followed a band of Indians from the mouth of the Kanawa, overtook them on or near the site of Columbus, and gave them battle and defeated them. During the fight, one of the whites saw two squaws secrete themselves in a large hollow tree, and when the action was over, they drew them out and carried them captive to Virginia. The tree was alive and standing on the west bank of the Scioto as late as 1845.* Howe)[51]

I had now reached a distance that was impossible for me to over-come. If I had made my escape that night, I knew not what the con-sequences might have been, but the probability is that they would have made a search for me the next day and found me. If not, I must either have fallen into the hands of other Indians or have perished.

We moved on again, traveling slowly day by day until we came within about two days journey of a Mingo village on the Mad River.[52] (*The village to which Alder was taken belonged to the Mingo tribe, and was on the north side of Mad River, which we should judge was somewhere within or near the limits of what is now Logan County.* Howe) Here we made a halt and two of the Indians left us and went on to the village in order to give them notice so they would give the prisoners a proper reception ac-cording to their rules and customs.[53] I was told that when we got to the village I would have to run the gauntlet.

We halted for a day or two then moved on, reaching the village in about two and a half days. We arrived within sight of the village about the middle of the afternoon. We halted and the Indians began to prepare for me to run the gauntlet.[54]

They picked a clear smooth piece of ground about four hundred yards from the village, and we all moved up to a place designated for me to start, once the word was given to run. We all sat on the ground while the entire inhabitancy of the village finished the preparations. All of the men, women, and children came out and formed two lines, single file and about two rods apart. I was made to stand up whilst twenty or thirty boys gathered round. From this crowd, they selected out six to give me chase and then the balance all took their places in line. These six was placed about two rods behind me, and all had keen-looking switches in their hands. My knees felt a little weak at times whilst this preparation was going on. After about an hour, I was made to stand up. The white man came to me to give the proper instructions. "Now," said he, "you see these boys behind you have switches." I told him I did. "Well now," said he, "look away up yonder on the hill. Do you see that woman standing there betwixt the two lines?" I told him I did. "Well now," said he, "when the word is given to run, you run with all your might right up to that woman, and these boys behind you will run after you, and if they can catch you, they will whip you until they are satisfied. Now, be sure to run right to that woman and start just as quick as you hear the word 'Run.'"

The Indians had been very manly with me in this matter. I examined the boys closely and they all appeared smaller than I was, but they all looked keen and trim. (*I examined the boys carefully; they were all fresh and active, while I felt sore and tired from my long march. But the boys were all smaller than myself, which gave me some encouragement.* Hill) First, I looked at the woman and then at the boys. Every little bit, the boys would cut the air with their switches, but after a great deal of preparation and maneuvering, they all got to their places and stood perfectly still. At last the white man stepped up and told me to be ready, and I began to try to get my nerve up for the race, which was to be a good long one. (*The boys were cutting the air with their switches behind me while the woman held out her hands and beckoned me cheerfully and hopefully to come to her; but it was a long way to her. However, I concealed my fears and determined to do my best, let what would come.* Hill)

All was ready and the white man gave the word "run." No sooner than the word was out, I started with the boys after me. As I would pass the Indians they would raise the war whoop, and the little fellows behind me would raise the whoop also.[55] I felt a little embarrassed in the start, but after I had gone about fifty yards it seemed as if every yell behind me gave me new strength, for all the noise was all behind me. All the Indians in front kept perfectly still and quiet until I passed them, then right away they would raise the yell. The farther I went, the stronger I got, for it seemed as if their cheering was all for my success. If there was ever a footrace run where the parties done their best, it was here, at least on my part. I could hear the boys cutting the air with their switches close behind. I kept my eye fixed steady on the woman and watched her every motion. When I got within about one hundred yards of her, I began to run uphill. She started to wave me on and, although I was slightly out of breath, my courage didn't fail. I reached the woman in triumph. She reached out her hand and took hold of mine. I took the liberty of looking over my shoulder for the first time and I saw the boys was a little farther behind me than they were when we started.

As soon as the woman grasped my hand, she ran with me for the council house which was about a hundred yards farther.[56] She went so swift with me that it was difficult for me to keep my balance, and I am sure that sometimes I went ten feet without touching the ground. We reached the council house without my receiving one stroke from their switches. (*I am sure she lifted me ten feet sometimes, without touching the ground, she ran so fast. Indeed, she thought I was a little hero and was very proud of my success.* Hill)

She took me in and seated me by her side in a conspicuous place set apart for that purpose. Meanwhile the little boys all dropped their switches at the door and also came in and seated themselves close by. They were puffing and blowing at a high rate, and their faces were very red and dripping with sweat. The other Indians also began pouring in and soon the house was crowded full. It was a long building and held a heap of people. It seemed as if there was no end to them, but finally they all arrived and sat down. In a short time everything was so still you could have heard a pin drop.

It was their custom on all such occasions that the head Indian got up and told the whole story in detail from the time they first started out until they got back, so that all could hear the story and none would have to hear it secondhand. He talked a long time, perhaps an hour and a half or two hours, while I sat there surrounded with a large collection of people, not able to understand one solitary word. When the Indian finished his story, the rest of them began going out. After most of them had left, the Indian that took me prisoner came and took me by the hand and led me away to his own wigwam. Here, I passed the first night in the village. On the next day, Mrs. Martin and I were separated. She belonged to a man of another tribe, so I never saw her afterwards until we met about two years afterwards down at Chillicothe at the salt lick. Nothing particular transpired for three or four days except that I began to get very lonesome until the white man told me that arrangements had been made, and that I was to be adopted into a certain family in a few days.

The Adoption

When everything was ready, I was taken to another Indian by the name of Succohanes. (*His Indian father was a chief of the Mingo tribe named Succohanes; his Indian mother was named Whinecheoh.* Howe) His wife and he had but three living children: Hannah, Sally, and Mary. They had also had one son, but he had died when young. They had requested to take and adopt me in place of their son that they had lost.[57] The day before the adoption, my Indian mother had gathered a large amount of herbs of various kinds, and that morning she put them into a large brass kettle and strained the water all out and cooled it to about blood warm. Then, she took and stripped me stark naked and commenced rubbing me with soap, some of the finest British soap that could be bought. She talked the entire time that she washed me, which perhaps consumed all of half an hour. I know that I never was washed so clean before nor since. Her ceremony was all in Indian. I couldn't understand one word of it, but it was all explained to me after I learned the Indian tongue. After she got through washing me, she brought out a new suit of clothes that I suppose she had been preparing for a week before. I was dressed all up from head to foot with the finest of goods in perfect Indian style: brand new moccasins very ingeniously made and covered with beads and silver buckles, and a silk handkerchief tied on my head. I was dressed equal to any chief's son or a young prince. There was no boy in town that was dressed equal to me. (*His Indian mother thoroughly washed him with soap and warm water with herbs in it, previous to dressing him in the Indian costume, consisting of a calico shirt, breech clout, leggings, and moccasins.* Howe)[58]

About the first words I learned in the Indian language was to call them father and mother, and I never called them anything else. Even though I couldn't understand it at the time, my mother explained the adoption ceremony to me after I learned the Indian tongue. She would also instruct me about the Indians' customs and chastise me if I met with her displeasure. (*His first lesson was from his Indian mother, who taught him to call his new parents father and mother, a lesson he never forgot as long as he stayed with the Indians. His mother frequently catechized him on his adoption after he learned to talk the Indian tongue, and explained the nature and importance of the ceremony. His father and mother, being of different tribes, spoke different tongues, though each could speak the language of the other and understand both. Such was their partiality for their respective tribes, that when Succohanes spoke to Whinecheoh, he used the Mingo language, and when Whinecheoh spoke to him, she used the Shawnee tongue, and when either of them spoke to young Alder, they did it in their native tongue, and in that way, he learned the Mingo and Shawnee languages at the same time. His father, however, was determined he should be a Mingo, while his mother was equally resolved in teaching him to be a Shawnee. The result of these desires was to stir up frequent family jars and disputes but no violence, especially on the part of Whinecheoh, who proved to be really the best woman he ever saw.*

In fact, he learned also the Delaware language, for there were many Indians of that tribe in the village, and many of the boys and girls with whom he played spoke all three dialects, so he learned them all about the same time. Hill)

(*They could not have used their own son better, for which they shall always be held in most grateful remembrance by me. His Indian sister Sally, however, treated him "like a slave," and when out of humor, applied to him, in the Indian tongue, the unladylike epithet of "ornery [mean], lousy prisoner!"* Howe)

(*His Indian sisters were all married. Mary was the wife of the Shawnee chief John Lewis;[59] Hanna married Isaac Zane, the half breed,[60] and Sally became the wife of an ordinary Indian. Jonathan went to live with the latter as a nurse, and she was very cruel to him, abusing and whipping the boy without any provocation and treating him "like a slave." After two years had passed in this way, one of his playmates told Whinecheoh, who immediately took him away from her cross daughter, telling him, over and over, how sorry she was that he had suffered so much cruelty. He subsequently went to live with Chief Lewis, who had no children.* Beers)

(*Having now reached the age of twelve, his Indian mother sent him to live with Sally, for whom he had no very great affection. He says: "I was kind of nurse* to take care of her children, which she seemed to produce as fast as I cared for, and a little faster than Indian women generally do. This nursing business was a new thing to me, and one that was by no means agreeable. I did not like it, for in addition to nursing, I had to do all the washing of the children's clothes, which was neither a clean nor pleasant work. There my trouble commenced. I suppose I was a little stubborn and contrary, at least from that, or some other cause, I received many a severe whipping from Sally. In truth, she treated me in every respect as a servant, and when she became angry, which was very often, she would call me 'a mean, low, saucy prisoner,' which hurt my feelings more than all the whippings, for it conveyed to my mind the idea that I was a degraded person, beneath the Indian race, and in no way the equal of my passionate sister or her children. This state of things lasted about two years. On one of these occasions, she gave me a merciless whipping. Her husband brought in eight or ten coons, and the next morning she divided them equally between herself and myself. We began skinning them. She was an experienced hand, and I was quite awkward and slow. She hurried me frequently, calling me a 'dirty, lazy dog.' I told her my knife was dull and I could not skin any faster with it. A young hunter standing by took my knife and whet it for me. It was very sharp, and I began to get along very well; but as soon as she finished, she tossed her knife near me, saying 'There, take my knife.' We were sitting on the ground near each other, and I picked up the knife and threw it back into her lap. Her limbs were bare almost to her hips, and the knife fell upon but did not wound them. She became angry in a moment, and sprang to her feet. Suspecting violence, I sprang up also and started to run. We had an exciting race for about one hundred yards. She broke a switch as she ran, and as soon as she overtook me she began to whip me and order me back. I turned and ran back—tried to out run her, but could not. She cut me with the switch almost every step, and when we returned, she ordered me to take the knife and skin the coons. She said she would teach me how to throw a knife into a person's lap. I sat down and finished the coons, but never forgot the whipping as I was sore for a long time afterward." Hill)

(It was the habit of the Shawnees to visit each other in the evenings to relate their hunting excursions and warlike exploits. On such occasions, they frequently remained until a late hour, and during the recital of these stories and adventures, young Alder often fell asleep where he was sitting. In this situation, his high-tempered Indian sister would halloo at him to arouse and get up. Of course he jumped up suddenly, well knowing if he failed to do so, his sister Sally would strike him with a stick across the head and shoulders. Upon the whole, he had but little peace while he lived with her. In fact, he became much disheartened under the severe treatment he was receiving.

He says: "One day about two years after I went to live with Sally, one of the neighbor boys came to pay a kind of visit. We were, at this time, scattered in the country for the purpose of hunting. The boy was there most of the day. Sometime in the afternoon he asked me to walk around in the woods with him. I told him I dared not do so, for if I did, Sally would whip me. He looked surprised and said he hoped not. I said she would not let me go out of her sight. 'Well,' said he, 'if she does, I will tell your mother. Let us go and see what she will do, and if she whips you, I will tell the old woman.' I then told him how she treated me. We started off and wandered some three or four hundred yards from the camp. I was not long until I heard her calling me and I answered, but she kept on calling until we got to camp. When she saw us coming, she started to meet us with a large switch in her hand, and when she came up, caught hold of me saying she would teach me how to stray off again. She gave me the severest whipping I ever had—indeed, she almost killed me. The Indian boy stood by amazed, but did not interfere or say one word in my behalf, but as soon as the whipping was over, he left for home. As he had promised, he went over and told my mother how badly I was treated. The next morning very early, I was overjoyed to see my old mother coming, and determined to tell her all before Sally, not knowing that the Indian boy had told her about the manner in which I had been used. My old mother came in and made herself quite easy, and after some little chat, told me I might go out and play. In about two or three hours, she called me to the camp. When I came, I saw from the appearance of Sally that she had been crying. My mother came and kissed me, saying, 'My poor, brave boy. I did not know how you were treated. You should have told your old mother, and she would have taken care of you. You shall now go home and stay with your old father and mother, and if you ever go away again, I will see you are treated well!' She picked up my bundle of clothes, which had been packed already, and we started without speaking to Sally, who sat with her head between her hands crying all the time as if something terrible had happened. To say I was glad to get home but poorly expresses my feelings. After we got home, my mother made further apology for neglecting me so long. She said she did not know that I had been so badly used, or she would have taken me away long before." Hill)

(*Jonathan for a time lived with Mary, who had become the wife of the chief, Col. Lewis. "In the fall of the year," says he, "the Indians would generally collect at our camp in the evenings, to talk over their hunting expeditions. I would sit up to listen to their stories and frequently fall asleep just where I was sitting. After they left, Mary would fix my bed, and with Col. Lewis, would carefully take me up and carry me to it. On these occasions, they would often say, supposing me to be asleep, 'Poor fellow! We have sat up too late for him and he has fallen asleep on the cold ground,' and then how softly would they lay me down and cover me up. Oh! Never have I, nor can I, express the affection I had for these two persons."* Howe, Beers)

(*In fact, they never seemed to weary in their kindness toward me, and it seemed a great pleasure to them to treat me kindly. The least accident, or pain, or suffering on my part was a source of regret and self-accusation on their part. They would say, "It would not have happened had we been more careful. We will never allow it to happen again!" Then they would commence applying remedies for my bruised skin, cut finger, or pain in my stomach with as much care as if they expected the injury to be fatal. My bitter experiences and treatment with my sister Sally made me love Mary and her husband and try to please them in all things. Their acts of kindness are among my pleasantest memories.* Hill)

Despite my adoption, I was frequently low and not satisfied. Mrs. Martin and I were separated and the white man had left. I saw him only occasionally afterwards. There was not one living soul that I could talk with or understand except occasionally when I would meet a white prisoner. In this condition, I got very lonesome. I would set and think for hours remembering my home, my mother, and my two brothers. I was so full of sadness that I would be ready to burst out and cry. I made it a rule every day for a whole year at about three o'clock in the afternoon to go down to the river bottom to a certain walnut tree and sit down and cry for an hour or so until I could give full vent to my feelings. Then, I would get up and wipe up, and wash to prevent their knowing that I was in so great trouble. It is surprising to think how much relief that gave me. Notwithstanding my efforts to conceal my troubles, my Indian mother could see it. As soon as she could make me understand, she would frequently talk to me and tell me not to be troubled. I learned very fast, for the boys and girls took a great interest in my welfare and would try to amuse me and learn me to talk. I was a great favorite with them. (*I could not have been treated better by my own brothers than I was by the boys and girls of the town.* Hill) (*The family, having thus converted him into an Indian, were much pleased with their new member. But Jonathan was at first very homesick thinking of his mother and brothers. . . . Childlike, he used to go out daily for more than a month and sit under a large walnut tree near the village and cry for hours at a time over his deplorable situation. They took pity on the little fellow, and did their best to comfort him.* Howe)

The Burning of Colonel Crawford

I had not been adopted for more than about three weeks when I was informed that there was a white man to be burned, which afterwards I learned was Colonel Crawford.[61] They gave me the opportunity to go and see the execution if I wished. It was not a great ways from where we was that he was killed, but I had no desire to see a man burned so I didn't go. (*In the June after he was taken occurred Crawford's defeat. He describes the anxiety of the squaws while the men were gone to the battle, and their joy on their returning with scalps and other trophies of the victory.* Howe) Pretty much all of the village went, including a great many of the squaws. I didn't learn much about the particulars at the time, only that it was an American officer, high in office, that had been captured. I have been on the grounds where he was burned hundreds of times.[62] Crawford was the last white man burned after I was taken prisoner, according to the best of my knowledge. I frequently heard the Indians argue against it, and the main reason was that when the whites took prisoners, they invariably treated them well.

(*Early in August 1782, a grand council of Indian warriors was held at Chillicothe, near the present site of Xenia,[63] at which Succohanes was present.* Hill)

(*During the early summer and fall, he amused himself in playing ball, running races and the like with the Indian boys and girls. These exercises constituted their principal recreations. He became very expert, and quite a favorite, but was* not exempt from the tricks and jokes of the youths of both sexes. They never really treated him rudely or in a way to intentionally wound his feelings. Their jokes and tricks were intended as pleasantries. No bitterness or strife was engendered. In all their sports and tricks, no matter what would happen, neither ill will nor malice was manifested. They were always cheerful, good natured, and happy, and this added much relief to his despondency. Hill)

The time slowly wore away. Their manner of living was so different from what I was used to and their food didn't agree with me. Most of their diet was meat. Occasionally, they would have hominy and beans, but bread was a thing I hardly ever saw. Salt was an article scarcely used in their victuals. Consequently, I became lean and haggard. My discomfort lasted about three years. But as time wore along, the foods, the language, and the lodging, all of which were very hard in the start, became more natural. (When Alder had learned to speak the Indian language, he became more contented. He says: "I would have lived very happy if I could have had health; but for three or four years, I was subject to very severe attacks of fever and ague.[64] Their diet went very hard with me for a long time. Their chief living was meat and hominy; but we rarely had bread, and very little salt, which was extremely scarce and dear, as well as milk and butter. Honey and sugar were plentiful and used a great deal in their cooking, as well as on their food." Howe)

(The first work required of young Alder was to skin and stretch the pelts of coon. That kind of work was always done by the squaws and boys. At first, he was very slow and awkward, but soon became adept at the business. He says: "I soon learned to skin and stretch a coon or other skin as quickly and as neatly as any boy or squaw in the village." Nevertheless, he regarded the task, at first, as very unpleasant, but in a short time found that he really enjoyed it, as it gave him something to occupy his attention and prevented him from brooding over his troubles. In a few years he became very expert, and concluded he could beat any Indian he ever saw skinning and dressing anything from a coon to a buffalo. By the end of the trapping season, he could understand a good deal of the three languages spoken in the village and was allowed by the young folks his age to take an active part in all the favorite games and sports. These games and sports furnished much diversion, and gave great relief to his mind. In truth, he became so much infatuated with their novelty and merriment, that he gradually neglected his old habit of going to the walnut tree in the bottom to weep. So great had been the change that he says: "I began to enjoy myself to a large extent." Hill)

(The work of the females, or squaws, is very different from females among the whites. The Indian squaws are expected and required to do all the drudgery, cut and carry all the wood, bring all the water, skin all the game including deer, bear, and buffalo, if brought to the camp unskinned. They skin and stretch all the furs, plant the corn and beans, and cultivate and gather the crops. The Indian hunter feels it beneath his dignity to give his attention to such matters. In addition to these extra duties, the squaws have the entire control of the family, girls until they get married and boys until they are twelve years old. The boys are classed as squaws or work hands until the age of twelve, during which time they are required to do all kinds of squaw work. They are frequently called squaws until they arrive at fourteen years of age, after which they drop the female character and are allowed to use and own a gun. I was of the right age to work with the squaws. During the summer, I worked in the garden, or patches as they were called, and during the fall, winter, and spring—at skinning time—dressing and stretching skins. To do this properly was quite a trade. The first thing was to shave off all the flesh that adhered to the hide, being careful not to cut the skin, and stretching it in a neat manner, so as to make it as large as possible and of good shape. This was one of the few things Indians seemed to take pride in doing well, and they certainly had some reason for so doing. If the peltry were not properly prepared, there would be a reduction in the price. I have thought the traders often took advantage of slight defects in dressing skins, more to make a bargain than from real injury. They examined every skin very carefully and appeared anxious to find some fault. Hill)

As I began to learn to talk, my father would flatter me that sometime before long I should be exchanged for other prisoners and that I would get home to my mother and brothers. I held very little hope that that would happen, but the thought still made me anxious.

About two weeks after my adoption, a white man came and had a long talk with me. He questioned me all about my folks and where I was from and how I was used, and if I thought I would be satisfied to live with the Indians. He told me that his name was Simon Girty and that he was also from Pennsylvania.[65] Said he, "If you are not satisfied to live here, I will buy you, which I can do for a small sum, and send you across the lake into Canada amongst the British, for it is most likely you would learn some trade." "But," said he, "if you stay with these people, you will be exchanged for other prisoners and get back to your mother. You will be more likely to get back to your people if you stay here than if you should go to the British, for it is most likely you would become attached to them and by the time you became a man, you would lose all desire to get back to your folks. Moreover, this war is not going to last a great many years. The whites will conquer the Indians and peace will soon be made between them. The whites and the Indians will live upon peaceable terms and then you can go where you please. You may stay with these people or go back to yours." He then told me to think on it, and he would be back in about two weeks. If I was not satisfied, he would buy me and send me across the lake to the British.[66] (*I knew Simon Girty to purchase, at his own expense, several boys who were prisoners, take them to the British, and have them educated. He was certainly a friend to many prisoners.* Howe)

At this time, the name of the British was almost hated as bad as the Indians, so I studied the thing over and over and put it in a great many shapes. I finally came to the conclusion that my chances might be better to get back home to my folks if I remained with the Indians than if I went to the British. In about two weeks, Girty came back to see me and inquired of me if I had made my mind up in regard to staying with the Indians. He then had a long talk with me and gave me a great deal of encouragement and good advice, namely to be a good boy and be kind to my Indian father and mother. If I did that, he claimed, I would be sure some day to get back to my mother. He shook hands with me and left. I frequently saw Girty afterwards and was glad to see him, for he seemed to like me and took a great interest in my welfare. Every time we met, he had a great many kind words for me and good advice.

After peace was made and I had got back among the whites, the first question asked me was if I knew Simon Girty. I told them that I did, and was well acquainted with him, and that he was one of my special friends. Well, I soon learned that above all names and men, Simon Girty was the most hated because of his conduct at the burning of Colonel Crawford.[67] I know nothing of his conduct there, but it was out of his power to save Crawford. Girty belonged to the Seneca tribe. Colonel Crawford was captured by the Delaware and Girty had no control over them whatsoever. The tribe's decisions regarding Crawford were entirely beyond Girty's ability to manipulate. I know that Girty's influence with the Senecas was very great and in several instances was the means of saving prisoners' lives. But it is an invariable rule amongst the Indians for each tribe to manage their own business, make their own laws, and punish their own criminals. (*There were exceptions to this general rule. In the case of Leather Lips, in Franklin County, who was executed for supposed witchcraft, much influence was brought to bear upon the tribe to save the old chief, but to no effect, for he was put to death.* Hill) The other tribes at Crawford's death minded their own business.

Girty saved the life of Simon Kenton when he was captured by the Senecas.[68] I had it by Kenton's own mouth. He said he was captured in a skirmish in which he was in command. After he was taken, the Indians held a council and he was condemned to be burned. He was painted black (done to all prisoners who are to be burnt) and seated close to where the preparations were being made. Girty, in passing round to see what prisoners had been captured and to see if by chance he might know any of them, came to Kenton and saw that he was already blacked and would be burned in a few hours. Learning that Kenton was an officer, Girty began asking him questions and trying to learn how many men Kenton commanded. Kenton was not going to tell the truth, and remembered officers enough to command a thousand men.

"Then," said Kenton, "he asked me what my name was. I asked him what he asked me for. Said I, you know me well enough. I know you, you are Simon Girty." "Yes," exclaimed Girty, "that is so. But I do not know you." "I told him that it was strange that he didn't know me. He declared that he did not." Said he, "Who are you?" "I then told him my name, Simon Kenton. No quicker had I said it but he recognized me and sprung at me, and caught me around the neck and hugged and kissed me, and went and cried over me. The excitement continued for some time and when he let go of me, he turned to the

Indians and talked for a long time. As he told me afterward, he told them that I was a namesake of his and a schoolmate, and if they ever done him a favor, to release this man to him. So I was finally untied and washed and then he very readily could recognize me. All of this took place in sight of the stake and the wood. So Girty took me off with him."

Let Girty be what he was, he could not have saved Crawford's life. Crawford had done something before that was held in remembrance by them, so much so that his fate was sealed. Girty may have been cruel in some respects to white prisoners, but as a man, he was considered true and honest amongst the Indians.

After I was grown, Girty told me that he had been captured by the Indians in a battle and had been held until he had learned their nature and gained their confidence. He became a trader with them and the whites once peace was restored. When the Revolution began, he was living in Pennsylvania. He and McKee and Elliott were all Indian traders and had Indian wives and all three held military offices under the United States government.[69] When the war broke out, the Americans held a council and decided that men having Indian wives would not be safe men to trust. They then held an election and elected other men to replace the three traders. Girty, Elliott, and McKee all took this action as a personal insult and immediately left the whites and joined the Indians. This was his excuse for the course he had taken. As for his acts of cruelty, I had no knowledge of them until I learned of them from the whites, but I think that the whites were greatly exaggerating.

(Jonathan took great pleasure in learning to fish and trap small animals. This was a kind of pastime which the Indian boys learned when very young. Neither fishing nor trapping was done from necessity, nevertheless, the boys were always proud of taking game, and were warmly praised by the Indians when they evinced skill and success. As among white boys, gathering wild fruits and nuts was a favorite amusement because it furnished an agreeable and profitable employment. The pleasure of cracking nuts around the fires of the wigwams during the long winter evenings while the elder Indians were relating their wonderful adventures, either in war or hunting, was eagerly seized by the young folks. They listened to *these stories as well as to some ancient oracle relating the history of his tribe and other marvelous stories that had been handed down from generation to generation. To the young and uneducated Indian, one of the greatest sources of pleasure, next to telling his exploits, is to hear some old sage of the tribe relate its history. It was in the midst of such scenes as these that the summer, fall, and winter months were passed. Sometimes, the Indian camps were enlivened by a white trader coming in, but this was a rare occurrence during the fall and winter. The principal period of trade was in the spring.* Hill)

(At the close of his second winter among the Indians, a white trader from Kentucky, with an Indian wife, made his appearance for the purpose of exchanging prisoners.[70] Jonathan was informed of the circumstance, and was delighted with the prospect of soon again seeing his mother and brothers; but his Indian boy companions, who had become much attached to him, told him terrible stories as to his future if he went with the white trader, hoping thereby to induce him to remain with them. His Indian father always told Jonathan that these tales were false. A few days prior to the time he was to start for Virginia, Succohanes took him to the agency, which was ten miles distant. The parting from his Indian friends was very affecting, for they all loved him well and wept bitterly over his departure. The same hour of his arrival at the agency, the agent, who was a rough man, began to abuse him. Jonathan resisted, and the trader's squaw came to the boy's assistance. This brought on a big quarrel, during which Jonathan "struck out" to overtake his father, in which he was successful. He was joyfully received back by Whinecheoh, as well as the entire youth of the village, the latter of whom made him the butt of their friendly jokes on account of his short stay with the agent, whose treatment completely weaned him of any lingering desire to return to his early home. Beers)

("My father, who had been always honest and true in his dealings with me, called me to him one day and asked me if I would like to see my mother and little brothers. I was very much astonished at first, as I supposed my mother and brothers had been taken prisoners. Consequently I hardly knew what answer to make, so I merely replied, 'Why do you ask me that?' He then told me that there had been a treaty made with the whites by the Indians for an exchange of prisoners, and all that wished to go back to their people could do so now, and 'if you want to go back to see your mother and live with her and your brothers, I will make the arrangements so you can do so. You can consider the matter and make up your mind, as it will be some time before you will have to start. We would like very much to have you stay with us, but if you wish to go, you shall do so, and your (Indian) mother and I will see that you have all that is necessary for you to take along to make you comfortable. Make up your mind so that you will be satisfied one way or the other. It will be very hard for your (Indian) mother to part with you, yet she must do so if you think it best. Now go and think about it, and let me know when you have made up your mind.

"The old man took my hand and turned his head away from me, and I thought I saw a tear in his eye—a very rare thing to see in an Indian warrior. This news from my father almost set me crazy. I was really wild with excitement, and the very thought of getting home made me nervous and sleepless. It was, however, a hope that had never entirely left me from the moment I was taken up to that time. I very soon made up my mind to see my mother. I was so overjoyed with the idea I could not prevent tears from coming to my eyes whenever they spoke to me about it. Even when by myself, the thought of once more having the pleasure of seeing my mother and little brothers so overcame me that I would burst out crying for joy. But very soon, an undercurrent was set in motion to destroy my hopes and expectations.

"As I have said, I had become a great favorite with the boys and girls, and as soon as they heard I was going to leave, they told me all manner of stories and bugaboos about the trader. The story that most influenced me was that the Kentuckian was not an agent, and had no intention of taking me home to my mother, but would take me to Kentucky and sell me for a slave, as he had done with several others. 'You will be a slave all your life and never see your mother or brothers in the world,' they said. They would take me by the hands, both boys and girls, look me squarely in the face, and talk to me in this manner until their eyes would be full of tears, begging me not to leave them to be a slave. 'Oh, they never could live to see me so badly treated.' Thus, for hours they would talk to me and cry, and beg me not to go. To such an extent was this carried, that I scarcely knew what to think or do.

"I frequently told my father what the young folks had said to me, but he assured me that there was no truth in it—all was false, that the man was a duly accredited agent, and would take me home and deliver me safely to my mother, and for me not to believe any of their stories. My Indian mother had but very little to say on the subject, but that which she said satisfied me that it would be a hard mat-

ter for her to part with me. Indeed, I knew the hour of separation would be a trying one for both of us. Not a day passed that the young folks did not coax or attempt to frighten me to stay. However, I placed full confidence in all my father
said concerning the agent, and felt easy in my mind.

"My father frequently visited the agent, and when he came back told me all he
said concerning his preparations about the time he would be ready to start. Thus,
time passed, but with a great deal of anxiety on my part. I was anxious to see the
day come, and equally anxious to see my mother and brothers; but sorry to leave
my Indian parents and the young people, and of course there was a lingering doubt
in my mind about the final result, for notwithstanding all my father had said,
there was still some fear in my mind that at least some of the many stories the boys
and girls had told me might be true. If any of them were true, it would be a bad
thing for me; yet my resolution was to go or make the effort, let what would be result.

"Finally my mother began to fix my clothes and get things ready for me to
start. She told me that in about ten days I would be taken by the agent that was
making the exchange, so that I should be ready. When this came to be known
among the young people, they doubled their efforts to frighten me into staying
with them. I did not fully understand the Indian character in such matters. In
many respects they are the most honorable and truthful people I ever knew, yet
when they have anything to accomplish that may add to their interest or pleasure,
they do not hesitate to carry their purposes by false or deceptive means.

"At last the day came, and I was told the agent would be ready to start in about
ten days, and that he wanted me about eight days beforehand in order that we
might become acquainted with each other. My father told me we would start the
next morning, and he would take me to the man, and for me to bid good-bye to all
my young friends, for I would perhaps never see them again as I was going on a
long journey and not to return. That farewell was by no means a pleasant one for
me. Such weeping, crying, and begging I never heard before or since. I felt very
sorry to leave them, for they had all treated me so kindly; yet I had made up my
mind to see my mother, and when they found their efforts were of no avail, each
one came and gave me some token of remembrance, and so we parted late in the
evening, I with a resolute but sorrowful heart, they sorrowful and hopeless."

After taking leave of his associates in the Mingo village, young Alder returned
to the wigwam of his Indian parents. With the bright anticipation of a speedy ex-

change and return to his mother and brothers in far-off Virginia, he retired to rest and pleasant dreams. His Indian mother awoke him early the next morning and began preparations for his departure. He was dressed in regular Indian style from head to foot, his clothing being all new and perfectly clean. His Indian mother was much depressed in consequence of the expected departure, but sufficiently collected to give him the necessary advice and directions concerning his future conduct. Just as his mother completed the arrangements, the boys and girls of the village returned to make another effort to induce him to change his mind and prevent a final separation. They came very early, and all had some new and astounding story to tell him, the principal of which was that the "agent was very mean, that he whipped and beat boys severely, and took all their good clothes away, and gave them mean ones in exchange, and did not half feed the boys. In fact several had starved to death on one trip he had made before." Alarming as the rumors were, he still relied on what his father had said, and tried to believe all would come out right. After he had been thus tried a second time, he resolutely adhered to the purpose of returning to his mother and again took leave of his companions and playmates with considerable regret on his part. He continues:

"All things being ready, my father brought up his horse and mounted him, and now the time came I was to part, perhaps forever, from a woman who had taught me to call her mother, and who really loved me as her own child, and had, in fact, been to me everything that a mother could be. She came up to kiss me and shake hands for the last time! When she took my hand, her usual stoical feelings forsook her, and she wept aloud. So deep was her grief that she was unable to utter a single word. She held me by the hand, firmly looking me in the face, and kissed me, crying all the time as if her heart would break, my father all the time sitting on his horse without speaking. It was a scene never to be erased from my memory. I can yet see the sorrowful but firm look of my father as he sat on his horse and hear the sobbing of my mother. My sisters and young associates were weeping, all of which was calculated to impress my mind very strongly—never to be forgotten. Finally my mother gave me one long and passionate embrace, kissing me over and over again, and then lifted me on the horse while my father turned its head away and started towards the agency. I could hear my mother's voice above the wailing of all the others when we were more than a quarter of a mile away!

"After we got out of hearing, my father commenced to talk to me. He told me he was old, but that I must be a good boy and maybe he and my Indian mother would come and see me sometime. He said I had been a good boy and he was very sorry to part with me, but that his nation had made the treaty, and he had to obey; yet he hoped that sometime, when I got to be a man, I would come and see him and my Indian mother; that I should always be welcome to the best they had. He requested me not to tell stories (lies) to my own mother, but to speak the whole truth and tell her just how he and his wife (Succohanes and Whinecheoh) had used me; that if they had ever treated me wrongfully, they did not know it, and was very sorry for it, if it were so. I told him they never had, but that they had been the best friends I ever had; that I would not leave them, only I wanted to see my own mother and little brothers. He said he did not blame me, for that was natural. He then gave me a great amount of good advice, to all of which I said but little, for the scenes through which I had just passed, together with his kind desires for my welfare, so overcame me I was scarcely able to speak at times."

The ride along paths and through glades from the Mingo village to the agency was about two miles, and his mind was occupied by various reflections during the whole distance, and time passed so rapidly that he arrived sooner than he expected. He continues: "When I got there, I saw about twenty white boys in the yard playing ball, and they could not have looked dirtier and blacker if they had been drawn up and down a chimney; they were as ragged as they could be. The very first sight of them brought all the stories of the Indian boys and girls fresh to my mind. Now, I thought, here are these little fellows, blackened and dirtied up, ready to be sold for slaves, for they really looked more like boys destined for slavery than for freedom. When we came up to the front of the house, we dismounted and walked in. After the usual compliments between the agent and my father, the latter said to him, 'Well, here I have brought this boy.' 'Very well,' said the agent, 'take a seat, my lad.' My mind was full of what I had heard, and the present appearance of the boys was not in any way calculated to allay my anxiety, but on the contrary, tended to increase it; consequently, I was very suspicious of the agent, of whom I had heard so much and saw so little.

"Somehow, I thought I saw something in the man that promised me no good. I did not like him. He spoke harshly and roughly—at least it appeared so to me. I took a seat where I could look down at the boys playing ball, and the longer I sat, the more I became alarmed. I thought to myself that just as soon as my father leaves, all my nice new clothes will be taken from me and I will be blackened just like the boys on the grass. In fact, I became satisfied that the stories the young folks had told me were true. I made up my mind that, come what would, I would not stay and be treated in that way. My father and the agent talked some half hour or more, and when he got up to leave, he turned to me and said, 'Be a good boy. This man wants to take you safely to your mother.' He held out his hand. I took hold of it and he held on for some moments, talking to me—shook it cordially, and turned and bid the agent good-bye, stepped out, got upon his horse, and rode off.

"I sat still a moment or two, but very uneasily. Finally, I got up and went to the door. I thought I would see which way he went. The agent ordered me to stop, but I kept on. He sprang to his feet, caught hold of me, pulled me back, and ordered me to sit down. I was now badly frightened, and began to cry and fight. I scratched and bit as best I could. He called his wife to help him, speaking to her in Indian, but I could understand both tongues. He told her to bring him a rope. Said he, 'I will tie the young rascal.' He wife, however, would not bring the rope; he insisted she should do so, but she still refused. He became angry and spoke roughly. She then got mad, and told him to let me go. One word brought on another until they got into a regular quarrel. She told him he frightened me, and that I would do no good under such treatment; nor would I stay with him if he did tie me. She ordered him to let me go, and he could go to the camp and see me and talk friendly, and by that means, I might, perhaps, be induced to stay with him, but as it was, it would be no use for him to try to detain me. He declared he would do no such thing; he would tie me.

"She then said he should not tie me but should let me go. He continued to hold me for some time while I was engaged in scratching and biting him. At last his wife stepped up and ordered him to let me go and he did so—and that pretty quickly. As soon as he let go, I ran off and followed the path my Indian father had gone. I struck out at my best speed following the trail as best I could. I ran about three miles before I came in sight of him. He was crossing a small prairie and riding slowly. I was about a quarter of a mile behind him and hallooed three or four times, but could not make him hear me. I ran some distance farther and hallooed again but could not attract his attention. I ran again, stopped and hallooed, and so on, several times before he heard me. When he did, he stopped and waited for me to come up. When I overtook him, he asked me what was the matter. I told him I did not like the man, and was not going to stay with him. 'Well,' said he, 'put your foot on mine and get up behind me, and I will take you back to your old mother.' I got up behind him and went back to the village.

His Captivity and Life with the Indians   61

"When my mother saw me coming, she came running to meet us and inquired the reason of my returning. I told her the same story I had my father; that I would not stay because I was afraid and did not like the man, and that I was going to stay with her. She could not have appeared more gratified if I had been her own son and had been lost and just found. She helped me off the horse, took me by the hand, and led me into the wigwam. She requested me to sit down, saying I must be very hungry, and she would get me something to eat as quickly as she could.

"She immediately began to prepare a meal for me with as much ado as if I had been some great personage she desired to honor. Indeed, it seemed she did everything possible so as to bestow all the kindness she could upon me. Right in the midst of this great ado, the young people of the village came to learn all the facts. My mother would not let them bother me, stating I was tired and scared, and they must go away and leave me alone; they refused to go, so I told my mother I would tell them the whole story. She consented, and I related the adventure to the boys and girls, being very particular to tell them how the agent wanted to tie me, and would have done it had not his wife prevented him; how ragged and dirty the boys looked; that I thought I had made a lucky escape. They all cried out 'Did not we tell you so? Did we not tell you that he was a mean man, and would sell you for a slave? That is just what he will do with all those poor little boys he had in his camp.' I said I believed every word they uttered concerning the agent. I told them I did not wish to see him again if I could help it, nor did I want him to see me. They said that he would never give up that way, that he would be sure to come after me, and I must watch and be on my guard and they would help me, and as soon as they saw him coming, they would tell me so I could run and hide.

"This little piece of advice, as I afterwards learned, was the occasion of much sport. They nicknamed the agent, and would frequently look and call him by that name and cry out, 'Here he comes!' Of course, I did not stop to look, but darted off into the thicket to conceal myself and remained there the rest of the day. Late in the evening, I would crawl towards the wigwam and watch to see if he was gone, and finding the coast clear, went in. This kind of sport was kept up by the young people nearly all summer.

"My mother frequently told me the young people were fooling me, but I thought it safest to keep out of the way of the agent. She added that before I fled again, I must look, and if I saw the man, I could run, but, as my eyes were as good as theirs, I need not run until I saw him. I thought this good advice, and the next time they told me that the man was coming, I started to run, but stopped and looked around and, seeing nothing, I asked them where he was, but all said, 'There he is, do you not see him?' I looked, but did not see anyone. So finding I would not scare until I really saw the man, they gave it up. That was the last of that kind of sport. I have been thus particular in relating these little incidents to show the Indian character. No people enjoy jokes and fun more than the Indian. The best friend is not exempt from their fun-provoking tricks. Every incident of their life, however serious or solemn it may be in the beginning, will, in the end, furnish the means of merriment and amusement." Hill)

Now there are a great many little incidences that I shall forget to tell and a great many more that are not worth telling. I will tell a great many little circumstances that may not be interesting to the reader, provided this narrative should ever go into print. But they were all more or less interesting to me at the time, and as for the dates and keeping the year, I had no means of keeping that, only by recollection. As a matter of course, my dates for these incidents may not be exactly correct. I may get some sooner and some later, and not all exactly in their correct place, but the circumstances themselves will be as correct as I can recollect them.

(Jonathan, with some other boys, went into Mad River to bathe, and on one occasion came near drowning. He was taken out senseless, and some time elapsed ere he recovered. He says: "I remember, after I got over my strangle, I became very sleepy and thought I could draw my breath as well as ever. Being overcome with drowsiness, I laid down to sleep, which was the last I remember. The act of drowning is nothing, but the coming to life is distressing. The boys, after they had brought me to, gave me a silver buckle as an inducement not to tell the old folks of the occurrence for fear they would not let me come with them again; and so the affair was kept secret." Howe)

(I got on the back of one of the large boys and locked my arms tightly around his neck. He then struck out and swam around for some time, instructing me in the art of swimming. After swimming in this manner for some time, he swam up above the riffle where the water was deepest. All at once, without giving notice, he dived in the deepest part, taking me with him. Not being aware of his intentions, I was, of course, strangled and let all holds go. He had to rise to get his breath, and supposed he would find me at the top of the water, but he was mistaken—I sank to the bottom! As soon as he found I did not rise, he became scared and commenced diving here and there all over the river, hunting for me. All the other boys came to his assistance and searched for me under the water for a long time (so they told me afterwards), but all was of no use, the water being deep and muddy. I could not be seen; so after a while, they gave up the hunt, came out, and commenced putting on their clothes; for they were all badly frightened and scarcely knew what to do. Just then, one of the boys observed something white in the riffle. They all swam out to see what it was, and found me.

They thought I was dead, but applied the usual remedy in such cases. The first I remember, after I began to rally, was that I was lying on my face with my head down hill, and the water was running out of my mouth. The boys were rolling me back and forth on the river bank. To die by drowning is an easy death, but it is very severe to come to again. When the boy first dove with me, I was strangled, but that was soon over. I became very sleepy and drew my breath easily. As I lay in the river, I looked at the sun as it shone in my face and that is about all I remember. The next was that they were rolling me on the bank, with my head down hill, and the water ran out of my mouth. The boys frequently pressed on my stomach; my breath was very short; it seemed as if I was smothering. Between the times of rolling, they stopped for a moment and spoke to me to see whether I could answer them, but it was some time before I could. I was in great pain, and vomited several times. Sometimes they put me on my feet and held me up, but I was unable to stand, so they laid me down on my face and rolled me again and again. I noticed I was improving, but it was very slowly. I could breathe easier, and the pain was less severe. About the middle of the afternoon, they made preparations to take me home. I had, by this time, so improved that I could walk around. The next difficulty was to so manage that the folks at home would know nothing about the occurrence; for the boys very well knew that if they were found out, it would be the last time I would be permitted to go with them. The boy who had done the mischief gave me a large silver brooch, and the other boys gave me other things by way of presents. They all begged me not tell the story to anyone, saying they would always be my friends, that they were only in fun when diving with me on their backs, as that was the way Indians were taught to swim!

It was the custom of the larger boys to take the smaller ones on their backs and teach them how to make the proper motions with their arms and feet, and then take them into deep water, cut loose, and let them help themselves. But the larger boys always remained near the smaller ones to render any assistance that might be necessary. I had sunk immediately, and did not rise. The Indians always rise to the top again. They declared no trick should ever be played on me again if I would only agree not to tell anyone about it. I took all the presents and made all the promises they desired, after which we all ventured to return home.

All our care did not do, for the watchful eye of my mother perceived something wrong. She questioned me very closely. "Was I sick?" "Had I got hurt?" I told her no, but that I did not feel as well as usual. She then inquired how I became possessed of the valuable brooch, beads, and other presents. For fear she would think I had stolen them, I told her the boys gave them to me. It seemed to please her very much to know I had got all of these fine things honestly, and that the boys thought so much of me as to make a present of their most valuable ornaments. These statements seemed to elevate me in her estimation over one hundred percent, though she could hardly believe the truth until I told her what boy had given me the large brooch and who had gave me the other things. She then asked them if it was true—they told her it was. Then she was really happy. Hill)

(During the latter part of the summer of 1784, his Indian father and mother, with many other Shawnees, visited the salt spring near the present site of Chillicothe in Ross County. He had the good fortune to meet his old friend Mrs. Martin, from whom he had been separated about three years. The Indians with whom she lived had gone there to make salt. This was their first meeting since they had parted in 1781. They recognized each other as soon as they met, shook hands, and both took a hearty cry. They remained at the salt springs about three months. Mrs. Martin was considerably shocked to find the head of her young friend covered with vermin. She carried a fine toothed comb in her pocket, which she used every few days until she had rid her young friend of his troublesome little pests. One day she took out of her bark basket a few little scraps, among which were pieces of the scalp of her child the Indian had killed. "She said after the Indian whipped her so hard, she saw him trim the child's scalp and watched where he threw the pieces, and when she had an opportunity, gathered them up when no one was looking, and had kept them to that time; intending to do so as long as she lived." This statement brought the scenes of the past vividly before them, and the result was they both wept deeply over their misfortunes. Mrs. Martin, on several occasions during her stay at the salt spring, exhibited these memorials of grief to young Alder, but never without shedding tears. Late in the fall, the Indians left the springs, and young Alder and Mrs. Martin were again separated, never to meet. She was exchanged sometime in 1785 and got safely home, as he afterwards learned. Hill)

(It was now better than a year after I was taken prisoner when the Indians started off to the Scioto salt springs near Chillicothe to make salt, and took me along with them. Here, I got to see Mrs. Martin that was taken prisoner at the same time I was, and this was the first time that I had seen her since we were separated at the council house. When she saw me, she came up smiling, and asked me if it was me. I told her it was. She asked me how I had been. I told her I had been very unwell, for I had had the fever and ague for a long time. So she took me off to a log and there we sat down, and she combed my head and asked me a great many questions about how I lived, and if I didn't want to see my mother and little brothers. I told her that I should be glad to see them, but never expected to again. She then pulled out some pieces of her daughter's scalp that she said were some trimmings they had trimmed off the night after she was killed, and that she meant to keep them as long as she lived. She then talked and cried about her family that was all destroyed and gone except the remaining bits of her daughter's scalp. We stayed here a considerable time and, meanwhile, took many a cry together; and when we parted again, took our last and final farewell, for I never saw her again. Howe)

(The Indians have some very singular notions about signs, and often dream of things they believe are about to come to pass, of both good and evil. They always have some plan of escaping the evil, or of possessing themselves of the good. These plans are either discovered while awake or in dreams. The flight of birds, the skin of fish, the entrails of game, and a thousand other things are used to interpret their dreams and tell them what to do. It was about the middle of winter and we were camped about one hundred and fifty yards from the banks of Mad River. One night, I was awakened about midnight by my father and told to get up because he had dreamed a very bad dream about me.

He said he had dreamed that I was out in the woods and a white bear got after me, and that after a long chase, it had overtaken me and torn me to pieces. He said he feared something very bad was going to happen to me if not prevented in some way, and he could not tell what the trouble would be, but it would be very bad and something must be done to prevent it. He requested me to take off my clothing, wrap a blanket around me, put on my moccasins, go down to the river, jump in and dive three times. This, I thought, would be rather a cold bath, but I made no *objections. I got ready and started, and when I reached the river, sat down and shivered on the bank a minute or so dreading the operation, arose, stripped off my moccasins and blanket, jumped into the river, and went under three times as quickly as I could. I then came up out of the water, drew on my moccasins, wrapped the blanket around me, and started on a full run for the tent. This performance, to be effectual, had to be done alone, no one else being present, and it took considerable resolution for one of my age to do as I had been requested. In my absence, my father had built a big fire for me to warm by, and my mother had a clean suit of clothes hung around the fire warming to wrap me in. As soon as I was dressed, she spread a warm blanket on the bed for me to lay on, and another over me. This performance lasted altogether about one hour. I soon fell into a sound sleep, and do not know that I ever slept better in my life. It is sufficient to say no evil ever befell me, nor was I ever chased by a white bear. Hill)[71]*

(Bathing is undoubtedly a healthy practice.[72] My Indian father made it a rule to bathe summer and winter regularly, and he was decidedly a healthy man. One winter, he kept a hole cut in the ice where he went regularly to bathe. I asked him one day to let me go with him to bathe. He took me along, and when we got to the place, he opened the hole, stripped me, and taking my hand, led me into the water up to my neck. He then lifted me up and helped me dress. I started on a run for the camp, and that was the last time I ever accompanied him to bathe in the winter. Hill)

Before I was old enough to go hunting by myself, sometimes one or another of the Indians would take me out with them if they were only going to be out for one day and back at night. Big Turtle asked me to go with him one cold winter morning when we were living near the Sandusky Plains.[73] We got ready and started out and wandered around considerably. Finally, he said we would cross the plains and so we did, finally coming to a wooded area on the other side. At last we killed a deer and skinned it and hung it up. We was too far from camp and it was getting too late to carry the meat in. The weather had been changing all day and by this time it had turned very cold, and while he was skinning the deer I began to get very cold as well. We started back to camp and hadn't gone far until Big Turtle killed a turkey. At about the same time, he noticed that I was getting very cold, so he gave me the turkey and told me to run, thinking to warm me up in that way. Presently, we struck the prairie and the difference in temperature was so great that even if I had stripped off half my clothes in the timber, I could not have felt the cold more intensely. We hadn't gone more than half a mile until I began to get very numb and threw down the turkey. I had gone some distance before Big Turtle discovered my trouble. He turned and ran right back and passed me and got the turkey but before he got back to me, I had fallen three or four times in the snow. I had become benumbed and was unable to keep my footing. When he reached me, he saw that I was freezing. We had about two and a half miles to go before we got to the timber. He took me by the hand and told me to run and he ran with me, carrying his gun and the turkey and encouraging me to hold out and help myself all I could. As soon as we struck the woods, there was so much difference in the temperature, it was as if there had been a blanket wrapped around me. Big Turtle never did let go of my hand until we got to camp. The Indians were very careful not to let me cross the plain any more that winter.

Freezing, like drowning, is not such a very hard death. I had been getting very cold for sometime, then my limbs began to get still and very much benumbed before I began to fall in the snow. I was getting quite sleepy and if I had been alone and saw some place to have laid down, I should have done so and slept my last on that day on the Sandusky Plains, but the Great Spirit that ever guarded and protected me carried me through for another day.

(*He lived with Chief Lewis until thirteen years of age, when Succohanes took him home, saying that it was time for Jonathan to be doing something for himself, that he would not have to work, but must become a brave man and a great hunter. The English gave his Indian father, annually, a keg of powder and a keg of musket bullets, so giving the boy an old English musket with plenty of ammunition, he said, "Now start and kill any game you see; it makes no difference what it is, so long as it is game."*[74] *Beers*)

(*When he was old enough, he was given an old English musket and told that he must go out and learn to hunt.*[75] *So he used to follow along the water courses where mud turtles were plenty, and commenced his first essay upon them. He generally aimed under them as they lay basking on the rocks; and when he struck the stone, they flew sometimes several feet in the air, which afforded great sport for the youthful marksman. Occasionally, he killed a wild turkey or a raccoon; and when he returned to the village with his game, generally he received high praise for his skill—the Indians telling him he would make "a great hunter one of these days."* Howe, Beers)

(*His first great feat was the killing of a large buck deer, when a big feast was celebrated over the victory, none being so proud of his prowess as his good Indian mother. He says: "Between Col. Lewis, Isaac Zane, Sally's husband, and my father, it was sometimes a tussle between whose knees I should sit and tell over my great deed of killing the deer. I really think I told it fifty times that evening." The next spring, his father gave him a new rifle, and his whole business was to hunt. He soon was second to no Indian youth in the camp, finally becoming the hope and support of his Indian parents.* Beers)

(*My father was getting old and, my success having been so much beyond his expectations, he, in a short time gave up the chase and, from that time forth, I was the hope and support of the old people. My father frequently talked to me about my success, and always remarked that it was very lucky for him and my mother that I was not exchanged at the time we had made the effort. He said the Great Spirit had interfered as his only son had been taken from him and had sent me to fill his place; that he had no doubt the Great Spirit intended I should remain with him and my old mother the rest of their life; that I would be their main support in their declining days, which were rapidly approaching. My health was remarkably good at the time, and I was gaining flesh and growing very fast, and began to feel that I was of some importance—almost a man, with a family on my hands. Save what we got from the British, I had to furnish all the necessities of life for myself and the two old people. We had many difficulties to encounter, and among others, the whites came from time to time to make war on us. The attacks gave us a great amount of trouble; sometimes a number of Indians would be killed and sometimes the whites would be driven back with loss. A number of these little invasions were headed, as I afterwards learned, by Simon Kenton. We were frequently compelled to run from him and his soldiers, and were often reduced to great distress from the burning of our towns and the destruction of our winter provisions.* Hill)

When I was about twelve years old, an Indian came into camp and said he had killed a large buffalo and wanted some help to carry in the meat. I had frequently gone out with them when they killed deer and they would give me the head to carry, which is a very convenient thing to carry when they have the horns on. So I told them that I would go along and carry the head. They laughed a little and said very well. Now, I had never been close to a buffalo before. When we got out to him, it was an old buffalo bull of the largest kind, and the head was so big that it was as much as I could do to lift it, let alone carry it. (*They all laughed and said, "Carry it! Why don't you carry it?" I felt very much ashamed, and really did all I could to carry it, but that was impossible. So after some merriment at my expense, they carried it. But my inability to carry the huge monster's head was quite an amusing scene for the Indians and boys, and for a long time they plagued me about the affair. My mother always took my part by saying, "Poor fellow, he did all he could, and if he would not carry such a big load, you should not tease him about it." After a while, they got a joke on some other person and the matter was forgotten; at least it was never mentioned again. I assure you I was not sorry, as I had become tired of hearing it laughed about among the boys.* Hill)

I never had any trouble with any of the boys who belonged to the different tribes except for one who belonged to our tribe. He was several years younger than me and so I was always able to handle him. He was smart, brave, and daring, but the greatest trait of his character was war. We would frequently be out in the woods together and he would make sham fights with his tomahawk and butcher knife, fairly lashing himself into a rage until he would act like a mad person. He would come up to a rotten tree or a stump and call it a Tawway, Chipaway,[76] or a white man, and sink his tomahawk or butcher knife into it. He would fly from one thing to another till I would get afraid of him and keep off at a proper distance for fear he might hurt me until his rage cooled off. In one of his sprees, he threw his butcher knife at me and stuck it in my heel, making me lame for a considerable time. I drew out the knife and stuck it in the ground and broke it in two. I tried to coax him up near to me to see what he had done, thinking that if I could get hold of him, I would pound him, but he was too smart for that. Before my foot got well, he made a great many apologies to me and promised never to do the like again. But once afterwards, when he was about fourteen years old and had commenced hunting, he had been out with his gun and had come in from the woods. Some few words passed between us and in a fit of passion, he jerked his rifle off his shoulder and pointed it right at me. He was standing only ten feet away, but before I could reach him, he snapped it at my breast well loaded and primed.[77] I grabbed the muzzle of his gun and drew out his ramrod[78] and whaled him with it until he begged like a good fellow. I then told his mother that if he ever attempted anything of the kind again, that I would kill him. She said she knew that he was a bad boy, but she could not help it. She was very determined to talk to him about it and told him what I had threatened to do. Afterwards, he and I was on the best of terms and had no more difficulties except for one time after he was grown.

The Indians are like all others of the human family. Periodically, they have their large gatherings where they govern themselves in councils. Each tribe makes its own rules and regulations. The decision to go to war is also made in council, often made up of the village chiefs.

One of their great gatherings is the green corn dance, which is held once a year about the time that corn is in the roasting ear.[79] The festival is held at some suitable place where it is shady and dry and where pure, easily obtained water is nearby. The chiefs and a few other important members of the tribe meet together about a month (moon) before the festival and make all the necessary arrangements. The dance is always held about the time of the full moon in August, for that is their only way of keeping time—by the moon and the four seasons of the year.

When I was about fifteen years old, I had been to many a green corn dance, but this year the arrangements were made to meet on the banks of the Maumee River. This meeting lasted three days. The green corn dance is a feast of fat things and the Indians all brought their green corn, beans, pumpkins, squashes, and everything that grew in the soil, along with their dried venison, bear meat, bear's oil, sugar, and honey. Several thousand Indians, big and little, attended this particular feast or dance. There were speeches on various topics and great thanks went up every day to the Great Spirit for their preservation and health during the last year. When there were no speeches, there would be singing and dancing and all manner of playing and games in every direction. Young and old, male and female, we all engaged in wrestling, running footraces, and other contests. Our religion placed no restraints on our activities. We were expected to feast and enjoy ourselves the best way we could, but not to forget to return thanks to the Great Spirit for past blessings and this privilege.

On these occasions, a select group of about fifteen or twenty of the most perfect and active young men came out every day. They were stripped stark naked except for their breechclout, which covered them from their waist about halfway down their thighs, and their moccasins, and their faces and the balance of their bodies were ingeniously painted in such a manner that their appearance would attract the attention of anyone. These young men are dressed, painted, and prepared by a committee that keeps them in a secret place. They remain hidden until they make their appearance in some remote part of the campground. First a musician, who is also dressed and painted, begins to make music and quickly they all begin playing and singing and dancing. Soon, the whole village is anxious to get close to them to see them and their dancing, which is very interesting. They will play and dance until the whole crowd gathers around them. The musician will then stop playing and dart right through the crowd. As soon as they see him coming, they will all give way and let him pass. The dancers all follow him single file, winding round through the crowd half bent so their heads can't be seen until their whereabouts is entirely lost to the crowd. Then, they dart out into the open ground and commence more music and dancing. Then another great rush is made to get to them. The music and dancing continues in that place until the crowd has about gathered and then the same thing is repeated. This continues for about an hour and a half and then the dancers will dart off into some tent and wash their paint off and dress themselves and come out, with but very few knowing who they were.

The last day of the festival was principally taken up with the distribution of prizes. In the morning, the Indians brought out hundreds of dollars worth of dry goods such as calico, cambric,[80] and broadcloth. They had various ways of awarding the prizes. In one, they placed a strong young man on the stand with the goods. Short plugs of wood, anywhere from four to six inches long, were marked so that they designated the prize for which the Indians would draw. When the contest was ready to begin, all those who wanted to compete for the prizes posted themselves where they thought best. The one on the stand told the crowd to be prepared and one of the stout men of the village took up one of the plugs and motioned as though he was going to throw it. The crowd all made a motion as if to run in that direction. He then motioned in some other direction, and so on for a number of times. At last, he let the plug slip with all of his might and the crowd ran and tumbled, scrambling for the prize. The smallest plugs win the finest prizes. I obtained one of them which drew me a pair of fine latch leggings. When he is through with the plugs, he next uses a number of balls, which he throws in the same manner. These draw a larger prize.

To award the last prize, he uses a bow and arrow. This prize is a whole suit made entirely of fine broadcloth and cambric and moccasins richly adorned with beads. There was no knowing which direction these arrows would go except that it would always be into the river. As soon as the arrow was shot, they all plunged into the river with such shouting and whooping and hallooing that they made the woods fairly ring. The arrow must have lit as much as four hundred yards in the river. The contest was exciting and delightful, but presently some began to fall behind and two young men took the lead. They swam side by side and straight for the arrow. The race was not a swift one like running on land—a man swimming in dead water does not go very fast—so of course it took some time for them to reach their goal. The two men swam on side by side each doing his very best, for the prize was worth at least fifty dollars. They both came to the arrow at the same time and each grasped for it at the same moment, and both got hold of it. Each made an effort to wrench it from the other and, as a result, the arrow broke in two. They both started back with his half of the arrow and when they came to the stand, each still holding his half of the arrow, the judge with but very little ceremony decided to divide the prize as equally as possible between them. His decision was satisfactory to both and with a few remarks from one of the speakers and a few thanks to the Great Spirit, the matter was ended and each made his way home.

(*Young Alder was now about fourteen years of age, and was becoming very active and useful as a hunter. It was the custom of the Shawnees from the upper waters of the Scioto, the Maumee, and Mad River to make annual excursions to the salt springs near Chillicothe to make salt. Young Alder, in company with a number of Shawnees, started on a hunting expedition through the Darby and Pickaway Plains in the direction of the salt springs.* He continues: "When we got down on Darby and Paint Creek, bear and deer were very plenty and quite fat. We spent several weeks—or rather moons—there hunting. Indians always count by moons, that being the only way they can conveniently keep time. Our camping places were along the streams wherever a good spring was to be found. On the oak run below the present site of London (Madison County), there is a very large spring, and another not far from it on Paint Creek. These were great camping places. There was also another good spring a few miles north of London on the headwaters of Deer Creek. On the waters of Spring Fork was another great camping place, and also a kind of burying ground. Several Indians were buried near the last-named spring. We traveled back and forth between Big Darby and Paint Creek, gradually moving toward Salt Springs, killing deer and bear almost every day. When we arrived at the springs, we put hunters to roam the forest in search of game so as to keep the salt-boilers in meat. We remained there one or two moons making salt, which was quite a slow process. Our kettles were small—nothing but common camp kettles that we carried with us when we left. The water was not strong, and it took a great amount of boiling to evaporate it and make a little salt. Some families did not make more than a peck in a whole moon. In general, each family had two kettles, one holding about three, and one about eight gallons. Many were there for weeks with but one small kettle. Of course, the process was slow; but whatever they succeeded in making would be their only supply until the next year. From one to one and a half bushels was about as much as one family desired to make.

"There were assembled at the springs several hundred Shawnees, large and small. The same people did not go oftener than once in two or three years. Their trips were regulated by the quantity of salt made when last there, as well as the number in a family to consume it. Many times we would get out of salt before the season to make it would return. In that case, we would either have to go alone to make it, or do without. The latter was almost always the case, as no one family wished to go to the springs alone. A little salt goes a great ways with the Indians. They do not use much salt on their meat, and often none at all; hence, their diet did not agree with the whites, and is at no time palatable to those who have been accustomed to the use of plenty of salt.

"After we got through making salt, we concluded to have a bear hunt. We roamed among the hills up northeast of the salt springs. The region was then the best bear country in the west. The fall was advanced, and it was getting quite frosty and cold. Consequently, it was just the time of the year they were very fat, owing to the fact that pawpaws were ripe and mast was abundant at that season.[81] No Indian will kill a poor bear unless driven to it from necessity. It is not so with deer, elk, and buffalo. Their meat is good for food whether poor or fat, yet, of course, much better when young and fat. One day when we were well up among the hills and bluffs, some one of the Indians treed a bear up a large tree where it had gone into a hole. The Indian's tomahawk was too small to cut down the tree, so we went up the side of the hill, or mountain, and selected a small poplar that we could cut and make fall against a large limb of the bear tree.

"The poplar was cut and fell as described, but when it struck the large tree, we heard it crack and waited some time to see if it would break and fall, but it did not, so we finally concluded it would be safe to ascend it. The next thing was to get someone to climb the small tree and drive the bear out, and as I was the smallest person in the company, it was decided I should go up. I did not like the job—not that I was afraid of anything except the bear. I consented and was instructed to climb the tree and go a little above the bear hole, and take my tomahawk and cut a stick and punch the bear out. I knew this would be a very easy job, for as soon as the stick touched him, he would come out. They told me that when I saw the bear coming, I must climb up the tree a short distance, and the bear would come and, seeing me, go down the tree, and they would kill it as soon as it came into view.[82]

"I stripped myself for the task, fastened my tomahawk to my belt, and began to ascend the poplar. After I had gone about fifteen or twenty feet, they told me to spring up and down so as to shake the tree and see if it was safe. I shook it all I could, and it appeared to be solid. I continued to go up. I got to a large limb and put my hand on it to rest. I looked down, and it appeared a long ways to the ground. After I had rested a few minutes, I again started; but just then, the tree broke off where I was sitting, and down I went with the broken tree! That was about the last thing I remembered until I revived, when I found myself lying on the hillside on my back. I looked up and saw an Indian away up the tree trying to put fire into the bear hole. One of the Indians told him to come down, adding, 'We have got one killed already with that bear, and that is more than all the bears in the woods are worth; we cannot spare another—you had better come down and let him go.'

"Just then, one of the Indians came to me and seeing that I was alive, hallooed back to the others that I had come to. They all gathered around me in a short time, and I never saw people so rejoiced as they were when they found I was not dead. In a short time, I began to talk and answer their inquiries as to how I felt. I told them I felt very badly and did not think I would live, but they all said I would live, and they would take good care of me. They said that after the tree fell, they could see nothing of me; but they cut the brush away and drew me out, and supposing I was dead, had taken me up on the side of the hill and laid me down. While I was lying there, they had cut another tree against the bear tree, and an Indian had gone up to put fire in the hole, but his pole was too short and they had given up, and bruin had, for once, come off with a whole skin after a hard day's work of a half dozen Indians and myself. This broke up the bear hunt so far as that day was concerned.

"The fall had injured my back to such an extent that I could not stand on my feet, so they made a litter for me to lie upon, and when we moved from place to place, they carried me. Sometimes two, and sometimes four Indians would perform that service for me. The litter was made by taking two poles of proper length and connecting them in the middle for about five feet with bark and buffalo robes, somewhat like cords in a bedstead, and on this they would spread bear skins, upon which I was laid. When we were ready to move, four Indians hoisted the litter upon their shoulders, one at each end of the poles, and in this way, carried me a whole day, and then put me down to rest for several days while they hunted, leaving someone to take care of me, and brought in game every day. In this manner, I was finally carried back to the town on Mad River. The Indians, during the whole trip, refrained from murmuring, and did not seem in the least to regret the necessity of carrying me; on the contrary, they performed this hard service with the greatest cheerfulness and treated me, all the time, with the utmost kindness and tenderness, and permitted me to share in the full benefit of the hunt, the same as if I had done my share of the hunting.

"My old mother was very much surprised when she heard I was hurt. She had heard of the accident a day or two before I got home from an Indian who, as usual, had gone ahead to report the approach of our party. She started my Indian father at once to meet our party; and during the whole time I was disabled, no parents could have given more care and attention that I received from them. I did not walk a step until the following March, and then very little. My back was so badly injured that I had to be careful of every step I took, for the least jar or twist would lay me up for weeks. It was several months before I could perform the least service. I, however, gradually outgrew the hurt and, in the course of time, became as stout and active as if it had never occurred.

"The spring of 1786 opened finely, and the Indians raised a good crop and harvested it nicely; but great havoc was made of it before we had time to enjoy the fruits of our labor. It was in the fall after I got hurt that Logan, with a large force of men, made a raid on us; they burned all the Mack-a-chack towns, with all our corn and beans; and made a complete destruction of everything we had; and it would have been a total surprise on our part, and many more Indians been killed, had not one of Logan's men deserted and given the Indians notice of his approach a few hours before."[83] Hill)

(The news of the approach of the Kentuckians was communicated to the Indians by a Frenchman, a deserter from the former. Nevertheless, as the whites arrived sooner than they expected, the surprise was complete. Most of the Indians were, at the time, absent hunting, and the towns became an easy conquest to the whites. Howe)

(All the women and children were sent further up the river to a little town where I was staying, while the warriors made preparations for battle. But when the whites came up, they were too strong for the Indians and consequently killed a great many and took some prisoners. Early one morning, a runner came to our town and told us that a very great army had attacked the Mack-a-chack towns, and that we must hurry and get away as soon as possible, or the army would be right on us. We packed up everything we could carry and commenced our retreat to the northwest. We traveled in that direction for two days and better. Our entire company consisted of women and children, the men having all stayed back to defend our homes and property. I was among the largest of the males and, of course, could carry but little. We retreated until the squaws thought themselves safe and then made a halt, which was beyond the headwaters of the Scioto River.

We suffered terribly for provisions, there was not a man among us and, of course, no person capable of furnishing such a large company with provisions. We stayed there some ten days and subsisted on pawpaws, mussels, and crawfish. The mussels were covered with hot ashes and roasted like potatoes, and when done, the shell was opened and the contents eaten; the tail of the crawfish was pulled off and broiled on the fire coals until the shell peeled off. With a little salt, they were very nice eating.

It was in this way we lived until the warriors came to our relief, and then we all moved to Zanesfield where we remained a short time, and then went to Hog Creek where we wintered.[84] Our chief living there was coon without salt, hominy, or corn, for we had lost everything we had in the way of food. Coon were plenty and fat, and not bad eating for a hungry person. Deer and bear were very scarce owing to the fact that there were so many tribes of Indians living in that part of the country; though sometimes a deer was killed. When we did happen to kill either a deer or a bear, it was quite a treat, and the meat was closely taken care of, and dealt out very sparingly.

In the latter part of the winter, we moved back to within sight of our old town at Mack-a-chack to make sugar, as that was the best sugar country in that region. Sugar is a staple article with the Indians, as well as with the whites, and no season is permitted to pass without making more or less of that article if it is possible to do so. When we arrived at our town, we found but little left; we saw but the ashes of our former cabin, all our choice, beautiful fields of corn had been burned. The ears were all lying in charred heaps; yet we overhauled it to see if there were not some that had escaped the fire that we could parch and eat; but nothing of the kind was found. We remained there during the sugar-making season, and made a good supply of sugar, which was a great help to us through the summer as our means of subsistence were very limited.

In the spring, we removed to the headwaters of Blanchard's Fork,[85] for the reason that we would there be more secure from the raids of the whites. Here we had a hard time indeed; for the camp had to be cleared and huts built, which took so much time that it was very late before we got a crop planted, and for that reason, together with the scarcity of seed, we raised but a small crop, which was more or less injured by the early frost, not having time to ripen before cold weather set in. During the summer, we suffered very much for want of food. With the exception of coon, game was very scarce. Coons were plenty, but very poor. A lean coon is very poor eating, as bad, if not worse, than a poor bear. When we had to rely on small game, it was very difficult to get a sufficient quantity for so large a company under the most favorable circumstances. In our case, it was even worse, for we were so busy preparing for winter that few could be spared to hunt.

Every preparation for winter had to be made during the summer, for as soon as fall came and game began to get fat, we would have to go off where there was plenty to procure our winter's supply. To such an extremity were we driven for food, that we did not even skin the coons for fear of losing some part of them that could be eaten. We generally threw them into the fire to singe off the hair, and then ate them skin and all. Some of them were suckled down so poor that I have frequently seen our dogs refuse to eat them. Yet, for months we were compelled to eat them or starve.

There was a kind of wild potato that grew plentifully in that section of the country which we used to roast and eat; though they were not very palatable, they sustained life.[86] It was owing to the abundance of this very inferior vegetable that we were influenced to stay in that locality. There was plenty of game south of us which we could have had by going for it. But we could not abandon our crops at that season for, in that case, we would have continued the miserable condition we were in the winter before.

It is an invariable rule among Indians to raise a crop of corn, beans, and pumpkins before the hunting season commences. The pumpkins are cut and dried, and put away for winter use, not to make pies as the whites do, but to boil with meat. Dried pumpkins boiled with fat deer meat are about as good eating as a hungry person could wish. After we cleared the ground and got the crop in and partly raised, and our huts built, the hunters scattered in all directions, wherever game was plentiful, to hunt, leaving the squaws to finish and harvest the crop and fill the crevices between the logs of the huts with moss to keep the cold out.[87] Some of the hunters went as far south as Big Darby and Paint Creek. Here they killed deer, elk, buffalo, and bear in great numbers, and dried and jerked the meat, and returned with as much as they could carry, which was no small quantity; for an Indian can carry a larger load of provisions than any other people I have ever seen.

It was in this way they finally got a supply. As soon as they prepared a load of *meat, they came back to the camp, left it, and returned to the hunting ground for another load. By the last of August, we began to live better, and during the fall, we were full and had plenty. Such is Indian life. It is either a feast or famine, as the whites sometimes say. They (the whites) live off the fruit of the farm, but sometimes their crops fail. Yet, if ever a people live on the game of the land when it is plenty and fat, that people are like the Indians. What more delicious eating could a man desire than fat deer, bear, buffalo, elk, or wild turkeys, all of which the Indians frequently had in abundance? Then they were happy, and for all this prosperity, gave thanks to the Great Spirit. Hill)*

(During my stay with the Indians and until after the great victory of Gen. Wayne, we were frequently attacked or disturbed by the whites. In fact, not a year passed without suffering some loss on our part by attacks of the white armies. The fall of the year was generally chosen as the time best suited to march against the Indians, for the reason, perhaps, that then we had our crop raised and preparations made for winter, and if our subsistence was destroyed, we would be reduced to a greater necessity at that season of the year than at others. When all was peace, we enjoyed ourselves freely, but these terrible troubles were attended by the loss of everything the Indian holds dear on earth. Driven from place to place, our favorite hunting ground taken from us, our crops destroyed, towns burned, women and children sent off in the dead of winter, perhaps to starve, while the warriors stood between them and their great enemy—the whites—like a mob only to be shot down. All these things engendered animosities and encouraged retaliation. But the whites were strong and powerful, the Indians were few and feeble. This state of things will account for many, if not all, the cruelties charged to the Indians. I was getting to be an Indian in the true sense of the word, and felt sorely on these occasions and acted as they do—revengeful and hateful to the race. Robbed of their land, their sacred graves desecrated, and the whole race driven farther back into the wild forest, from land that the whites never could have had any claim to whatever. Even the theory of purchase was but another pretext to rob. We had no choice left us but to sell and take what they chose to give or be driven off and get nothing. The price offered was always governed by what it would cost to drive us off, and if the latter cost the least, it would always be resorted to. Beers)

When I was about sixteen years old, the Indians made up a party to go over into Kentucky in the spring to steal some horses from the whites. *(In the spring of 1790, Alder went with a party of Indians into Kentucky*

to steal horses "in retaliation for the destruction of our town and property."
Beers) They coaxed me to go along, flattering me and by saying that I
could get a horse. I had never owned a horse and thought that I
would like to have one, and would also like the trip. (*I had never owned
a horse, but was very desirous of doing so, and did not reflect upon the mode proposed to obtain them. To me, nothing seemed wrong so far as the whites were concerned. We had suffered so much at their hands that all seemed to be fair. I was assured the whites would steal our horses, or anything we had, if they had a chance
to do so. They had several times taken or destroyed all we had, whereby we were almost reduced to a state of starvation. Hence, I felt somewhat like retaliating if I
should have the opportunity. I knew I would like the trip, even if we failed in getting horses. Under these considerations, and with the consent of my old Indian father and mother, I concluded to go with them.* Hill) In the end, nine of us in
all started from Meccocoche [Mequashake] and passed down from
what is now Logan, Union, Madison, Pickaway, and Ross Counties.

We stopped for a day or two on the Pickaway Plains and then
moved on slowly, hunting and drying some meat to pack with us after
we crossed the Ohio River. We came to the Ohio near the mouth of
the Scioto where we stopped for a day and made bark canoes and all
crossed over. This was the first time that I had seen the river since I
had crossed it as a prisoner. As soon as we got over, they took their
tomahawks and cut holes in the canoes and shoved them into the river in order that there should be no sign left that the whites might by
chance discover and then we struck out into the countryside. We
camped that night without fire and we traveled the next day and
night very cautiously. The next day, in the forenoon we came to the
settlement. We could hear the axes chopping at many houses. The
leader of our raiding party said, "Tomorrow is the day. They are all
now out chopping wood for the Sabbath, which is tomorrow. Their
horses are all turned out and in the morning, the men will all be inside about the house." The whites were not out working the following day and so we gathered up thirty-two of their horses and took
them back and tied them in a secret hiding place before nightfall.

We had planned our raid to take advantage of the full moon, and
now had the benefit of its light. By nine o'clock that evening, we had

our horses selected and bridled, and ready to mount. I had taken a mare, a two-year-old colt, and a yearling colt. The leader of our party said that if anyone was not satisfied with the amount of horses that had been taken, then he would give them time to get more, but we all declined. We all mounted and, with the raiding party's leader in the front, rode off in a westerly direction to where he knew a large wagon road would lead us back to the river. We hadn't rode more than half an hour before we struck the path. (*It was what I suppose is now called the Maysville road.* Hill) We started in a full trot and sometimes rode at a gallop. We passed several houses and some of the folks was not yet gone to bed. At one of the houses we passed, there was a big light in the window and the dogs there made a wonderful fuss as we were passing. The man came walking out bareheaded and scolded his dog. The Indians hallooed, "Get out! Get out!" He walked on and came to the yard fence and put his hand on the gate and stood there until we had all passed. We kept that road until about three o'clock in the morning, when we left it and went in a northeasterly direction.

We traveled all that night and throughout the following day when we stopped for the night. We had been now three nights without sleep. After we had eaten, we were preparing to lie down, but a hooting owl commenced howling. The leader of our party also began to hoot. Soon, another owl joined them and all three hallooed thirty-odd times before they finally quit. Our leader thanked the owls over and over very gratefully and then got up, went to his tobacco pouch, took his pipe, and filled it, and then lit it. As he began to smoke, he drew out a few coals from the camp fire and threw some tobacco on them and called upon the Great Spirit to take a smoke with him, frequently thanking him for his great kindness in informing him of the danger that he and the rest of the party were in. After he finished smoking, he got up and told us we must leave. Thirty-odd whites were following us and if we stayed, we would be overtaken; perhaps some of us would be killed. The Great Spirit had been very kind to tell us of our danger, he said, and it would never do to stay there after his warning.[88]

Very reluctantly we bridled and mounted our horses and moved

A History of Jonathan Alder

on. None of us had slept and I got so weary that I would go to sleep on my horse and came close to tumbling off several times. I would get off at every stream and throw water in my face and let it run down my back. But it was all to no purpose, sleep I would. At about eleven o'clock at night, Big Turtle called a halt and said he was not going any further that night, that he was not afraid of owls himself and if there was any that was afraid, they might go on, but he would go no further. I got off and soon so did the rest, one after another. Black Foot, our leader, finally said that if they were all going to stop, that he might as well too, so he dismounted. We haltered our horses and wrapped ourselves in our blankets, and every fellow just laid right down where he dismounted. When I awoke in the morning, the sun was shining and we found our horses all close by, not one more than two hundred yards off. We ate a bite and bridled our horses and started for home, feeling refreshed and like new men.

Crow, one of the Indians that had gone on the raid, had captured a fine, well-gaited, valuable horse. Skunk, another of our Indians, asked him to let him ride the horse that day, saying that he would like to try his gait because the horse seemed to carry himself so well. Crow told him that he might do so and they changed horses for that day. Skunk spent the day gaiting and making the horse show off to the best advantage. Both seemed very proud of the horse. When night came on, we halted and turned our horses loose. After eating a bit and an hour or two of chat, we wrapped ourselves in our blankets and went to sleep. We woke up in the morning and found our horses all close except for Skunk's. Skunk bridled Crow's horse and lashed on his blankets. Then a parley arose about the horse. Crow told him that he couldn't ride the horse that day. Skunk said it was the horse that he had ridden yesterday and he should have him today, and that it was the horse he was going to keep.

Black Foot told them to hunt for the missing horse and to do so quickly, for he wouldn't wait long. Crow started out and sauntered around but didn't go out of sight. He came in directly looking mad. He walked up to Skunk and said to him, "You say that is your horse, do you?" "Yes," said he, very short, "that is my horse." No sooner had

Skunk replied than Crow shot off his gun and hit the horse right through the body behind the shoulders. The horse dropped immediately. Skunk fell to work as fast as possible to get his blankets off, for they were getting bloody. Said he, "Why didn't you tell me you was going to shoot your horse? I would have taken my blankets off and not got them bloody." Crow walked off and made no reply. Skunk got his blanket off and straightened up. Said he, "Men, wait a little till I look for my horse." But Black Foot said, "There lies your horse; you have got no other," and ordered the men to mount. We freely offered our spare horses to Crow and Skunk to ride, for it relieved us of the burden of having to lead them. We all had two and three horses apiece, except for them two, so them two poor fellows came back without a horse.

Later that day, we got to the Ohio River. About noon, we rushed the horses down the bank at a very suitable place to cross where it was hemmed in on all sides. The horses were tired and so gaunted that they seemed to have no disposition to be contrary. We took off all of our blankets and halters and led two or three of the horses into the water. The rest of us got behind the horses with whips and drove them all into the water. Three of four guns was fired and then every horse struck for the other side of the river. We watched them and saw every one go out safe. Then we went up on the bank and peeled an elm, and made a bark canoe. We all put our blankets and guns and clothes in it and one Indian tied a piece of bark to one end of the canoe and put the other end round his neck and struck out for the other side. We all plunged in one after another, so as not to swim in a huddle for fear of getting entangled with each other.

I considered myself a good swimmer but I had never swam a long distance or any deep water, so I was the last one starting in and the last one to cross. I was the youngest one in the company and wished to have the way clear, so I waited until the last one before me had got about four feet from shore and I started in feeling a little timid, but full of faith that I could swim the river. I swam with great ease and it seemed as though I had hardly wet my back. We all came out safe on this side of the river, men and horses. We dressed ourselves and emptied the canoe and sunk it, and then went up on to the bank. We ate a bite and then moved our horses into a suitable place for them to graze a proper distance from the river and then kept a watch back at the river to see if there was anyone after us. After a few days rest to ourselves and horses, and a good supply of fresh venison, we took up our march again for the Indian town on the Mad River. We passed up about the same route that we had went. When we got into what is now Madison County, we lingered along through that area very leisurely, for it was a good chance to graze our horses. So finally we arrived home and, as usual, a meeting was called and the story with our success or misfortune must be told.

My Indian father and mother were greatly elated over my success. I had to give them a full history of all the little particulars that took place. They thought it was a great thing swimming the Ohio River. They seemed to be overjoyed that I had made the trip so safely and so successfully. They also seemed to set great store to the horses, not because they were so valuable, but because they had a son that could venture out so and be so successful, and they were proud of this.

There was one John Bricke that I got acquainted with.[89] It was several years after I was taken prisoner that I saw him. He was taken by the Delaware tribe of Indians. John Bricke was a quick, active boy and fell into the hands of a mighty good family and fared mighty well. The first time I saw him, they came into our town on the Maumee River. I saw quite a large group of these Indians that day and there seemed to be a great deal of excitement among them. I walked up to where they was and they had formed a ring. This white boy was wrestling with the Indian boys and he was throwing every-thing of his size and age and some that was older and bigger. It seemed to please the Indians wonderfully to see the strength and ac-tivity of the little fellow, and he seemed to take a great deal of pride himself in the matter, but made himself in every way very friendly and sociable. They stayed around there several days and him and I got quite intimate. I saw him frequently afterwards until after Wayne's treaty.[90]

Although his home was down in the valley where Columbus now

is, we frequently met one another during our hunting expeditions. After Wayne's treaty, I saw him no more until I met him again in Franklinton.[91] He had left the Indians and gone home and, in the meantime, had learned the hatter trade and came back and set up hatting in Franklinton, and was dressed in the white style. I yet wore the Indian dress. We soon made our first acquaintances and every time we meet yet, we have a talk in the Indian tongue.

Afterwards, he bought a piece of land some eighty acres or more where the Indian village was on the side of the river and moved over there and set up his hatting business, and afterwards sold eight acres of his farm to the state and now the state prison was built on it. He frequently calls and stays a night with me and when I go to Columbus, I either stay with him or Jeremiah Armstrong, another white prisoner that I got acquainted with while a prisoner with the Indians.[92] Armstrong was also taken when a boy from Pennsylvania and brought to Ohio. I got acquainted with him soon after he was taken. Jerry didn't fall into the hands of a very good and kind family. He was not treated like myself and John Bricke. He was taken by the Wyandots who had quite a large village on the east bank of the river right where the new state prison now is. After a time, he was exchanged for other prisoners and got back to his people, and I saw no more of him until I met him after the treaty and peace was made. I also met him at Columbus and we soon renewed our old acquaintances and, like John Bricke, him and I never meet on the street but we have a little chat in the Indian tongue. He bought property in Columbus when it was first laid out and erected a hotel.

Robert Armstrong, a cousin of Jerry's, was also captured in Pennsylvania and raised with the Indians.[93] I became acquainted with him soon after his captivity. He fell into the hands of a mighty good family, stayed with the Indians and, after Wayne's treaty, married a squaw, raised two sons, and had them educated by the whites. One of them was admitted to the bar and practiced law. Robert Armstrong was a man of great intellect. He learned most all of the Indian languages of this section of the country and after peace was made, he frequently served as an interpreter betwixt the Indians and the government. A man of great worth and true integrity, he lived and died with the Indians.

James McPherson was a prisoner and served the Indians in an honorable capacity, both under the British government and after Wayne's treaty.[94] He was strictly honest and kept a store in Lewis Town.[95] The Indians had such undoubted confidence in him that no other man could buy their furs but him.

Traders had frequently cheated the Indians before he went into business as storekeeper and agent, but in a few years, they would buy from no other man nor sell their furs and skins to no other trader. Traders would call on them to buy their furs but they would tell them, "No, we always sell to the agent." If they had offered them ten cents more apiece on coon skins, they couldn't have bought them. They was afraid they would be cheated in the money or in the count. Their confidence in McPherson was such that they never lost it. You could no more make them believe that McPherson would cheat them than a mother would withhold the necessities of life from her small children. When he was removed in 1830, it gave the Indians great dissatisfaction. He married a fellow white prisoner girl and lived and died with them. He died about two or three years after he was discharged as an agent.

It was in the fall four or five years before Wayne's treaty that my Indian mother took sick and died. She was quite elderly, reckoning herself to be somewhere about eighty years old. Her death was a sore loss to Father and I notwithstanding they were both very old. Father and I then lived alone. It doesn't discommode a man amongst the Indians to lose his wife as it does amongst the whites, provided they have no small children, for an Indian man can cook just as well as a squaw.

(*During the border wars between Kentucky and the Shawnees, I have seen many white scalps in the council house after a battle. I have frequently been asked if the British paid the Indians for the scalps they took according to a specific agreement. Had it been true, I certainly would have known of it; but to the best of my knowledge, there was no such agreement, nor did the British pay for the white scalps. I do not know that these scalps were delivered to the British, or even shown* to them, for I saw them stuck up in the council house and remain there until eaten up by worms. After a battle or any other way in which an Indian could take a scalp, there was always a meeting in the council house, and each man exhibited his scalps. They were then counted and the story of each scalp told, how it was obtained, and all the circumstances minutely detailed. Then, the scalps were all stuck up in the roof of the house or hung on a pole, and there remained until they were destroyed by worms or otherwise. The only object I could see in producing scalps was in the name. If an Indian produced many scalps in his wars, he got the reputation of being a great warrior, as that is an Indian's greatest honor. I heard an Indian boasting one day how many scalps he had taken. Tecumseh, the great chief, turned on him and told him he was a low, mean Indian; that more than half the number of the scalps were those of women and children. Tecumseh said to him, "I have killed forty men with my own hands in single combat, but never yet have I taken the life of a woman or child." Hill)[96]

(I was well acquainted with Tecumseh. I sold him a keg of rum one day for a horse; the horse got sick and died, and shortly afterward I told him he ought to give me another horse. He said he had drank the rum up and it was all gone, and he supposed I was about as well off as he was. He said the rum was of no use to either of us, and that he had suffered all the bad consequences of drinking it. He reasoned that the horse had done me as much good as the rum had done him, and perhaps more, but as it was, if I was satisfied, we would quit square, and so we did. This great chief was a man of wonderful intellect; brave, fearless, and of pure integrity. He would do nothing but what was right and would submit to nothing that was wrong. Beers)

It was about one year after my mother died that we took in head to go over into Kentucky to see if we couldn't get us a horse or two apiece, and in making up our company we took in the same Indian, Shawmosh, that I had so many difficulties with. He had now got to be a man and was a shrewd, daring fellow, and they proposed to make him leader. I didn't much like the idea but nonetheless he was chosen, and all things being ready, we started. We hadn't gone but two or three days until we saw that we would have trouble with that fellow. He was lazy and overbearing all the time and always trying to shirk out of duty. We traveled on until about the fourth or fifth day when myself and two of the others began to talk the matter over and to think that we would have to separate. Although we had gotten along so far without any problems, he seemed so ill-tempered and over-bearing that we was afraid we would have trouble with him. One evening we stopped before night and after roasting and eating a hearty meal of fresh venison, he addressed us in about this language. "Now," said he, "you would all like to know what kind of luck we are going to have." We all told him that we would. "Well," said he, "if you will all do as I tell you, I will tell you in the morning what our luck will be." So we all consented to obey him. About sunset, he went out about four rods from our fire and stuck up a stake about ten feet long and then he cleared off all the leaves for about two yards. About dusk, he told us that he was going out to his stake to commune with the Great Spirit and that he didn't want any of us to speak to him after he came in until he first spoke in the morning, nor did he want much talking in the camp amongst ourselves after he came in. If we obeyed him, he would tell us in the morning all about our trip.

About dusk, he got up and walked out to his stake in a very solemn mood. There, he turned his face upward and sang in that po-sition for some minutes. Then he knelt down and prayed to the Great Spirit for protection and information. When he was through, he walked back into camp, laid down, and wrapped himself in his blankets. After he went out to his stake and commenced singing, there was not another word spoken by any of us until the next morn-ing. Like Shawmosh, we all soon laid down and wrapped ourselves in our blankets and fell asleep and there slept soundly until the next morning when we were awakened by Shawmosh telling us to get up. We all arose and seated ourselves to hear what he had to say.

The first thing he told us was that we would separate, that we would not all stick together and that there had been talk already of separating, which was so, and that our trip would be all for nothing. He said the party that he was with would take a prize but that they would lose it again; he said he couldn't tell exactly what kind of prize it would be, some way or another he said he couldn't see it plain and could not tell what it was, but said he would lose it. As for the other party, which would be the largest, they will get nothing—they will have taken their trip all for nothing. But, said he, we will all get back safe, that there would be none of us killed but we would get nothing for our trouble.

We got ready and started on again as usual. Later, we had a private talk, again about the separation and we decided that we would stick with him, let the trouble be what it might and make him out a liar, for we didn't think he knew anything about the future. Some way or another, he seemed to be more cross and ill-tempered and had but little to say in a pleasant way. I soon saw that we had better separate. For the rest of the trip, we divided off in the morning so as not all of us would travel together and would have a better chance of killing game. We also designated where we would meet in the evening. One evening we dropped in one after another at the place designated and Shawmosh was the last one that came in. This was the first day that we had all failed to kill any game but when Shawmosh came in, he had a fresh deer hide. I said to him, "You killed a deer," and he replied, "Yes." "Well," says I, "why didn't you fetch in some of the meat, we have not killed any." Said he, "It was poor, and not fit to eat." I went and picked up the hide and unrolled it and there was fat sticking on the hide. I told him he had lied. Said I, "Here is fat on the hide. It was nothing but laziness not to carry it." He grew very mad, but attempted no violence.

We ate our dried meat that we had intended to eat after we had crossed back over the Ohio River. Later, a few of us talked the matter over in private and concluded that we would separate the next day and that we would not meet at night at the designated place, but Shawmosh got wind of it and in the morning, after we had all got ready to start, he turned and faced us and said he supposed it was arranged for us to separate today. "I don't know who is going with me," he said, and as he turned to go, I saw tears running down his cheeks. He started from camp and there was only one other Indian that followed him; the rest, five in number, stayed back until they was out of sight and then we turned a little more westward and struck the river lower down, and crossed over and made our way out into the settlement. After we got into the settlement, we prowled round there a part of two nights, but there appeared to be no horses turned loose to the commons. We gave up the hunt and made our way back and crossed the river without a single horse. This time we crossed the river on a raft made of dry logs, floating down the river a long distance before striking the other shore. Then we made our way back slowly, hunting as we went. Deer was plenty and fat, and we stopped at all the Indian towns and villages we passed to sell our hides and furs as we had no horses to pack them on.

We got back to our town late in the fall, all without any serious trouble or difficulty. In ten or fifteen days after we got in, Shawmosh and his man came in and, as usual, called the village together and told of their trip. They crossed the river and made their way out to a different settlement than the one we had been through. Shawmosh said they searched around for two nights, but could find no horses running at large. Then, they tried some of the stables but found them all locked. They got discouraged and started for home. In passing a new settlement they found by the noise of axes and hallooing that the whites was raising a new house. It was then close to noon, so they concluded they would wait and waylay the path and as soon as the whites went to dinner, they would catch a Negro. Shawmosh said that the whites would go ahead and the Negroes would be some considerable distance behind; so they found the trail and secreted themselves close by. Not long after, the woman bellowed, "Hoo-Hoo," and all the men at the building hallooed, "Hoo!" and directly the men all came stringing along. After they had passed a hundred or two hundred yards, the Indians saw two Negroes coming. They ran ahead of the two and caught one, but he was a very stout fellow and he fought and hallooed so they had to let him go.

Because they had made themselves known, they thought it best to get back across the river as soon as possible. Now, a slave amongst the Indians or taken prisoner by them was a great prize. He would go to a chief or a great warrior a great deal readier than a horse. Many Indians considered slaves more valuable than horses, not because they were more useful, but because of the honor of having a slave.

Shawmosh was killed a few years afterwards in a battle. He was the making of a great warrior.

During my stay with the Indians, we was harassed and disturbed with armies more or less every year until after Wayne's great victory, generally in the fall of the year. In the fall of one year, a considerable force came out from Kentucky and attacked the towns at Macochec [Mequashake]. The women and children were run off and the Indians stood a fight, but the whites proved too strong and the Indians had to retreat. During the fight, there was six Indians that barricaded themselves in one of the houses and when the Indians fell back, it was not easy for them to fall back with the others. More than that, they seemed to be doing a very good business in the way of their own defense, but after the rest of the Indians had been dispersed that was not taken prisoner, the whites surrounded this house and had them six Indians completely cooped up, but the great trouble was to get at them. When they tried to storm the house, some were picked off every time. At last they resorted to a little stratagem and shot fire into the roof of the house. The Indians were compelled to break out, but instead of surrendering themselves up, they tried to make their escape. Four was shot down, but two got between some logs and killed six of the whites before they were killed. The loss of the whites during the battle was considerably more than that of the Indians. During their retreat, the Indians carried off their dead and wounded, all except the six that was in the house. As soon as the fight was over, the whites were in a great hurry to get away for fear of a reinforcement of the Indians. Not wishing to leave their dead unburied, but having no (or at least very insufficient) tools to bury them with, they went to one of the large quagmires near by there and cut the turf around, making a hole about five feet in diameter, and dropped their dead all in that hole, both whites and Indians. This story we partially learned from the prisoners the whites took after they were exchanged. The balance of the account I got from Simon Kenton, who was commanding officer in the fight, which I will speak of hereafter.

I was now drawing towards manhood and I had become accustomed to all their ways and habits of diet and lodging and had become perfectly reconciled and satisfied with my fate. I had lost all desire to return to my native home. My health was good and I was growing stout and active, and had the universal goodwill of all that knew me. I was also getting very expert in hunting, in which I took a great delight, for in some instances, it provided a great deal of sport. In the fall of the year, after bear would become fat, it was not uncommon to come upon an old she-bear with four cubs, which is usually the number she raises, and shoot the old one and then take a ramrod and take after the cubs and commence whipping them. They will immediately tree and then you go to loading and shooting, and so you would have the whole litter all done in the space of half an hour. Sometimes, if there would be two of us together and we came across an old she and her cubs, we would shoot the old one, throw down our guns and draw our tomahawks, and then see who could tomahawk the most cubs, which, at the time, was great sport.[97]

Another practice that we used to take deer in the forepart of the summer was to make a deer blate and blate up a doe that had a fawn, which was a very easy thing and very common amongst young hunters, but I got completely cured of that one day.[98] I was out on the Maumee River in one of the large spice brush bottoms. I had my deer blate, and I commenced blating. Now a doe will leave her fawn when it is quite young after hiding it in some secret place and go off to feed. After some considerable time, I noticed the spice brush shaking some distance away. It would stop and then I would blate again, and it would start and come a little further and stop. I would blate again and so on until it got quite close. I squatted down behind a large bush in order not to be seen until I could call it up close to me. It seemed to come very cautiously, more so than common. I would blate a little every now and then, and it came right to the opposite side of the same bush that I was behind. I could see the brush shaking, but the deer didn't appear to be moving. The brush was so thick that I couldn't see it, so I gradually raised up and, to my great horror, there was a huge panther, his tail whipping from side to side. This was what had kept the brush shaking. His feet were all on the motion, just as you have when a cat is about to pounce onto a bird. In less than a minute, if I hadn't risen up, he would have been on me. I was so scared that I never thought of shooting, but hallooed with all my might. I guess the panther was about as bad scared as I was for his first leap must have went twenty feet. He went off in a hurry and I left the chase for that day. There was no more deer blating by me that summer.

This country that is the state of Ohio (for I believe I never was out of it after my captivity) abounds with all kinds of game and wild animals. There was none that was particularly dangerous except that which was wounded and you crowded onto him. The wolf was the most likely of any to attack a person. The wolf and the rattlesnake was two that an Indian didn't like to trust. I once went out with Swank to keep camp for him while he hunted. One evening in the dead of winter, he was late coming in. He had gotten far off that day. He had killed some game and in skinning and hanging it up out of the way of the wolves, he was delayed. I suppose that it was ten or eleven o'clock at night before he got in. Directly after dark, I heard the wolves begin to howl and bark. They were a mile or more off when I first heard them, but I soon found that they were coming closer. I expected Swank every minute and kept a very anxious lookout for him, but no Indian appeared. The wolves, though, came closer and closer.

I was quite young, this was before I had commenced hunting by myself, and of course I had not a gun. I had no weapon at all except my bow and arrows, which all boys have as soon as they are large enough to draw the bow, which is quite young. This was a poor thing to fight the wolves with. They finally came up within about a hundred yards and set up a wonderful yelling. I could hear them snapping their teeth and occasionally one would come so near that I could see the shine of his eyes. I shot away all my arrows and don't know whether I hit any or not. I finally covered up the fire (which was the wrong move) and tore down my tent and doubled up the cloth and stretched it out full length. Then I lay down on one end and rolled over and over until I had rolled the whole tent-cloth round me, thinking it would take them a good while to tear it to pieces. I had not laid long until I heard Swank coming. There was a heavy crust on the snow and I could hear him walking three or four hundred yards off. I then began to unroll myself. Presently he hallooed to know if I was alive and I answered. He told me to stir up the fire and soon he came up and fired off his gun into the thickest of them and threw some firebrands at them, and they soon left. He wanted to know how the tent came to be torn down and I told him what the object was. He laughed at me and told me I had taken the wrong course. Instead of covering up the fire, he said I should have built up a large one and thrown firebrands at them. He told me then that if I was ever caught in that fix again to build up a large fire and go to throwing fire at them and there was no danger, for a wolf wouldn't stand fire. That was the closest attack that the wolves ever made on me. They would frequently strike my trail late in the evening when I was out hunting and follow me for miles, barking and howling on my track.

The Indians have a great many superstitions and prejudicial notions about things and one is in regard to the wolf. In all kinds of hunting, you are liable to shoot at game and miss. If an Indian shoots at a bear, deer, or buffalo and misses, he thinks nothing of it, but if he shoots at a wolf and misses, he thinks that the wolf has put a spell on his gun that will last for five or six moons—your gun will shoot wide for about that length of time before the spell wears off. You are liable to miss and lose a great deal of your game in that time unless you unbreech your gun and scour and wash it thoroughly clean. I have often seen them unbreeching their guns and asked them what was the matter. The answer was "Well, I shot at a wolf the other day and I guess I must have missed him, for my gun hasn't shot right since." I believe I have done the same myself and that is one reason that they hardly ever shoot at a wolf, for fear they might miss him. This is one reason I think that wolves are a little more bold than they would be otherwise. Another thing that I often noticed was that a squaw with a papoose in her arms, if she is going out after night, in passing from one camp to another or from one camp to home, will invariably go to the fireplace and take up a little dry ashes and sprinkle them on the child's head. What this was for I cannot tell, for I never asked.

There is a great many different kind of feasts they make and one is a feast to the dead.[99] This feast is calculated to be made about once a year. Sometimes a single family will make the feast if it is not convenient for several families to join together. They will pick some convenient ground and stretch up a large tent, and then, in the afternoon, they will cook and prepare their victuals, for these feasts are all eaten after dark. They are firmly of the opinion that their dead relatives come and feast with them just as they do when they are living. How often I have went to these feasts with my father and mother and witnessed the solemnity of them. The victuals is all prepared, and generally a good variety of it. A fire is built at this tent to make light with. A committee is appointed to make all the preparations and to see that there is no dogs about. About dark, the Indians will commence gathering in with their supper already cooked.

After they have all got in, some old man will get up and state the object of the meeting, something like this. After thanking the Great Spirit for the many blessings they have received since last they feasted with their dead relatives and friends, he says, "We have now met together again to feast with our friends that are dead and gone; we can't meet and see each other and talk face to face, for we can't see a spirit with the natural eye. But they can see us and hear us talk, and we can eat and feast with them while they can hear and see all what is going on." He then appoints a few to take a smoke and talk about their relations that have died and their friends generally, which, in fact, makes it quite a solemn meeting. After the victuals had set out in the dark for perhaps an hour or two, the head Indian gets up again and tells them that he reckons the dead has had time to eat and now we will eat what is left. He appoints someone to carry in the victuals and place them before the seated company and then he bids them all eat. For fear that some of the young folks might be a little skeptical about the spirits eating (the bowls and dishes was always as full when they was brought back as when they was taken out), he tells them that the spirits can eat and be filled and still there will be no less victuals in the bowls and dishes. After supper was over, the old man would return thanks to the Great Spirit and then dismiss us.

My Indian father enjoined it upon me to make him a feast every year as long as I lived, if I should outlive him, and said he would always come to my feast. I frequently think of it but after I became naturalized with the whites, I have never made, nor gone, to a feast of that kind. I would gladly do it if I thought he would meet with me.

We took it in our heads one fall to go over into Kentucky again and see if we couldn't capture some horses. After making up our company, which consisted of five Indians and myself, we started from the Mad River, passed down the usual trail from Upper Sandusky to the saltworks, and from there to the Ohio River. We crossed over in bark canoes and struck out through the countryside for the settlements. We passed a cabin a long distance this side of the settlements, but passed round as we didn't wish to disturb anyone. The day before we came to the settlement, we passed another cabin in the woods, but went around it as we did the other and got into the settlement before dark.

We began to look for horses, but somehow we were discovered. The first thing we know, the whites were on horseback and we struck for the woods and entered a cane patch. We stayed there a while, but the Indians soon left me as they were all men and I was but a boy. The cane was very tall and it was difficult to run a horse through it. The whites came so close to me that I could hear their horses' feet right behind me. I stopped and set my gun down and turned around to give myself up, supposing that they would see that I was white and take me prisoner, for it was not yet quite dark. But when I looked back, they were not in sight. The road had forked a couple of hundred yards back and the front ones had taken the other fork of the road.

I jerked up my gun and ran again, and didn't go far until I saw the cane shaking where the Indians had turned out of the path, so I turned out and followed the shaking cane and didn't go more than six or eight rods until I came up with them all standing in a huddle very much scared. I had just reached them when the whites and their horses passed round us on both sides in a full gallop. We sat right down where we was until after dark. A short while after dark, we heard a bell rattling. We all got up and got back into the path and listened to the bell for a while. "Now," said the head Indian, "that is all a trick to catch us, one that has often been played. They will take an old, worthless horse out and spangle him and then surround him and watch.[100] If we were to go there, we would be shot down. The best thing that we can do is to make our way back to the river as soon as possible. The whole settlement is now watching that horse, so we can make our way out of here with safety for they are not watching any place else, only there." So we took the path and struck out.

We traveled on until a late hour, finally lying and sleeping until the break of day when we rose and moved on. A while before dark, we came to this last cabin that we had passed as we was going in and so we halted and counseled a while. The Indians concluded that, as they had been discovered and had missed their object, they would wait until after dark and kill the folks in the cabin. There was some objection to that as it might be hazardous and some of the Indians might also be killed, but the head Indian said that if you rouse a man out of a sound sleep, then he was only half a man and that it would be an easy matter to overcome them. They said that they would do something that the whites would remember them by, so it was settled that the family should be murdered that night.

Some of them slipped up about dark and reconnoitered the house and premises and then slipped back about half a mile. There, they waited until about eleven or twelve o'clock getting ready before starting for the slaughter. I dreaded what was to come and hated being a part of it, but I saw no way of escape. It had grown cloudy just before evening and it was very dark, so we crept along very cautiously and sly until they thought that they had gone far enough to be near the house. Then, they wandered around the house for half an hour or more in a huddle to council. Being a boy, I never engaged in their council. The head Indian made some remark like this: "If you recollect, it was a clear day all day until just before sundown and then it clouded over. The Great Spirit doesn't intend that we shall kill these people, so we may as well leave, for we will not find them."

I was standing about a rod from the crowd and heard the cabin door screak and open as plain as I ever heard anything. In about the space of a minute, I heard it screak again and shut. Well, I must acknowledge that I fairly shook and trembled for I expected in two minutes or so to witness the horrid and bloody dead. But the Indians kept talking and I was soon satisfied that none of them had heard the noise. We had already passed to one side of the house and beyond it in the direction that we was going. Finally, the head Indian gave the word to move on. If I had told them what I heard, that poor family would have all been butchered that night.

We moved on and was soon out of hearing. We traveled a mile or so and laid down to sleep, as we didn't wish to be near the cabin, in case we overslept and then we might be caught and harm would befall us. We arose up early in the morning and passed on. About noon, we came to the other cabin that we had first passed going out. When they saw it, they made no halt, but all started running. When they came to the door, they kicked it open and ran in. I stopped outside at the yard fence, but there was no one there. Everything looked as if the settler had just left that morning. The Indians took the straw bed out and ripped it open and carried off the tick and bed clothes.

We traveled on that day and, just at night, we came to a lick where it seeps out a little brackish salt water. Here, we found some horses that had strayed off from the settlement and, with a good deal of stratagem, we caught us a horse apiece though none of them were very valuable. We came to the river, which was very low and drove the horses in on a ripple. They waded a portion of the way and swam the balance. We gathered some dry logs and made a raft by lashing them together with grapevine. We paddled over and caught our horses, and all was safe.

We spent the balance of the fall in hunting. We passed through the west side of the Scioto River stopping awhile on the bottoms where Columbus now is. There was large fields of corn and an Indian town on the east side of the river where the new state prison is, which I will speak of hereafter. Then, we struck up betwixt the river and Big Darby. There was a great beech crop that fall and bear was very fat and fine. We killed bear and deer and by the time we got back onto the Mad River, our horses was well loaded with skins.

We had arrived back safely without any serious trouble and the one thing that gave me great consolation was that we had made the trip and they had neither killed nor hurt anyone. I was very careful never to tell them how I heard that door open and shut for fear they might think I was not a true partner.

I was now bordering close onto manhood. One morning my old Indian father called me and told me that I was now near the age that young men should be free and doing for themselves. I now had the right to come and go and stay where I pleased and was not under any restraint whatsoever, particularly from himself and my mother. "But," said he, "if you choose, you can stay with us as long as we live and then we may eat of your venison and bear meat and oil, which will be a great consolation to us in our old days. But all the profits arising from the sale of your skins and furs shall be yours. I shall still draw my rations of clothing, and blankets, and powder, and lead from the British government and you shall always have what we don't need."

I thanked them both very kindly for the liberty they granted me, but told them I had no desire to leave them; that I preferred to stay with them as long as they lived if I should outlive them; that they had been very kind and good to me and that I would feel an obligation to them as long as I lived. "My white mother I have almost forgotten and, of course, I shall never see again," I told them. "I accept you as my parents. I acknowledge myself to be your son by adoption and am under all obligations to you as such." My mother came up to me and held out her hands. She was so overcome that she did not speak, but I saw that her eyes were full. My father came forward and shook hands with me without saying anything more. I must acknowledge that my feelings were greatly agitated, for everything had happened so unexpectedly. To avoid any further outbursts of feeling I picked up my gun and shot pouch and went off hunting. I must confess that the thought that I was now my own man, free to go and come, and act, and do for myself agitated my mind more or less all day. I had been free before, but this seemed to be a new era in my life. I killed a deer in the afternoon and carried it off. Everything seemed to be cheerful and pleasant, but there seemed to be a different feeling with us such as I cannot express. From this time on when I would sell my skins

A History of Jonathan Alder

and furs, I had a purse of my own and kept the money and bought my own clothes.[101]

I had become a great favorite amongst the young folks, both male and female. I was very active on foot. I never saw but three Indians who could outrun me running footraces; hopping and jumping was also a great sport with the boys and young men and even the old men engaged in footracing. Singing and dancing was a great amusement amongst the young squaws and young men. I was counted a good singer and always was called upon to sing at their dances, which both sexes commonly hold. There are also other amusements, such as gambling. In the game "pay of ponds," they will take six moccasins and place them in a row. One of the players will take a bullet between their fingers and run their hand into every moccasin and leave the bullet in one. The other player has the right to pick up two of the moccasins; if they get the bullet, then they have won the wager (whatever it is) and if they miss, then the one who handed the bullet has won the pond, or wager.[102] When both sexes are engaged in any of these games, they place little burdens, or duties, on each other, such as bowing, kneeling, or kissing each other, anything to make the play amusing or interesting. There is, perhaps, as great a variety of different games amongst the Indians as there is amongst the whites.

There is a great many of their customs and practices that are similar to those of the whites, but their mode of courtship and marriage is very different from ours. A squaw is just as likely to go sparking as is a man and it is just as respectable as it is for the man. She will make her business known to you and if it is acceptable, when bedtime comes she goes to bed with you. There is no setting and losing sleep. And the same thing happens when a man goes to see a squaw. He makes his business known to her and she makes the necessary arrangements, and the two lies together. Some might suppose from this that they were not so virtuous as white folks, but that is not the case. Illegitimate children is not a common thing with them.[103]

After their marriage, they are not bound to live together any longer than they can agree.[104] Separations frequently take place, but I think not oftener than with the whites. If a young squaw's husband dies, you will not see her out at any of the feasts or large gatherings for a whole year. After her year is up, she will be out at the next feast all dressed in her very best. Some other Indian that is in the habit of speaking will take her onto the stand with him and relate the circumstances of her loss and announce that she is ready to receive the company of anyone she wishes.

An Old Indian Dies, 1792

My father, now somewhere near ninety years old, was getting quite old and his health was failing him fast. He thought he would like to take a trip with me down to the saltworks thinking that perhaps it would improve his health, though he said he would not live long, and that a year or so, or even just a few moons, might end his days. We got ready in the latter part of the summer three years before Wayne's great victory and started.[105] We traveled slowly, frequently staying six or eight days at one place. We traveled in company with others that had a pack horse to carry our kettles and tent cloths. We passed down through what is now Madison County and camped at the big spring below London. We remained there half a moon and killed a heap of deer, dried jerk, and stretched and dried the skins. Finally, we passed on to the salt spring and commenced boiling salt.

We had been here, I reckon, about two moons. I saw that my father was getting more feeble and more helpless. His limbs were swelling and he was bloating up. One morning he told me that he was out of tobacco and that I would have to go to Upper Sandusky and get him some more, as he could not do without it. He was a great smoker. The Indians never chew tobacco, but some of them are great smokers. I started immediately that morning, but I was satisfied that he was not going to live a great while. I took my gun, tomahawk, butcher knife, and blanket and started on foot. It took me about fifteen days to make the trip, but when I got back, my father was dead and buried. He died with the dropsy about two days after I left.

I was now left comparatively alone in the world. I had no one to care for, nor no one to care for me. I had lost a warm and kind father and mother and I missed them very much. My father and mother had taken a great deal of close attention and care for my welfare and they have always been held gratefully in my remembrance. I stayed at the saltworks until the crowd got ready to go back and went back with them.

After my father's death, I wandered far and wide, more than I had done before. The number of my acquaintances was greatly extended and I became a great favorite with both the young and old, and I attended all their feasts and dances.

Barshaw, the sister of Big Turtle (she was somewhat older than I), was a squaw of great ingenuity and handy with her needle on all kinds of fine work. She made and sold a great many moccasins that was very ingeniously covered with beads and porcupine quills of different colors. She would make pictures of birds, squirrels, deer, or bear and then very readily sell them to the French and British at a high price. I began to occasionally pay my respects to her when I would be in the village at Upper Sandusky. But as her occupation required her in the village and mine in the forest, we didn't get to see each other very often.

I decided to seek out a location for hunting operations in the fall and as the Darby Plains seemed to be the best for all kinds of game, I struck out for the Big Darby alone. I started about the time that acorns was getting ripe. I had got down into what is now Union County, taking the Indian trail from Upper Sandusky to the salt springs. Along about noon, I spied a monster of a bear up in the top of a large white oak, picking off and eating acorns. I didn't wish to kill him, as bears were not yet fat and their fur was not yet come to its full growth, so I sat on the ground about a hundred yards from the tree to watch his motions. It was amusing to see him get around in the tree top. As he would move from place to place, the whole tree top would shake with him. Finally, he slid down the tree and commenced picking up the acorns that he had scattered off. All at once he looked up and came straight towards me, straight as a line. I had my gun laying across my lap and I saw he would run right over me. I hadn't time to get out of his way. I raised my gun and cocked it as quick as I could and fired. He was then almost on me. I shot him right through the brains as he was making his last jump. He fell right across my lap; I tell you I was scared. I kicked and scrambled to get out from under him, but I had shot him so dead that he never kicked and he was so heavy that I had hard work to get from under him. I didn't stop to see if he was dead until I got loose from him. I camped at the nearest water and skinned my bear and feasted a couple of days on him.

Next, I passed on down into what is now Madison County and pitched my tent near where Pleasant Valley now is, a little higher up the creek near a spring. I remained here during the fall and it proved to be a fine hunting ground; deer was plenty and there was a fine mast of oaks and bush betwixt Darby and the Scioto, a fine bush country. Deer got fat and bear got fat, and I would carry my skins down to the village where Columbus now is and there I could always find traders to buy them.

I had made a fine fall hunt. Late in the season, I went back to Upper Sandusky. I was now doing for myself and was able to dress myself in good Indian style. I remained there during the winter and joined in the sports and games and feasts and occasionally spent an evening with my Barshaw.

The next spring, I bought me a pack horse and started early while the furs was yet good. I packed up my tent cloth and my beaver traps, as I had discovered that beaver was very plenty along Paint Creek. I went immediately down into Paint Creek a few miles below where London is, to a fine spring where I pitched my tent and went trapping for beaver. I done a fine business here in the way of catching beaver and otter and hunting throughout the day for deer, which was also plenty. I remained here throughout the trapping season, occasionally taking a trip over to the village on the Scioto to sell my furs and skins. When the summer season came on, I moved up on Darby to fire hunt in the creek.

There was a kind of moss that grew in the head of the creek underwater as round as a woolen roll that comes from a carding machine. The deer was very fond of this, and it grew very plentiful. We would make bark canoes and then fix what we called a shade board in front and put a lighted candle into that, and then sit behind it. We could push right up to a deer, frequently within ten or fifteen feet of them. Of all the ways to take deer, this was the easiest and the surest. We generally calculated to shoot at the first convenient distance. As we shove up to them, they can see nothing but the light. If we got very close, it blinded them and they frequently made right for the light. I have frequently had them jump right into the canoe onto me and sink me in the creek. It is always warm weather when we fire hunt and I would very often have my leggings off and my thighs and legs all bare. The first thing I would know, I would feel a snake running across my thighs. They would see the light and make for it and come to the canoe and swim right up into it, and across, and out on the other side; many a one I have killed with my pushing pole when I would see him coming.[106]

This time I concluded to stay on Darby all winter. Coon was very plentiful between Darby and the Scioto and by staying, I would be ready to trap them early in the spring. I moved my tent down the creek and onto the east side. There was a very good spring at this site, down at the water's edge and a little below what is now the Foster Chapel and graveyard, but on the opposite side of the creek on the farm that is now owned by Knowlton Bailey. I pitched my tent right on the same ground where Bailey's house now stands.

Along during the winter, there came a little light skift of snow. It was very clear and the moon was visible about noonday. At night, it was almost as light as day. I had pulled off my moccasins to go to bed when I saw an otter coming swimming down the creek. While I was in the door of my tent, I reached and got my gun to shoot him, but as soon as he saw me move, he dived under the water. I knew about what distance he would be under the water, which was about a hundred yards. I hadn't had time to put on my moccasins, but I run down the creek about the distance that he would naturally come up for air. He came up, but he was so quick that he went under again before I could shoot. So I run again and the same thing happened again. That otter took me down the creek about half a mile in the snow bare-footed to a high bank and there I lost him. Well, I never felt my feet being cold until I had lost the otter, then I discovered that my feet were getting very cold. My excitement was so great that I had not felt the cold during the chase. I made my way back to the tent as fast as possible, but by the time I got back, my feet were almost frozen.

A few days after my otter chase, I stepped on a honey locust thorn and ran it into my foot. It swelled so bad and became so painful that I was not able to walk on that foot for about fifteen days. About the same time, it commenced snowing and the snow fell about half a leg deep, and it was only with great difficulty that I could get to the spring and back for water. After it had snowed, it rained and then turned very cold and froze a thick crust on the snow. At about the same time, two Indian boys dropped in my camp. I readily took them in, for I was in a very helpless and sad condition. In preparing my tent and fixing for winter, I had neglected hunting and my stock of provisions had got quite low. These two boys were not more than about fourteen years of age and were not well experienced in hunting. In fact, the crust was so thick and hard on the snow that it made so much noise in walking that it was impossible for them to get near enough to a deer to kill when they hunted. They hunted for ten or fifteen days without killing a single deer. We were on short allowances for five days when our provisions run out and for the after, we had nothing to eat.

The third day of our fast the boys came in about the middle of the afternoon very much fatigued and very much discouraged. I told them that I had killed a wolf the day before that had come trotting along up the creek on the opposite side. I was sitting in my tent door and saw him coming up the creek. I reached and got my gun and fired at him, and he dropped right in his tracks. The boys said they had heard an old man say that a wolf ate tolerable well when one was hungry, so they went over and skinned the two hind quarters and brought them over. We sliced off some meat and stuck it before the fire to roast. The boys were so hungry they began eating theirs as soon as the blood was out of it. I roasted mine thoroughly done and took it up and tried to eat of it, but it was so strong that I couldn't swallow it. Then I scarified it both ways and thought I would roast it into a crisp and perhaps that the strong taste would leave it. Before I got ready to try it again, we heard a deer begin to blate up the creek. In a moment, the two boys grabbed their guns and started. I told them to stop. "There is a wolf who has got a deer," said I. "He will soon kill it. But if you go now, you will scare him off and perhaps you will not get the deer." So they stopped and presently the deer began to blate weaker and weaker. In about fifteen minutes, the boys left and returned with a spike buck. They said the wolf had just got it killed and torn a hole in the flank and commenced eating when they got there. When he saw them coming, he stepped off a little, looked at them and then trotted off. They didn't offer to shoot him.

There is a large pond just east of Thomas Timmon's house in the bottom betwixt the creek and the hill. After the snow, this pond had frozen over and the ice was smooth and slick. As the deer attempted to cross it, he slipped and fell and the wolf caught him. According to our notion of things, the Great Spirit provided this deer for our relief, for which our thanks was duly returned and the wolf, who was an instrument in his hands, received his share.

Before that venison was eaten up, there came a thaw. The boys could now kill deer and my foot got well, so I could also hunt. We had no more trouble about meat. The boys stayed with me until spring and then left. I commenced preparing my coon traps towards the latter part of winter, so as to be ready as soon as there was a general thaw.

We made a kind of deadfall trap along the small branches and around the ponds where the coons resort for the purpose of catching frogs and crawfish. An Indian, if he traps for coon, plans to set about one hundred traps beginning about the first of March. Throughout March and April, he will catch about one coon for every trap. I got my traps all ready early and in good order by the time spring opened.

I also used my beaver traps along Darby for otter, of which I caught a fine lot. I also done a fine business in catching coons and found a ready market over at the town on the Scioto. (*Their traps were of the deadfall construction, and a good hunter could set about one hundred traps a day. These traps were expected to average about one coon each, sometimes more, owing to the location, the luck, and the experience of the hunter setting and attending them. The deadfall was placed on a log leading into a pond and supported by a figure-four treadle, upon which a piece of frog or other meat was fastened as a bait in such a manner that, when the animal attempted to pass or remove it, the trap would fall upon, wound, kill, or hold it until the hunter came up. Coon were very fond of frogs, and would approach the center of ponds on fallen timber to capture them. But by the wiles and inventions of the red man, they became the victims. Hill*)[107]

The word Scioto is not the proper name for that river. Its proper name is Scinutu, but because it is difficult for the whites to give it the right sound, they called it Scioto.[108] The Indians' original name for Little Darby was Sycamore Creek, from the great quantity of sycamore trees that grew there. Big Darby's name is Crawfish Creek, from the large quantity of crawfish that was in its waters. It was named Big Darby by the white surveyors who named it after an Indian of that name who they found living on it near its mouth. When they commenced entering and surveying the land and came to Little Darby, they also named it, but their true Indian names are Sycamore Creek and Crawfish Creek.

I remained hunting on Big Darby, Little Darby, and the Scioto until fall, when runners came saying that there was a probability that a large army would be brought to bear against the Indians.[109] It was necessary that all the Indian forces be collected together. All the Indians from this section was leaving for the scene of action, which would probably take place soon, somewhere on the Maumee River. I gathered up all of my effects that I had not already sold and went up to the Macache town [Mequashake], and soon found that there would be a conflict betwixt the whites and the Indians.

The Indians had been so successful against General St. Clair that they had made no other plans but that they were going to have the same results with General Wayne. But it turned out to be very different. Little Turtle and one other chief was for making a treaty of peace, but the majority overruled them, and were now quickly completing their preparations for war.

The Indians never insisted on my taking up arms against the whites, but always left that to my own choice. Consequently, I never was in any battle except a little while in the first conflict of this great battle. They had flattered me that it was going to be an easy victory and but short duration, and that Wayne was rich with horses, blankets, and clothing of all kind. If I didn't wish to take part in the fight, I needn't do so.

When our army got ready to move, I started with them. General Wayne had been moving gradually upon us, but cautiously and safely. There hadn't been a night after he got within a hundred miles of us but what there was Indian spies within his pickets. They said when he was on the march, every evening he would so fortify that there was no chance to even get a horse out of his camp. We had reports every day from the spies and the runners. He would chop down trees and so build them up into a fence sufficient to hold his whole army, horses, baggage, and everything. There was no possible chance to get anything out without removing the logs which was whole trees, and that would have required a number of men and some time. But when our Indians got into Fort Recovery, they thought that this was the proper place to attack.[110]

Chief Blue Jacket was commander in chief and decided to move upon General Wayne's encampment.[111] When we got within about two or three miles of the fort, the first thing I heard was exciting. I heard the whites hallooing, "Indians! Indians!" We had come onto about two hundred of Wayne's light horsemen, and the Indians on horseback made for them.[112] Now, there was a mighty rush by all the American horsemen and footmen towards the fort and the Indians run them so close that there was, I reckon, as many as fifty horses that the whites sprung off of and got into the fort as best they could. These horses was left running at large outside the fort, and was finely equipped with saddles, bridles, and horse pistols.[113] The fort was soon surrounded and a furious fire kept up on both sides for an hour or so. (*Simon Girty and the McKees, father and son, were in the fight, and Thomas McKee killed Captain Hartshorn of the American forces.*[114] Beers)

I thought here was my chance to get a horse already equipped, if I could only catch one. I got within about two hundred yards of the fort behind a tree. These horses were very much frightened and running in every direction. Several times they would come and stop close by me, almost near enough for me to reach the bridle, but whenever I would move towards them, they would be off. I saw several other Indians who were running half bent over after the horses who would go up within fifty yards of the fort and then take a circle round and out again.

An Indian that stood behind a tree close by asked me why I didn't shoot; he was loading and shooting as fast as he could. I told him I didn't see anything to shoot at. "Shoot those holes in the fort," he said, "you might kill a man." I told him I didn't want to shoot. "Well then," said he, "you had better get out of here. The first thing you know, you will be shot." Said he, "Didn't you see the bark fly a little above your head there a little bit ago?" "Yes," I told him. "Well," said he, "if you ain't going to shoot, you had better fall back out of reach before you are shot."

He kept loading and shooting, but all at once as he poked his head out to shoot, down dropped his gun and I saw him clasp one hand to his chin and then stoop and pick up his gun with the other. Then he run half bent as far as I could see him. The Americans had made a flesh wound on his chin. I stood there alone and it wasn't but a few minutes until I heard a cannon go off away out behind me. I began to feel pretty badly scared. I thought that we were surrounded. While I was in this quandary, I heard another cannon go off in the fort and directly a shell burst right over my head and the pieces flew all around me. Then I understood what the report was out back.[115] Finally, I started and ran back to the crowd. After a little council, they decided that they was not able to take the fort by storm, but they would try to take it by surprise after night. We moved off down the river about a mile and camped. In wandering about to find some of

A History of Jonathan Alder

my company, I came across one of Wayne's pack horses, so I haltered him and concluded that at least I had a horse, come what may.

We built our fire and lay in a circle.[116] About midnight, I was awakened by the roar of the guns. It was such a continuous roar that I couldn't hear one gun from another. I arose and looked around. I could see but five or six Indians lying in the circle where I lay, the rest had all got up and had gone to take the fort by surprise. The roar of the guns lasted for about an hour and then I could begin to hear one gun from another. In about an hour more, they began to come in and all the firing ceased. I could hear them talking and I found they hadn't accomplished anything, but had got a good many killed and wounded.

The next morning, the old chief that lay in the same circle where I lay arose early and called for our attention. He told us that they had been out last night and had made an attempt to storm the fort, but had been unsuccessful. When they broke off the attack, they had left one of our men behind. He had lain in our circle and was now wounded and lay near the fort and must be brought away. The old chief said that it would be an everlasting shame and disgrace to the nation to let that man lie there and be massacred, as he would be by the whites. The Indians had abandoned the idea of doing anything with Wayne in the fort, there was no chance to take him by surprise and we had decided to let him make the attack upon us in the open ground. "Now," said he, "someone that knows exactly where he lays will have to go so there will be no time lost in looking for him. Who will that be?" Big Turtle arose and said, "I will go for one, I know right where he lays." "Well, who next?" said the chief. No one spoke. He looked right at me and said, "Young man, you will go, and you for another, and you for another," pointing out two more. Said he, "Nary a one of you was out last night and have run no risk. Now go fetch that man away."

We arose right up and started with Big Turtle leading the way. The brush and small saplings were all cut off for two hundred yards around the fort, and just as soon as we got in sight of them, they commenced firing at us. We would run a little piece in single file, one behind the other and stop at every tree that was near our line of travel. We would stand there maybe half a minute and when we would start out again, the bullets would fly like hail. We had made several stops and was now standing behind a large tree when Big Turtle says, "We are doing wrong in stopping. That is giving them time to load." Said he, "When I leave this tree, I shall not stop any more until I get to the man and in order that there be no confusion in taking hold of him, when we come to him, we will go out in the same order that we are going; the ones in front going in is in the most danger and the ones behind will be in the most danger going out. As I am in front in going in, I will be foremost going and as soon as we come to the man, I will grab him by the right arm." Then he says to me and the two others, "You will take him by the left leg," and so forth. "When we start from this tree, we will lead first to the right and then to the left, as I shall give commands, and the same way as we go out. By so doing, we may escape some of their bullets."

When we started from the tree, there came a shower of bullets. We ran straight for the man, only dodging first to one side and then the other as Big Turtle would halloo, "Right!" and "Left!" We ran pretty swift and it seemed to me that we was going smack up to the fort. I don't think that he laid more than sixty yards from the stockade. As soon as we came to him we all seized him according to our instructions and ran, dodging first to the right, and then to the left, as Big Turtle gave the word. As we picked him up, his shirt was a little up and I saw that he was shot in the bowels and that it had turned green around the bullet hole. I then thought we are four live men risking our lives for one dead one.

As we moved out, there was a perfect shower of bullets that followed us, whining by on the right and left and cutting up the dirt on both sides of us. How four men could ever pass through such a scene and come out safe was always a mystery to me. Big Turtle was the only man touched with a bullet. One grazed his thigh just enough to make a little blood seep out and he had four or five bullet holes through his hunting shirt that swung loose. The wounded man groaned wonderfully as we ran with him, but we didn't take much pains for his ease or comfort. After we got out into the woods and they ceased firing, we stopped and laid him down to rest. Of course, our silent thanks went up to the Great Spirit. We carried him on to the army and when we got there, they had a litter prepared for him and other men to carry it.

Our army was all ready to march. Before we started for the wounded man, I had lashed my blanket and brass kettle to my horse. The Indians in camp had let him stray off and now there was no time to hunt for him, so I lost my horse, blanket, and kettle. We moved off down the river and about noon, our wounded man died. They had taken him to where a large tree had blown up and scratched out the leaves and dirt and laid him in and then scratched enough dirt off the roots to cover him. Then we moved on down the river to Fort Defiance.[117] We remained here for about two weeks until we heard of the approach of Wayne, for he was very closely watched. We packed everything and started for the old English fort at the Maumee Rapids. Here, we prepared for battle at the lower end of the long prairie.[118] Our camping place was about two miles below the prairie. The women and children were sent down the river about three miles below the fort. As I didn't wish to fight, they sent me over to Sandusky to inform some warriors (about twenty in number) that was there of the great battle that was about to take place. (*I remained at Sandusky until the battle was over.* Beers)

The Indians who waited for Wayne were camped about two miles below the foot of this prairie, but they chose their fighting ground right at the foot of the prairie, expecting to fight Wayne in the open ground and they in the timbers. The Indians estimated their forces at eight thousand and five hundred. The probability is that it was not so large, but it was a very large army. There was more Indians than the whites had any knowledge of. There was in that battle four hundred friendly Indians from the state of New York that the whites never knew anything of.[119] They happened not to get into the fight and as soon as it was over, they made their way back to their homes, and that was always kept a secret. Wayne came on down the river and halted at the upper end of the prairie, perhaps expecting for the Indians to attack him, but they did not choose to do so.

The Indians have a great many peculiar notions about themselves and perhaps some of them are very good. If an Indian expects to go into battle, he will eat nothing that morning, as they claim that if a man is wounded in the bowels when he is empty, his internals is not so likely to be cut as when they are full. When Wayne made his appearance at the head of the prairie, the Indians were all ordered to be at the foot of the prairie the next morning early and without anything to eat, as they expected Wayne to move upon them the next morning. Accordingly, they were all on the ground early and in good order and full spirits, for they expected it to be another St. Clair victory. They stayed all day until dark. When Wayne didn't make his appearance, they fell back at night and ate their supper and lay on their arms ready for a night attack in case it should take place. The next morning, they went as before, without eating anything. The result was the same. Wayne didn't make his appearance. The Indians fell back at night as before and then called a council of the chiefs.

The Indians said that eating but once a day would weaken their men and then they would not be fit for action. There was no knowing how long Wayne might hold off. If Wayne waited ten days or so, he would weaken their men so that they would not be fit for action and there was no knowing how soon he would attack. They thought that this might be one of Wayne's stratagems to weaken our men, for he had no doubt learned from his prisoners our mode of going into battle. Because we did not know when Wayne would make his attack, we decided not to be in such a hurry the following morning and have our men eat their breakfast before they started out for the battleground. Accordingly, our men went to cooking and preparing their breakfast and to eating and as soon as they were through, they would start back for the battleground.[120]

This was the third morning that the Indians had been waiting for the attack. Some were on the ground by daylight, but others were yet in their beds. Just as they were seeing the sun rising, they saw Wayne's army coming down the prairie in the direction they expected, but a little sooner in the morning. When the firing commenced, there was not more than one-third of our army on the ground; some were eating their breakfast, some were yet cooking, and a large portion on the road. Those that were on the ground commenced firing before Wayne's men was in reach of them, thinking to check them until their men could get on the ground, but Wayne made no halt and, at the same time, he sent his light horsemen around on the right of the Indians. At about the same time that they opened fire on them, the light horsemen began to blow their horns in our rear, which cut off the balance of our army. Those that were on their way and those that were yet at the camp when they heard the firing all started on the run for the fight. Those that were on their way all found that they were cut off by the horsemen and started to run back. The Indians were running both ways, meeting with one another, some breaking right through the horsemen. It became a perfect confusion. Of those that was surrounded, some broke for the fallen timber while some plunged into the river. What did not get shot swam across and made their escape, while others who stood their ground and fought were either killed or taken prisoner.

The slaughter was very great and they was so terror-stricken that they never attempted to rally their force, for the principal part of their chiefs were taken prisoner. The battle was very decisive and short. The Indians flew down the river while Wayne pursued them a piece. The Indians flew for the British fort and when they came to it, the British stood there in the entrance with their muskets and bayonets fixed and wouldn't allow one of them to enter in. They told the Indians that Wayne would attack them, and this very one thing done more towards making peace betwixt the Indians and Americans than any one thing. For weeks before this fight had taken place, they had been promised aid and protection and when they were in the most wonderful excitement and flight, the British refused them protection. It was an act that the Indians never forgot. From that very time, the Indians looked for and sought protection from the Americans.

A treaty was now held by Wayne and his staff and the different chiefs. In that treaty, arrangements was made for all the white prisoners that the Indians had taken when boys and was still with them should have a reservation of land to themselves, separate from the Indian reservation.[121] All the captives that attended that treaty and gave their names got reservations of land. I was notified of the arrangement, but was taken so young that I had no knowledge of land titles whatsoever, and so did not attend the treaty and my name was not taken down. Therefore, I failed to get my portion of land which was about one mile square. I made two attempts afterwards to obtain my amount of land or reservation through Congress, the last time by Sampson Mason of Springfield, but each time happened to be the year of a presidential election and local matters like that was thrown aside.

I received a letter from Sampson Mason while at Washington, and he said that he had shown the matter to several of the members and they all spoke favorable of the matter, but that the presidential election was so close that there could be nothing done then. But, if it was brought up the next winter, he thought there was no doubt but I would get all of my land with interest, and that was a larger quantity than any other prisoner had got. Mason's time expired that term and another man was sent in his place and so the matter was dropped.

I still claim that the land is due me from the government: I claim it in honor of my tribe and to my chiefs. In that treaty, Wayne told the Indians that the Great Spirit was on his side in all these battles and it would never be of any use for them to try to fight against him. "If you ever take up arms again while I am living, I will be the commander and you will be whipped, and it makes no difference whether I be dead or alive; if I am dead and you rise up against the United States, my spirit will be with the army and I will be their commander, and you will be defeated." And this the Indians believed. They thought that he was more than a common man, for during his sieges and battles, they said he never slept; he was always awake and you never could take him by surprise. They supposed him to be something supernatural.

And the Indians taught this to their children, that Wayne was more than a common man and that they should be careful never to go to war against the United States, for if they did, Wayne would be there, even though he had been dead for a hundred years. "Look," they say, "we just used every stratagem and we failed in every attempt.

We was successful in nothing. There was no other general that ever came against us that could succeed in everything. What a wonderful man he was." This was frequently talked over by the old men.

Arrangements were all made now for a final and great treaty, which took place some time the next year.[122] As soon as that treaty was confirmed and made, I concluded my arrangements with Barshaw and we was finally married according to the Indian custom. We immediately prepared to move to Darby, as this was the greatest and best hunting ground of the whole Indian territory. We got us a broodmare apiece and packed our goods, finally landing safely on Big Darby, or Crawfish Creek as it was then called, a little below where Pleasant Valley now is. There, we commenced life in good earnest. Our cabin was built near a spring on what is now known as the Jeremiah Dominy farm, exactly where he built his house afterwards.

It was only a short time after the peace until white people began to make their appearance amongst us. I think the first white men that I saw was two that was lost. It was the better part of the first winter that we were there. I had been out hunting on the east side of Darby and as I was coming in late in the evening, I struck the trail of two white men (they wore shoes, and I knew they were not Indians). I followed their trail some distance and soon discovered that they were lost by the way they wandered. It was dusk, so I left the trail and went into my camp and told my woman that there were two white men a little back in the woods lost. She remarked that I should have brought them in. I told her it was late and I did not see them, but I would go out early in the morning and bring them in.

I started as soon as it was light the following morning and struck their trail, and soon overtook them. When they saw me coming towards them, they took down their guns and cocked them. I walked on up within a few rods of them and saw that they were very much scared. I sat my gun down by the side of a tree and then walked on towards them. They then sat their guns down and I walked up to them and held out my hand. They both shook hands with me, but nary one of them could talk Indian, nor could I speak a word of English. They made signs that they wanted to go north and spoke the word "Sandusky." Then I spoke the word "Sandusky" and made signs to them that the trail was on the other side of the creek.

They then made signs that they wanted something to eat, so I made signs that I had plenty of bucks at the camp and took them in with me. I told my woman to put on some venison and boil it for them. She done so, and it hadn't boiled but a few minutes till one of them went to take some out of the kettle and I stopped him. They talked a little together and one took out his knife and cut off two slices of a raccoon that was hanging there and stuck it on sticks and stuck it up before the fire. I stepped up and pulled up the sticks and threw them away. They turned very red in the face and talked a little together and picked up their guns and was for leaving. I caught their guns and made signs for them to sit down again.[123] They done so and after a while, my woman told me to take out some of the meat in the bottom of the kettle and give them it to eat. I done so and their countenance changed very much all at once. After they had eaten, I took out a little more and after they had eaten that and sat awhile, I took off the kettle. The meat was well done and I gave it to them in a wooden bowl.

They ate very hearty and after they was done, I made signs to them to wrap up the remainder and take it with them, and they done so. By this time it was nearly noon. They wanted me to show them the Indian trail to Sandusky, so I took them down to the creek, right at the same ford where you cross now from Jeremiah Dominy. The creek was a little up and the water was cold. I made signs to them to wade across and right on top of the bank they would find the Indian trail. They waded into the water pretty near to their hips and they stopped and I made signs for them to go on, but they stood awhile and turned and came out. I tried every way to induce them to try it again. I couldn't get them into the water, so I started in and waded across and then made signs for them to come across, and they done so. Then I took them up on the bank and put them on the trail. They seemed now to be every way satisfied. One put his hand into his pocket and took out a silver half-dollar and gave it to me. Then he made signs to me that if ever I came to Sandusky, he would give me all the whiskey that I could drink. They shook hands with me and thanked me over and over and we parted, but I never saw them afterwards.

We remained here for awhile, but the pasture was so much better on the west side of the creek that we moved there a little about where Pleasant Valley now is.

Soon, the white people began to move in here. Amongst the very first settlers was Benjamin Springer and his family, and Usual Osborn, his son-in-law. (*He subsequently removed to the site of Plain City, on the west bank of the stream, and there was found by Benjamin Springer and Usual Osborn in 1796, who settled on Big Darby on land now owned by John Taylor, near the north line of Canaan Township.* Beers) They both soon became warmly attached to me and Osborn took great pains in learning me to speak English, first giving me the names of things, and then a word at a time. After I got a little start, I learned it very fast. After a little while, it seemed to come almost natural.

The next spring, Richard Taylor, Joshua Ewing, John Story, and a number of other white settlers came in.[124] They brought hogs and cattle with them and I soon went into the stock business, raising horses, hogs, and cattle. It was very little trouble to raise hogs and cattle and horses. We never failed to have a full mast of some kind every year, either of white oak, burr oak, hickory, or beech. Pasture for cattle and horses was abundant. All you had to do for them was to cut wild grass, which grew on these prairies as high as man's head on a horse, enough to take them through the winter. I soon had a fine stock of hogs and cattle and horses. I could almost beat any of my white neighbors, for I had the great advantage that when any of my stock strayed off, it was no trouble for me to find them. I began to sell horses and hogs to the white settlers as they came in and we sold milk and butter to the Indians, and furs and skins to the traders.[125]

I was now, in a manner, happy. Here, I could lie down at night without fear, a thing that had not been common with us, and I could rise up in the morning and shake hands with the white man and the Indians, all in perfect peace and safety. I had my own white race for neighbors and the red man that I loved, all mingling together. Upon the whole, I felt proud. I acted as an interpreter between the two races and became a great favorite with the first settlers. There was many of them that would have almost suffered, or at least went without meat for the first spring and summer, if they had not got their supply from me. Deer was plenty and it was no trouble for me to kill them. I had no use for the meat, only what was necessary for my own family. The balance I gave to my neighbors. As for work, I done but very little, for I did not know how to work. I pretty much hired all my work done and was forced to hire white men, for the Indians was like myself, they didn't know how and couldn't work. But even if they had known how, they wouldn't, for it is not natural for an Indian to work.

Right here, my first trouble came. My squaw didn't like to cook for white people. She was opposed to having them about. She became peevish and fretful and would often say to me that I had better get me a white woman if I wanted to live like white folks and have white men work for me. She finally got contrary and refused to cook for my hands. Finally, I came to the conclusion that I would rather live with the white people and own property the way that you could not do to any extent with the Indians. (*Being dissatisfied with his squaw—a cross, peevish woman—he wished to put her aside, get a wife from among the settlers, and live like them.* Howe)

In the meantime, she had two children, but they both died very young and I had got a notion that the Great Spirit was opposed to the two races mingling together. (*According to Mrs. Sarah Norton, an early settler yet living who is the daughter of Daniel Taylor, deceased, Barshaw had two children when Alder took her for his wife, viz. Sarah and John. Mrs. Norton says that she often played with them ere Alder and his wife parted. She also says that the squaw thought a great deal of Jonathan, and was afraid that he would leave her and marry a white woman, which fears were subsequently realized. During his stay with Barshaw, she bore him two children, both of whom died in infancy, and this, they believed, was a manifestation of displeasure by the Great Spirit at the intermarriage of the two races.* Beers) If we had been prosperous with children, we should have never parted, but that, with the other things, made us agree to separate. She saw that I had taken a great fancy to civil life, which was a thing that she would never reconcile to, and so we separated in perfect friendship. At the time, we had fourteen head of milk cows, nine head of horses, and a large stock of hogs. When we separated, I gave her all the cows and seven horses. I kept two of the best horses for my own use, as I had made up my mind to go back and see if I could find any of my people living.

When we had everything arranged, I took her, the horses, and the cattle to Upper Sandusky to her people.[126] After we got there, we spent the night. The next day when I was about to leave, I told her I wanted a little trunk of silver that she had owned when we went together, a little tin trunk about six inches long, and about four wide, and four deep. The trunk was as full of silver as it would hold, silver that we had saved from time to time, but she told me no, that the trunk was hers before we was married and she intended to keep it and all that was in it. I saw that I could not get it without a fuss (she was very determined) and I dared not get into trouble with her on account of her relations and the other Indians. They might have sided with me, but I did not know and wished to leave her in good friendship. I told her that if she would promise never to disturb me hereafter, she might keep the money, which with the horses and cows, would amount to over a thousand dollars. She promised me faithfully that she would not and so we parted in good friendship. But she didn't keep her promise altogether good, for she passed my house once afterwards on the way from the saltworks to Upper Sandusky. Finding no one at home, she stuck her butcher knife three times through the bottom of a tin cup and cut up a fine silver-mounted bridle that I had paid thirteen dollars for. (*At other visits, she destroyed whatever she could find in the cabin and Mrs. Norton says that she threatened to kill his white wife if she ever found her alone.* Beers) I made it a rule to visit my Indian friends once every two years at Lewis Town where my sisters lived. I would always hear from my wife at Upper Sandusky, but never visited her. She was living as late as 1830, but I have not heard of her since.

Usual Osborn and Benjamin Springer were among the first white settlers on Big Darby Creek, and Osborn took a great interest in learning me to talk and to farm. Osborn was a very kindhearted man and would discommode himself to accommodate his neighbors. He was a regular old bruiser; if you crossed his path, he was ready for a fight. Fisticuffs amongst one class of the first settlers was a very common thing, especially among the class that used whiskey to excess. Osborn was a stout, muscular man and I never knew him to get whipped.

He was a hardworking man, but rather a poor planner and of all the families, white or Indian, that I knew, I thought that his lived the hardest. The first winter that came on, they hadn't a sign of a bed in the house. He had a large store box that was long enough for him to lie on and wide enough for him and his wife both to lie in. In the fall, they gathered dry leaves and filled the box. They had two blankets and would spread one on top of the leaves for a sheet and cover with the other. The two oldest of the boys would carry in a back-load of prairie hay in the evening and put it in one corner of the house, and the three little fellows would crawl in under the hay and sleep there. The next morning, they would gather it all up clean and give to their milk cows. The next night, the same thing, throughout the whole winter.

Osborn's wife was one of those "do-less" women. She was, for a large portion of her time, without soap to wash with, a thing there was no need of for the material to make soap them days was very plenty. I have frequently known her to take honey to wash her clothes with. Osborn was a great bee hunter and always had plenty of honey. Honey makes a good lather, but not equal to soap. In right cold weather, I have known that woman to drive her cow into the house to milk. They were always scant of clothes. Osborn himself was one of those hardy pioneer men; he would go all winter with nothing but a pair or two of linen overalls and a linen shirt, a pair of moccasins or shoes, and a wool hat or coonskin cap, and that was his dress for years until sheep got plenty. I never heard him complain of being cold or hungry.

I spoke of him being a hardworking man. I don't mean that he was a sturdy worker, for he was not. He could do as much work in one day as two common men, but instead turned a great deal of his attention to trade and traffic in a small way. He was a stout, hard, robust pioneer, and if anyone was anxious for a fight, or to try his strength in any way, he was always ready, but not quarrelsome. But it was nothing strange to hear of Osborn having a fight.

Once there was a difficulty got up between him and one Chard. Chard came in on him one day in the winter. Osborn had on quite a large fire and had his shirt off mending it. As soon as Chard stepped in, he told Osborn there was a little difficulty betwixt them and he had come to settle it. "Very good," says Osborn. He threw his shirt down and sprang to his feet and they made a few passes at each other. Osborn clinched him and, being a powerful man, threw him onto the fire. There happened to be a neighbor man there and he sprang up and pulled Chard out of the fire before he was much burned. As soon as Chard got off the fire he run, so that ended the fight for that day.

Not many days after, Chard made it in his way to pass Osborn's house and met Osborn out on the road with a yoke of oxen going for a load of hay out on the prairie. Chard was on horseback and had a good, stout cudgel in his hand. He spoke to Osborn, but Osborn said, "Damn you, that is what you are." Chard got off his horse and while he was hitching it, Osborn stepped to one side and bent a bush down and drew his butcher knife from its scabbard, cutting off the bush. By this time, Chard had got his horse hitched, but when he turned toward Osborn and saw him trimming his bush for a cudgel, and seeing the butcher knife in his hand, he made for his horse, untied him, and mounted before Osborn got to him, and put spurs to the animal. Chard had to pass Osborn's house and so Osborn took after him as fast as he could run, and when he came to his house, he ran in and got his gun. Chard spurred his horse even more. Osborn followed him some distance and then fired off his gun up in the air; he said he did not want to hurt Chard, but to scare him. (*When Chard turned toward Osborn, he saw him trimming the bush with his butcher knife and, conscious of the power of the man, he trembled. The butcher knife and cudgel were, in Chard's eyes, as powerful as the fire, and having no desire, as he afterward expressed it, "to be butchered, roasted, and eaten," he sprang to his horse, mounted, and put spurs to him to make his escape before Osborn could catch him. However, Osborn pur-*)

sued Chard as fast as he could, and as the latter had to pass Osborn's house, Osborn ran in and got his gun, and fired it off in the air. Osborn said he did not want to hurt the "varmint," but only scare him to death. Beers)

Chard made good his way out of sight and halted in the midst of one of the large prairies. He was there, sitting on his horse looking in every direction, when one of the neighbors went out hunting, saw him sitting there on this horse and went to him. Chard inquired of him if he had seen anything of Osborn. The neighbor said that he had not and asked him why. Chard went on to tell what had taken place and requested his neighbor to go with him until he was entirely out of danger, and so ended the fight between Osborn and Chard.

Osborn managed to buy a small farm on the spring fork and farmed and wagoned considerable. He used to supply the neighbors with salt. In the fall, he would take two or three yoke of oxen and would load up with cheese, butter, and honey, and go to Zanesville. There, he would sell his load and carry back salt and glassware. But the country got too thick settled for him and he sold out about the year 1835 and moved west.

(Osborn finally bought a small farm on the east bank of Little Darby, now in Monroe Township and the property of Jonah Wood. After his settlement in Monroe Township, his neighbors soon discovered that he was not a man to be trifled with. One winter, hay and feed for stock was very scarce, there having been a short crop the previous summer, and considerable stock was really in a suffering condition. George Fullington had a better supply than most of the neighbors, and sold to them till he could spare no more, when he gave out word throughout the neighborhood that no one could be supplied with hay from his stacks. Osborn owned a pair of old oxen and a cow at this time, using the former to haul loads and travel around with. His animals becoming very poor and in an almost starving condition, he saw he must have hay or they would die. Mr. Fullington would sell no more, so Osborn hitched his oxen to his sled, drove to Fullington's haystack, and, with the assistance of his son, loaded on all he thought his animals could haul, and ordered the boy to drive home. He immediately walked to Fullington's house, called him out, and directed his attention toward the stack, whence the owner saw Osborn's son driving with a load of hay. He told Fullington that he could not let his cattle starve while hay could be found. It is said that Osborn was not very particu-

A History of Jonathan Alder

lar, when out of meat, whose hog he shot, and was therefore mixed up in a great many lawsuits, out of which he usually came victorious. Beers)

Benjamin Springer, one of the first white settlers of Darby, and Usual Osborn, his son-in-law, settled on Darby about the year 1798. Springer's family consisted of himself and wife and three children. Osborn's wife and his two sons, Silas and Thomas, and Benjamin Springer built the first mill that was built on Darby Creek, about a mile below Pleasant Valley (now Plain City), but it was poorly constructed and only run about six months. The first high water that came swept his dam out and he never rebuilt it. He lived to be eighty-odd years old and died on Darby. The last time I saw him was about 1825. He came to my house and took dinner with me. After dinner, we walked out together and as we were parting, we shook hands. He said to me that this was probably the last time he should ever call and we would not see each other again. I made light of it, but he said he was not going to live but a short time. This was during warm weather. In the fall and before winter set in, he died. He wanted to convey the idea to me that he had some supernatural knowledge of his death, but I supposed it to be the weakness of his mind.

White people suffered a great many more privations in the first settlement of this country than did the Indians. I have saw them two boys, Silas and Tom Springer, go till December without shoes on their feet.

Tom had a great notion of hunting and would frequently go out with me. One morning we started out early and crossed over Little Darby and Spring Fork. Late in the evening, Tom killed a large buck and by the time we got it skinned and cut up, it was night. Tom wanted to know what we would do. I told him we would have to camp for the night and he seemed very well pleased. We struck and built us a large fire, for Tom was quite industrious and willing to do most of the drudgery. We sat by our fire and roasted the venison and ate to our fill. At a late hour in the night, we began to talk about sleeping and Tom said as he had no blanket, we would have to lie together. I told him no, that two grown Indians never slept together. In that they were like he-bears. Said I, "You will never find two grown he-bears in the same hole or tree." "Why?" said he. "Well," said I, "they would fight, and one or the other would have to leave." "Well," said he, "what am I to do, I have no blanket." "You ought to have thought of this when you started out," said I. "You never see an Indian start out without his gun, tomahawk, butcher knife, and blanket."

He said that he did not know what he was to do if I wouldn't let him lie with me. "Well," said I, "we will fix our beds and you must cover over with your buckskin." He said he would never have thought of that. I had noticed a dead tree with dry, loose bark that was nearby earlier in the evening, so we went to the tree and peeled and carried bark sufficient to make us a bed to lie on, so as to keep us from the cold, damp ground. After we got everything ready, Tom stretched himself out and rolled up snug and tight in his buckskin and I done the same in my blanket. It was now quite a late hour in the night and Tom was soon snoring. I woke up in the night and found it was snowing very fast, but Tom was still snoring so I did not disturb him until he woke in the morning himself. There was about six inches of snow on us and when Tom awoke, he threw up his buckskin and let the whole flake of snow in his face. He said that was the first he knew of the snow, when it fell in his face. He said he never slept warmer, nor was more comfortable in his life, so we roasted our venison, ate our meat, and started for home. That was the proudest night of Tom's whole life. He never got done talking about it and telling it to all that he thought had not heard it.

I started out one morning before daylight with my dogs to coon hunt. This was a year or so before our deer hunt and there was one of those large, white frosts, almost equal to a light snow. After daylight, I met Silas and Tom Springer. Tom was entirely barefoot and his feet were very red. I asked him if his feet was not very cold. "No," he said, "not very." How the fellow could stand it to go through such a frost and not freeze his feet, I couldn't tell. After Tom became a man grown, he shifted off west and I saw no more of him. After Silas Springer became grown, he married Margaret Kilgers, a very fine young woman that moved in here with her parents in an early day. He bought him a farm on Big Darby and lived on it until about the year 1825. Then, he sold it to Israel Brown and went west. He was quite a pious and religious man and would sometimes preach. After he went west, he joined the Mormons.

I had not seen my sister Sally for some years as she was living at Upper Sandusky and me on Big Darby, and I had not put it in my way to visit her. One time she had been down to the salt springs and on her way back, we happened to meet right about where Pleasant Valley now is. We shook hands, and she was very friendly. We entered into quite a chat and talked in regard to each other's welfare. When she was about to leave she said, "Jonathan, I see that you stand in about the same relation amongst the whites here, when I inquire of them about you, that you did when you lived with us. Everybody that knew you seemed to love you, and I see it is the same with the whites. That speaks well for a man."

"Yes," says I, "but Sally, I would think a great deal more of you than I do if you had not abused me unreasonably when I was a boy and living with you. I respect you very much, but I can never love you as I do Mary and Hannah, they always treated me so kind." I saw the tears start in her eyes and she turned and walked off about ten steps with her back to me. I stood there for a minute or two and saw her wiping her eyes before she turned to come back to me. When she turned around, I saw she had been crying. She walked right up to me and said, "Jonathan, I am sorry you have any hard feelings towards me. You ought to think more of me than either of your sisters. You was wild and disobedient, like all other boys. I corrected you and brought you up right. If I had let you run at will and pleasure, you might not have been thought any more of than a great many others. You are now a man and you can reason these things in your mind, and you ought really to respect me the more for the way in which I brought you up." I told her it might be so, but I couldn't see it in that way. She told me that she had made a man of me and it was all owing to the way in which I had been brought up while young. "You are now respected by both Indians and white people," she said. We shook hands and parted, but I saw she was somewhat cast down.

In the early settlement of Darby, I frequently had a good deal of trouble to keep the peace betwixt the whites and Indians. Both the whites and Indians would come to me whenever any difficulty would arise between them. After I got so I could speak the English language, I was their only interpreter.

Joshua Ewing moved in on Darby in a very early day and brought on four sheep, the first sheep that was ever brought onto Darby. One day, he caught an Indian dog on one of his sheep, and before he could get the dog off, it had killed the sheep. Ewing took down his gun and shot the dog. Ewing made a fuss about the sheep and said to me that the Indian should pay for it. The Indian came to me and wanted me to talk to Ewing and have him pay for the dog. I done all the talking between them, but nary one was willing to pay anything. The Indian was quite angry and so was Ewing, and the Indian told me to say to Ewing that if he did not pay him ten dollars for his dog, he would shoot one of Ewing's horses. I knew it wouldn't do to tell it in the same language that he used, for they would be fighting directly, for Ewing was very spunky and he was no coward. I told Ewing that the Indian had said that if he did not pay him for the dog, he would kill something for him. "Well," said Ewing, "you tell him if he kills anything for me, I will shoot him." But I knew it would not do to tell the Indian that, for he would be for a fight immediately. I told the Indian that Ewing said his dog killed his sheep and that he had killed the dog, and that the sheep was worth as much as the dog and they now could quit even. I told the Indian he might as well give it up, for I guessed he would get nothing for his dog. He still insisted that if Ewing did not pay for the dog, he would have some satisfaction. I was uneasy for some time for fear that the Indian might kill something of Ewing's, but he finally gave it up and moved out of the neighborhood and the strife ended without anything serious.

The laws of the two nations were very much alike in some respects. I had become naturalized to one and was becoming subject to the other, and I frequently thought that the verbal law or rule of the Indian was better in some things and more just than the white man's written law. We had two parallel cases right in the neighborhood. There was an Indian who had a stallion which got loose and killed a mare that belonged to an Indian woman. The woman came to the man and told him he would have to pay for her mare. He said he had nothing that he could pay with, but if she would take the horse, she was welcome. She took the horse and that ended the matter, and that was in accordance with their custom in such cases.

In the same summer, one of my white neighbors owned a bull that he allowed to run at large. The bull hooked a horse belonging to another white neighbor of mine and I was forced to put the horse out of its misery. The matter run on for some time, and there seemed to be nothing said about it. One day, I asked the man that owned the bull if he wasn't going to pay the other man for the horse that his bull had killed. He said no, it was an accident, the bull was not known to be cross and that he couldn't help it. It was not his fault and he said the law would not make him pay. I told him he ought to give the man the bull anyhow. No, he said, he couldn't afford to do that. I thought that the law was very unjust.

When one Indian owes another a just debt and doesn't pay it in a proper time, the creditor can take anything the debtor has that he can get hold of and hold it until he is paid. If he is not paid, he keeps the property even though it might be worth more than the debt.

I soon began to learn the white man's laws, for as soon as the state of Ohio was organized into a state, there was an election held for state and county officers. I voted at the first election that was held on Big Darby and so voted regularly until 1840. That year, the Democratic party challenged my vote because I had not been naturalized, but the challenge was overruled and I voted again in 1844. My vote was challenged again by one Samuel Flint. I asked him why he had done so and he said he done it in retaliation because the Whigs had challenged his vote. I asked on what grounds they made the challenge. He said that he was taken prisoner by the British in 1812 and whilst in Canada, he did bear arms under the British government and guarded some American soldiers that had also been taken prisoner, but he also said that he did not bear arms for the British willingly, so Flint and I became friendly and the judges took my ballot.

We had an early settler on Darby, John Graham, that was a great annoyance to the people. He was a large-boned man, nearly six feet and two or three inches tall and rather fleshy. His weight was about three hundred pounds and there was but few men that could outrun him in a footrace, and as for a fisticuff fight, there was none able to whip him. The whole neighborhood hated him and was always trying to pick a quarrel betwixt him and someone that they thought might be able to whip him. Graham was not a quarrelsome man at all, not for fighting, but he was always feuding with his neighbors about his trade and business. At last a man named Ware came and settled on Darby. He was also a large, fleshy man weighing near three hundred pounds and as soon as he came into the neighborhood, they began to lay plans to get him and Graham into a fight.

It was something like a year before they accomplished it. We had a large gathering to raise a barn, and all through the day there were hints thrown out that Ware was a powerful man, but Graham took no notice of them. There had been some words some months before between Ware and Graham, not altogether friendly, and a great deal more carried back and forth than was true. Finally, the crowd got the thing started. Graham told Ware not to step up until he could talk to him. Ware walked to him and Graham said, "Ware, I have nothing against you, nor you against me, but your friends here are arguing this thing on. They want me whipped and there is none of them that is able to do it, and they want you to whip me, but you are not able to do it. My advice to you is to drop it." They had a little more talk and Ware turned and walked off, and I thought the matter was dropped, but Ware's friends got round him and talked a while and Ware turned and came back to Graham and said he guessed they had better fight it out. "Well," said Graham, "if nothing but a fight will do, strip and get ready," and so they did. They came together and made a few passes at each other. Graham clinched Ware and threw him on the ground and made a few licks, and Ware hallooed "enough." Graham got up and turned to Ware's friends and said, "Now men, I suppose you are satisfied," and that ended the fighting with Graham.

The year before I went back to Virginia, Graham bought a drove of hogs and drove them to Detroit. When he came back, he claimed

A History of Jonathan Alder

that he had lost a large portion of his hogs which had returned to Darby and were now held by his neighbors. Some of the hogs had returned and his neighbors did not hesitate to deliver them up to him, but he claimed a great many more than actually belonged to him. Graham had bought a lot from John Taylor and when he came back, Taylor had five or six fat hogs in the pen already fatted for his meat. Graham came and claimed they were his. Taylor told him they were not his, but Graham insisted they were and said that he would have them. For fear that he might have trouble, Taylor got three of his neighbors to come early the next morning to butcher the animals. Just as they had got their water hot and was ready to go to killing, they saw Graham coming. He was armed with a rifle and two horse pistols hanging in his belt, and about two-thirds of an old sword hanging to his side, and a butcher knife in his scabbard. He came right up without speaking a word, threw down the pen and drove the hogs off and butchered them that day himself. John Taylor was an honest, peaceable man and would suffer a loss any time before he would have a lawsuit or a difficulty with a man.

Graham sent me word that he had lost a number of the hogs that he had bought from me and he wanted to see me, so I went up to his house and found him at home. When he told me that he had lost a number of the hogs that he had bought from me, I told him if any had come back, he was welcome to them, but that I had not seen any of them. He said that he had lost quite a number and he would take enough of my hogs to make up the loss. I then began to get mad. We soon got into a quarrel and both used very angry words. He began to threaten me and said he would make every man fear him or love him. "Graham," says I, "I never loved you, and as to fear you, I don't." He moved a little towards me, but I had my gun ready in my hand. He kept moving around towards a plow coulter[127] that lay in the yard until he got it right betwixt his feet. He stooped twice to pick it up and each time I raised my gun, and then he would straighten up. All this time he was quarreling and when he raised up the second time, I said, "Graham, this is twice you have stooped to pick up that coulter. Now make another attempt and you are a dead man." I cocked my gun and

I felt as though I would as leave shoot as not. When his wife heard me, she sprang out of the house and put her arms around his neck and took him into the house and shut the door.

Presently, he came out with his gun but turned and walked from me and tried to fire off his gun, but he had got the load wet, and his gun wouldn't go off. He went back into the house and took the barrel out of the stock, unbreeched it and took the load out. Then he cleared the barrel, put it together, and reloaded. In the meantime, whilst we were quarreling, John Moore rode up in time to hear the most of it. After Graham had reloaded, he commenced knocking the chinking out of the house beside the door. Moore discovered Graham's actions and told me to get down behind the fence, for Graham was going to shoot. I squatted down in the joint of the fence and when Graham got his chinking out, he could not see me. Presently, he flung the door wide open and out he came without his gun, and I arose up knowing that the trouble was all over.

He came walking right towards me and spoke. Said he, "Jonathan, this is a damn shame. You are the last man that I ever expected to have a quarrel with." "Graham," said I, "who is to blame about this?" "I am," said he. "I know I am too passionate and I got mad before I thought. But now I want this all dropped and that you and I be friendly." I told him then (it was late in the evening) to go with me and my hogs would all be in their beds, and I could show him every hog I had and if he found another among them, he could take it. He got on his horse with his gun and I walked before him. I took him round and showed him every hog I had left and he said there was none of them his.

"If you can find any others in my drove, you take them," said I. "No," said he, "As you are going away and will be gone a year or more, I will not take a hog till you come back, even if it is five years. I will not take a hog without you are here, for if I should, the neighbors would tell you all sorts of stories." So he did not meddle with my hogs till I came back. We were always very friendly afterwards.

He called and stayed all night with me after I came back from Virginia, and in talking over our quarrel that night, he told me that he was so mad that he would actually have shot me that evening whilst I was taking him round to show him the hogs, if he hadn't been afraid. He said it came in his mind several times, but he thought his gun might snap and in that case, he said he knew he would be killed. "But," he said, "if I had known my gun would not have snapped, I would have killed you."

Before peace was made and while I was staying on the Darby Plains before there was any whites here, I went out one day to make a ring fire and capture a few deer. The grass was very nice and dry for burning. I went out two or three miles southwest from Pleasant Valley and commenced my fire. I cut some of the long grass and made a torch, and set it afire. Then I ran with it, circling around and taking in three or four thousand acres. Then, I got inside of my ring and it soon made a fine fire all around. Very soon I saw deer running from one side to the other. In my ring, I killed seven deer. When I would kill one, I dragged it into a thicket where there was no grass and scraped the leaves away so as not to have the hide injured by the fire.

At last, the fire began to close in on me, and it burned very rapid. I could see no good place of escape. I looked me out a good piece of ground where there was no brush and when the fire began to get pretty warm, I put my powder horn under my arms and fired off my gun, then leaped. I had wrapped my blanket tight around me—head and face all covered. I could not see a particle. I was perfectly blindfolded. I turned my face in the direction that I wanted to run before I covered it. The fire was then a perfect blaze ten or fifteen feet high, and I started and ran through it. The main blaze was not more than thirty or forty feet wide, but I ran about two hundred yards before I uncovered. I was out of the main fire, but it was still burning and I had to run further to get entirely out of the fire on account of my powder horn. My moccasins was entirely ruined and my leggings and blanket was nearly spoiled. I hunted up the deer and skinned them. Some of them had their hair pretty well singed off, but the hides were not injured. But that was my last ring fire.

There was an old tradition that I used to hear the old Indians tell and talk about that had been handed down, I suppose, from generation to generation. After I heard a passage read in the Bible, I suppose that it must have been taken from that and handed down from generation to generation. They would tell of the circumstances of a great battle that had been fought in a beautiful valley. The slaughter was so great that the whole valley was literally covered with the dead and that they lay there without being buried till the bones became dry and white. After many years, the Great Spirit came and gathered them bones all up and after he had got them all properly arranged, he stepped off to a large tree and gave it a push and hallooed with a loud noise to rise and run or this tree will fall on you—and that they all arose upon their feet and was again alive, a mighty great army.

In quite an early day, one or two years after peace was made, the district surveyors began to make their appearance surveying and locating lands. Lucas Sullivan was the first one that I got acquainted with.[128] He made a number of entries and location on Big Darby and the Scioto River and very earnestly solicited me to go with him as a cook and a hunter, and to show him the choice lands of the country. He said he would give me land for my services, but being ignorant of the value of land or land titles, I declined going with him from time to time until he had finished his locations. He was very generous and surveyed me off a small tract of land that I was living on, one near Pleasant Valley. But soon afterwards, I became acquainted with John Moore and him and I entered into a partnership in hunting. I moved off my land and went farther down Darby and erected a house right east of Foster Chapel on the bluff of the hill near the pond where the wolf killed the deer that I spoke of earlier. During my absence of a few years, other surveyors came along and enclosed my piece of land that Sullivan had gave me, and I neglected to contest my right and so lost my land.

One memorable, pleasant summer Sabbath whilst I was living at this new residence near Foster Chapel, John Moore was lounging about in the shade. He commenced asking questions about where I was taken prisoner from and said I might find some of my people living. My name, Alder, I had never forgot. He asked me if I could remember the names of any places, and I told him that I could recollect frequently hearing them use the word "Wythe," but did not know what it meant. I also remembered that they lived near a place called Greenbriar, and that there was a lead mine nearby, and that I used to go there and watch the hands dig ore. He then asked me if I could recollect the names of any of the neighbors and, after a good deal of reflection, I recollected a family by the name of Gullion. When I mentioned the name, he dropped his head for a short time as if buried in thought and muttered "Gullion, Gullion," several times to himself. At last he raised his head and said, "If there is any of your people living, I can find them. My father and myself were out traveling through that country and stopped and stayed overnight at a man's home by that name in Wythe County and Greenbriar Township. I know where the lead mines is in Virginia and I am going back on a visit next fall. It is but a little out of my way to pass through that part of the country."

That fall, Moore returned back to Virginia and passed through Wythe County and inquired for Alders and for Gullions, but Gullion had left that part of the country and he could hear neither of the name of Gullion nor Alder. Moore was a good scribe and he wrote several notices giving the facts, my name and my whereabouts, and my address, and passed on somewhat discouraged. He returned back here the next fall and related to me his unsuccessful search, but told me what he had done and that if there was any of them living, I might hear from them yet. I gave up all hope of ever seeing any of my folks. I had had a great deal of anxiety for the last three or four years of finding some of my relations and had made inquiry of all the newcomers if they knew anybody by the name of Alder, but without any success. I now made up my mind to make no further inquiry. All hope was now gone.

In the fall after Moore had come back, I happened to be in Franklinton and was told that there was a letter for me at the post office. I happened to meet Moore, and when I informed him of the fact, he said, "That is from your folks in Virginia," and so he went with me to the Post Office and opened the letter. It was from my brother Paul and contained the joyful news that my mother was yet alive and well, as were all my brothers. Not one member of the family had died since I had been taken prisoner. It fairly made me feel light-headed to hear from my family and to know that they were alive and well. It had been over twenty years since I had saw or heard from them. This was about six months after Moore had passed through the country. It took a letter them days about three months to go and come. The mail was carried on horseback and, in some places, on foot. The mail then came round through Kentucky. I got Moore to answer my letter back and we exchanged several letters back and forth. I now began to arrange my business to go back to the old homestead. Moore and I had entered into an arrangement to hunt and be together that summer, so for our convenience, we built us a snug log cabin on Big Darby just a little east of the Foster Chapel and followed hunting there all season. He read and answered all my letters for me and told my family about what time they might look for me the next fall.

In September 1804, I began to prepare to take my long and tedious journey back to the place of my early boyhood. One of the first things I did was to buy up a lot of dry goods and be dressed up in the order of the whites. I went to Franklinton and laid in goods sufficient for three suits, and took them to Richard Taylor—he was a tailor—and he made them all up for me in the style of that day. One of the suits was of very fine cloth.

I dropped the Indian costume that I had been accustomed to for the last twenty years entirely. My new suit changed my appearance very much and I must acknowledge that it was not near so handsome as my old clothes. I also disposed of all my large hogs and all of my skins and furs, and equipped myself with a new saddle, bridle, and saddlebags, as they called them. I owned two good horses, and if all went well, I knew that my stock hogs could take care of themselves for the coming year.

John Moore, his brother Nicholas, and I set out in November 1805. Nicholas rode one of my horses and I bore all the expenses. We traveled over rough roads, hills, valleys, rivers, and mountains, and arrived at my brother Paul Alder's home on the first Sunday after

New Year 1806 at about eleven o'clock. We dismounted, hitched our horses, and walked up to the house. We passed ourselves off as strangers and travelers, called for our dinners and to have our horses fed, which was very readily granted, and inquired who lived there. The man of the house said Paul Alder. I had concluded not to make myself known for sometime and I thought that when I would see my mother, I would know her by a mole on the side of her face. I wanted to make all the close observations I could before I made myself known, to see if I could recognize any of them. There was an old lady sitting there, and I eyed her very close to see if I could recognize her as my mother. When I was taken prisoner, my mother's hair was black as a crow, and this old lady's hair was almost white as wool. I supposed she was my mother, but could not tell. I then eyed my brother as close as I could but could see no features that I could recognize at all.

There was two young women in the house at the same time. One of them was my half-sister that I knew nothing of. My mother had been married in my absence and had had one child, which was one of the young women present. I noticed that they were scrutinizing me very close and soon commenced whispering together. I heard one of them say he looks very much like Mark, that was my brother. I saw that they were about to discover me so I turned my chair round to my brother and remarked to him, "You say your name is Alder." "Yes," said he, "my name is Paul Alder." "Well," said I, "my name is Jonathan Alder."

It is hardly necessary to undertake to describe our feelings at that time, but mine was very different from those I had when I saw the Indian coming with the scalp of my brother David in his hand shaking off the blood. When I told my brother that my name was Alder, he arose to shake hands but he was so overjoyed that he could scarcely utter one word. After giving me a hearty shake by both hands, he left the room to give vent to his feelings. My mother arose from her seat and threw her arms around my neck and kissed me. She too was not able to speak for a short time, but the first words she spoke was, "Jonathan, how you have grown," whilst the tears freely rolled down her cheeks. I have heard them read in the Bible about some brother that sold one of their brothers to some merchants, and was carried off into another country, and after many years was brought together as strangers. The circumstances were very different, but I reckon the payoff was somewhat alike. I was then introduced to my half-sister and the talk became common and general. My mother told me of a dream she had had. She said she dreamed that I had come home and that I was a little, ornery, mean-looking fellow, and that she refused to own me as her son. But, she said, she was entirely mistaken for the reverse was true. She was proud to own me as her son for I stood a little over six feet tall, and was as straight as an Indian.

I told my mother I would relate a few circumstances that took place before my captivity that she would probably recall so that she might know that I was her son. Amongst them was Mrs. Martin that was taken at the same time, and her exchange back, and the digging of lead ore close to where we used to live. Another was the Negroes passing our house on Saturday evening to spend Sunday with their wives and how they would beg pumpkins of us and get her to bake them, so they would get them to eat on Monday as they returned to their masters. I also told about the Indian that passed through the field, and how she clapped her hands, and how he ran, and how John took down the gun and ran out to shoot him but he was out of reach, all of which she well recollected. She said then that she had no doubts and was fully satisfied that I was her son.

We then passed the evening in agreeable conversation. I then commenced to relate to them that memorable morning and the tragedy of my captivity, and the killing of my brother David, and of my wearisome journey over hill and mountains, sailing down the Big Sandy in a bark canoe, our travels up through the country and running the gauntlet, my lonesomeness and my homesickness, and my poor health for three or four years.

From time to time I gave them my whole history of adversity and prosperity, which appeared to be very interesting to them. During my stay, I also visited the old homestead and also the spot where I saw my brother reel, stagger, and fall. They told me that about a year after my capture, they found the bones of David and gathered up what they could find and buried them. I traveled out a piece on the route that we went. I could show the place where we camped the first night. I also visited the house where Mrs. Martin was taken. Mrs. Martin had married again after she got back and had moved off, so I never saw her after we parted at the salt springs.

I found my brother living on fifty acres of poor mountain land. I hadn't been there long before I began to persuade them to sell and come to Ohio. The more we talked about it, the more excited they got. I had intended to come back the next fall but my brother made me the proposition that if I would stay one year longer, he would sell his land, and he and mother would come to Ohio with me. I agreed to it and stayed there a part of the next two years. My brother Mark was sent for and he came to see me, but my brother John had moved off so far that I did not get to see him.

While roving around, I fell in company with Mary Blont, and, as I thought that she was a rather handsome girl, I fell in love with her and proposed to take her with me to Ohio, to which she consented, and we were married in the winter of 1806. In the meantime, my young sister was also married to Henry Smith and they also felt an anxiety to see Ohio, so we all commenced making preparations for the long journey by wagon. We bought one large wagon and harnessed six horses to it, and set out the latter part of August 1806. We took the most direct road from Wythe County, Virginia, to Gallipolis. We traveled over wonderful hills and mountains. In a great many places, we had to lock both rear wheels of our wagon and then cut down a tree and chain a log to the hind axle tree of the wagon because the hills were so steep and long. We ferried the Ohio River and then took the road for Chillicothe. From there, we took the road for Sandusky passing up the Scioto to the mouth of Big Darby, and up that to our landing place, the house that John Moore and I had built a few years before. We had been eight weeks on the road. Although the road was rough and hilly, no serious accident had happened.

The land upon which my house stood was the same as that upon which Foster Chapel now stands. In my absence, Lewis Foster had meandered along up the river from Chillicothe and up Darby in search of a tract of land to buy. Finding a house on this side, he went back to Chillicothe and bought the whole survey—one thousand acres. I had not been in the house more than two months until his son notified me that his father had bought the entire tract of land, including the house that stood on it. I went to Franklinton to see my esteemed friend Lucas Sullivan, and he informed me that he owned the tract of land adjoining, so I immediately bought it from him. I gathered up some help, my brother Paul and Smith were both good hewers, and we went to work. In eight days, we had my house ready to move into. This was the same house that I am now living in and want my children to preserve as long as possible. My brother Paul and my brother-in-law Smith soon made selections of land on the Three Mile Run, and built themselves houses.

We had not been landed on Darby but a few days until I killed a fine fat bear. I thought now we will have a great feast on bear meat, but behold! There was not one of the women that would taste it except for my wife. Some said it looked like a dog; some said it had a foot and a paw like a Negro. They believed it was part human and nothing I could say would induce them to eat any, but that prejudiced notion vanished away in a few years.

At this time, there was two or three Indians living on Darby for every white citizen. During my absence, my hogs had got very much scattered and I was away from my house a great deal the first two or three years gathering up my animals. Frequently, I was away all night and it was almost an everyday occurrence for the Indians to call on me, more so because I had been gone so long, than if I had remained with them. When my wife would see them coming in my absence, she would close the door and keep them out. They would frequently complain to me of her ill treatment and I would have to apologize to them, saying that they were strangers, and she was afraid of them. Sometimes they would get into the house before she would see them, and notwithstanding all of her signs and entreaties, they would stay.

The first one that stayed in my absence got into the house before she saw him. She made signs for him to leave, but he would not. She

A History of Jonathan Alder

then gave him his supper and, late at night, she went to bed, but not to sleep. The Indian put on a good fire and stretched himself out on his blanket, and soon commenced snoring. She said that along about midnight, he woke up and raised up, and took out his butcher knife. She thought, "He is going to murder us," but there was a basket of turnips sitting close by, and he reached and drew the basket up to him and commenced peeling and eating them. When he was done, he wiped his knife very carefully and put it back in the scabbard, and then stretched himself out again and went to sleep. Just before daylight, he stirred up the fire and at the dawn of the day, he gathered up his blanket and gun and off he went. During that entire time, she never closed her eyes. That was the only time that she got to stay awake all night when I was away.

For several years, the Indians used to camp close around my cabin during the fall of the year. They would hunt for several months and the squaws would make baskets and moccasins to sell to the whites. After a few years, they gradually began to camp nearer to their reserve in the north.

I had a man and his wife camp on my place down by the creek where there is a fine spring. They had been there all summer when the man began to act a little strange at times. One morning, his squaw came up to my house and told me that her man had got up and gone off. She had made a search for him, but was not able to find him and she wished that I would call in some of my white neighbors and see if we could find him. I done so; I got two or three, and we made a thorough search up and down the creek but was not able to find him, and so gave up the search. I went back to the camp late in the evening, and he had come in and was sitting there, but looked quite wild. I asked him where he had been and he said he was up the creek a little piece, and said, "I saw you two or three times when you were hunting for me. I was sitting down up there." I told his wife the next day that she had better fix up and get him off up to the reserve where her people was because he might get worse and kill her when they were alone and, in a few days, they fixed up and left. I heard no more from them for about two years.

The first time after that that I was on the reserve for a visit, I asked about my Indian and they told me he had got very crazy, so much so that they had to keep him tied, and that he became so much trouble they took and tomahawked him. "My," said I. "Was not that rather barbarous." "No," they said. "He had got so they had to keep him tied. He was very dangerous and was liable to get loose at any time, and so they had to keep a watch over him all the time. Still, he was liable to get loose and might kill some good person, and as for him, he never would be of any account, and now he is out of the way. He is better off, and the people are safe. It was the best thing that could be done."

Lewis Foster and his family moved into the house on his new purchase as soon as I moved out, and he divided up his survey into hundred-acre plots for his children. Francis Downing married his daughter Elizabeth and he took the south hundred-acre plot. John Fowlinson had married his daughter Rebecca and took the next; his son Thomas Foster was also married and took the third; and his other children, Joshua, John, Benjamin, Joseph, and Rachel, all married and settled together on the thousand acres. Thomas Foster was drafted in the War of 1812 and died in the service. Lewis Foster was by nature a fine man, a good neighbor, and a Christian. He was a Methodist preacher of considerable ability. His house was open as a place of public worship for the church for several years until he donated two acres of land to the congregation for a burying ground and to build a church upon. The church was built and appropriately named Foster Chapel. He remained on his farm for many years and preached to the neighborhood gratis. He also taught in our school for years. He was one of our most useful men. He preached and taught school until he got too old for service. He was also a blacksmith—a person much needed at that time. He was one of the most industrious men; the sun never rose while Lewis Foster was in bed. His lady, Nancy Foster, was one of the purest of women and a devout Christian. She acted the part of a midwife for many years, lived to a good old age, and died and is buried in the Foster graveyard.

Joseph Downing moved in next with his family. His son-in-law,

Henderson Crabb, was a Methodist preacher. Crabb was an able speaker and had been a circuit rider for several years. Foster and Crabb lived side by side and we seldom failed to have preaching every Sabbath. Between the two, they built a large church. When Foster ceased teaching school, Crabb took his place. He was one of the finest penmen and arithmeticians around. Crabb sold his farm when he grew older and went into the dry goods business. Lewis Foster's family, one after another, began to sell out to go west. Finally, Foster himself sold and went west. There is no one from his large family in these parts now.

Blair came on in an early day and set up a distillery on Little Darby just below where Hampton is, and ran it for several years until it blew up. His son, John, set up a hatter business and went to farming. An honest man, John.

The next fall after I came back from Virginia, I took it to visit my special friend Peter Paugh living over on the spring fork. I was anxious that my neighbors should see my wife. On a Sunday morning, I convinced her that we should visit the Paughs. I saddled two horses and, as usual, took my gun along.

Mary carried our ten-month-old child and after we got into the plains about four miles from home, we ran into a bear. It was the first live bear my wife had ever seen. I took a shot at him and missed, then headed him off and drove him back past my wife. I came up on him, fired, and missed again. I drove that bear back three or four times past my wife before I hit him. As soon as I hit him, he made off for Little Darby and he ran into the water. I got off my horse and took a steady aim and hit him in the head, then went back to hunt for my wife. I found her away in one of the big prairies standing on a big stump holding her horse. The first thing she said was "This is the last time I will go visiting with you when you take your gun." I told her I had killed the bear, but she wouldn't have given six pence just then for all the bears in the woods. Her horse had got excited and wanted to join in the chase and so she was obliged to get off. I got her on again and we went on to the Paughs. Peter and I went back and skinned the bear and carried about half the meat in with us, and had some cooked for dinner. In the evening, I packed the remainder home with me, but that was the last time my wife ever went visiting with me when I took my gun.

The bear and wolves were very plenty in them days. The bears were very destructive to our hogs, especially the young pigs. They were fond of hog meat after they got a taste. The wolves was more destructive to the sheep. But the bear, wolf, and the deer are like the Indian; they can't stand civilization and are about disappeared.

Samuel Davis

Late one evening soon after I had moved to Darby, a rugged, stout-looking man called to stay all night. Through the course of the evening we commenced discoursing about the Indians and he began to speak very disrespectful language of them. I took their part and that seemed to rough his ambition, and finally both of us got out of humor. I told him they were as human as us in a great many respects and, in some ways, more so. I told him I knew all about Indians for they had raised me from a little boy and I had been with them for twenty-four years. He then wanted to know if I was the prisoner Jonathan Alder that there was so much talk about. I told him I was. He then cooled down and told me his name was Samuel Davis and that he was a prisoner by the Indians for a short time, and that they had used him very rough.[129] He went on to tell me how he and another man was out hunting and trapping on the Big Sandy River and had been very successful catching otter and beaver, and was slowly making their way back, trapping as they went. One night, as they had camped on an island they kindled a little fire, a thing they had seldom done before. A party of Indians came floating down the river after they had gone to sleep and slipped in on them, and took them by surprise. When they awoke, they was completely surrounded, and surrendered without making any opposition. The Indians immediately tied them and packed all their traps and furs and guns, and took them into their canoes.

"We pushed on," said Davis, "until we crossed the Ohio River and there struck out through the country in a northerly direction. We traveled several days during which they kept my hands tied and a strong tug around my body tied to an Indian. The last day I was with them, it rained and the tugs around my wrists swelled so that it was paining me very much, and so I hardly slept any that night. Along towards day, I requested through the interpreter to have the cord loosened a little, as it was troubling me very much. The Indian that I was tied to gave me a dig with his elbow and bade me lie still. Just as day began to dawn, I made the request again. By this time there was several Indians up who had stirred the fire. One of them ordered a boy to loose me and he, not understanding, loosed my hands and loosed me from the other Indian.

"No sooner was I loose than I arose to my feet, determined to make an effort to escape. I looked in every direction to see the safest way to make the start. Their guns were all stacked together and I quickly made up my mind to run in the opposite direction so that they would have to step back to get their weapons and, by so doing, I would gain some time. I knew that if I ran past the guns, all they would have to do would be to start with me and pick up a gun as they ran. In the opposite direction was an Indian who stood between me and the fire, but my mind was already made up.

"I drew back my fist and with one powerful lick, I knocked the Indian down into the fire and, at the same time, sprung over him and the fire. Then for a race. I put down my best licks, and so did several of the Indians after me. I gained a little time by the excitement of the Indian that I knocked into the fire, but I suppose the race was a pretty one for the men that saw it. I expected to hear the crack of gun or two every jump I made for a considerable distance, but they either depended on outrunning me or outwinding me, or else they dared not shoot on account of their own men that was just behind me."

Davis said that he thought several times they were just about to take hold of him, but it was now life or death and, after a long, good race, he could hear no more of them. Finally he looked back and, to his great satisfaction, there was not an Indian in sight. He began to slack his pace a little but did not cease running. He traveled on all that day until he found his feet was getting terribly cut and bruised as he had not taken time to put his moccasins on in the morning before he had started, and was running in his bare feet. He stopped and tore his waistcoat in two and wrapped his feet in it, and then pushed on until night.

It was January, and he did not dare travel in the dark for fear that he might loose his way. Seeing a large hollow log, he crawled into it and lay there a while but found that he was freezing, so he crawled out and took a circle round and jumped on the log until he warmed himself. Then he rested a while, and then circled round and jumped again, keeping that up till daylight. Then he struck out again for the Ohio River. On the third day, he struck the Ohio, all this time without food or sleep.

Once at the river's edge, he began to look for some dry logs to construct a raft. To his great satisfaction, he saw a boat floating down the river and he bellowed and beckoned to them, and told his sad story. But they told him that his story had been told too often.[130] He followed them down for miles and at last he told them to row their boat as near the shore as they felt safe and he would swim to them, and to this they consented. When they got about as near as they dared, he plunged into the water and began to swim towards them. Their fears all gave way, and they rowed their boat, met him, and lifted him in. He said he was very much exhausted, being three days and two nights without food or sleep and then forced to pass through the cold, chilly water. He found his rescuers very kind. They cared for him in every respect and landed him down the river where he wished to go.

Davis's story was about the same as the story the Indians told when they got back into Sandusky, except that they said that when he knocked the Indian into the fire and then sprang over him, they knew it was no use to run after him and burst into a roar of laughter, whooping and hallooing. The other prisoner with Davis was brought into Sandusky and I do not know what became of him, but he was not burned or killed. Davis and I had a very agreeable chat and were always very friendly afterwards.

Chief Leather Lips

The Indians are great believers in witches and witchcraft, in supernatural things, and in supernatural power. It is not uncommon for them to invoke supernatural power and supernatural knowledge as did the Prophet and Tecumseh in the War of 1812.[131] (*I was very well acquainted with The Prophet. He was no warrior, but a low, cunning fellow.* Beers) He told them that in battles, the white soldiers would fall before them like harmless flakes of snow and a great many believed it. It was also not uncommon for an Indian to be put to death for some alleged evil that he had done as a witch.

I was acquainted with several cases of that kind whilst I was with them. One, the case of Chief Leather Lips, took place after peace was made in 1810. Leather Lips was chief of the Wyandot tribe and lived at that time on the Scioto River about twelve miles above Columbus.[132] He was an Indian that I was well acquainted with. He was quite aged and his hair was almost perfectly white. He was an Indian of superior talent and ability, harmless, extremely pious, and was recognized as such, I suppose, by all that knew him, both white and Indian. He was too aged to be a practical chief except in council, and for some imaginary evil that had been done he was accused of the crime of witchcraft by a party of five or six Indians from Tippecanoe headed by Chief Round Head.[133] They found him encamped on the bank of the Scioto and made their business known to him. They went out a piece from their camp to hold council. The accused spoke calmly and with great firmness earnestly denying his guilt, but the sentence had no doubt been decided upon before his accusers had left Tippecanoe. After the sentence was reaffirmed, Leather Lips asked time to eat his regular meal, which was granted.

He leisurely walked to his wigwam, partook of a hearty meal of jerked venison, then washed and arrayed himself in his best robes that he had formerly worn when he met in council as chief of his tribe. He looked very grand and dashing. Then he painted himself and they all took a slow march while the chief sang the death song. Keeping pace with the tune, they went seventy or eighty yards from camp and came to a new, shallow grave that, unknown to any of the whites, had just been dug by the Indians. The whites all followed and marched in procession with the Indians. After the death sentence had been passed, the whites tried to interfere and buy the old chief. One of the Sells offered them a valuable horse if they would spare the old man's life, but they told him no.[134] They said you have laws to punish your bad men and the Indians do not interfere. This old man is a bad man, and we have our mode of punishing bad men, and the white man must not interfere. They tried hard to save the old man's life, but all to no purpose.

They came to the grave and the chief knelt down at the graveside and prayed very fervently and solemnly to the Great Spirit. When he was through, the captain that knelt by his side also prayed to the Great Spirit with great solemnity. They then arose to their feet and, after a few moments, the chief sank down onto his knees and prayed again as before and when he was done, he buried his face in both hands and told them he was now ready to die. The whites was at a great loss to know how the Indians were going to execute the old man for they had left all their guns and weapons at the camp, so far as they could see. But the captain that had knelt with the old chief stepped forward and drew a new, glittering tomahawk from under his capote.[135] Brandishing it a few times in the air, he brought it down on the crown of the old man's head with great force. The venerable old chief fell prostrate at his feet. While struggling there for a few moments, the sweat came out on his face and neck. The Indians pointed to that as a sure token of his guilt and one remarked, "He in Hell now." At that, the captain stepped up and gave him a few more blows with the tomahawk and in a few moments, his life was extinct, whereupon they hastened to place him in the grave with all his gorgeous apparel on his person. Thus ended the barbarous and horrible tragedy.

In a Drunken Row

Indians are not liable to quarrel or fight except when drunk. I have frequently known them, when they would get sober after having committed depredations or assaults upon their fellow Indians, to come back and ask pardon and make restitution for all the damage they had done, claiming that they were not to blame but rather the firewater that they had consumed.

Once, two different tribes were camped close together when an Indian trader, laden with whiskey, also camped near them. The two tribes both began drinking, and through the course of the night, an Indian of one tribe killed an Indian of the other. The fight continued until they had killed five in all, not killing the one who had started the fray but those whom they could slyly lure across to the opposite side. In the morning, the leader of the tribe that had committed the first depredation went to the other tribe and told them, "We are killing innocent men. If you kill another, we will have a general war and one tribe or the other will be destroyed." The other tribe then made a demand, "Give up the man that committed the first crime and let us kill him, or we will have a general war." The first tribe held a council and agreed to do so if they couldn't buy off their man. They went around the tribe and collected a considerable amount of wampum and presented it to the second tribe, but they refused to take it, telling them they wanted the man. The first tribe counseled again, and after a while they doubled the bounty. The second tribe again refused to take it, and they went back and doubled it again. It was now worth about one hundred dollars. They brought the bounty and the man and presented them both, saying, "Now take your choice. There is the man and there is the ransom. This is the last offer." The second tribe counseled a while, and then counseled with the murdered man's wife. She preferred the ransom rather than being left with nothing, so they told the first tribe that they would take the ransom and spare the accused man's life. That ended the strife, and the guilty man could have walked through the other tribe the next day with all safety if he had saw fit.

Captain John was as tall and fine a specimen of an Indian as you would see out of a hundred, full of mirth and fun and a great lover of whiskey, which very often led him into trouble and difficulty.[136] A half-breed by the name of John Cushen killed one of Captain John's warmest and best friends in one of their drinking frolics, which roused up the ire of Captain John. He told Cushen that he had killed his best friend and for that he would kill him one day. "But," he said, "I will not take advantage of you as you did of my friend. I will let you know when I go to kill you. So that you can have a fair chance for your life, I will give you a chance to kill me if you can."

Cushen left the country and was gone about three years, knowing that Captain John was in earnest and meant just what he said. While gone, he got into a battle and was severely wounded, so much so that he expected to die. When he returned, he came back a mere skeleton and told Captain John to kill him if he saw fit, but the Captain told him he was not going to kill a sick or wounded man, that if he died from his wounds, it was all well. But if he got better, he meant to kill him. Said he, "I want you to suffer all you can."

After a few moons, Cushen began to improve and finally saw that he was going to get well, and so slipped off again. He was gone about a year and supposed that the Captain might give it up by this time. He was staying and working a part of the time down around Chillicothe when an Indian trader, loaded with liquor and buying skins and furs, stopped on Darby where Captain John lived.[137] Cushen, hearing of him, also came up. There were several other Indians there trading and drinking, and the first night, Captain John and John Cushen both got drunk and got into a quarrel that turned into a fight. They were separated by the trader and the other Indians, but their ambitions were aroused up to such a pitch that there was no such thing as to pacify them. The old grudge came up, and Captain John told Cushen that now was the time to settle it. They agreed to fight the next day, and parted for the night.

They met the next morning and agreed to fight with tomahawks and butcher knives, so Captain John went and bought the tomahawks and knives and threw them down at Cushen's feet, telling him to take his choice. Cushen made his selection and they walked to a log and stuck up a stake, and then cut a notch in the log some distance from the shadow of the stake. Both agreed that as soon as the shadow of the stake came into the notch, then the fight should commence. Each fellow took his position on the log; one on one side of the notch and the other on the opposite side. There, they sat watch-

A History of Jonathan Alder

ing the shadow of the stake as it slowly crept along towards the notch, glancing at each other occasionally and looking as ferocious as tigers, but not speaking a word until the shadow of the stake fell in the notch. At that moment, both sprung to their feet. The ground was a little uneven and Cushen was uphill from Captain John. He came tripping down on the Captain as light as a feather. They came together and made a few passes at each other when Captain John's tomahawk sunk into Cushen's head and he fell lifeless at his feet. This ended another savage strife.

The next morning, Captain John went down to one of the Runes', and when he approached Mr. Runes he clasped his hand to his breast and exclaimed, "Me big man. Me Captain John. Me kill John Cushen. Me want a mattock and shovel to bury him." Runes let him have the mattock and shovel. Captain John buried Cushen and carried back the tools, but felt very proud of the deed he had done.

It was along about 1806–8 that the Indians began to fall back on their reserves. They were scattered pretty much all over the state before the treaty of 1795 and frequently a tribe would sell their right to their land in Ohio for a small portion of land somewhere else in the west and a certain amount of money to be paid yearly. In these treaties, the Indians was very often made drunk and very badly cheated. In nearly every case, an agent accompanied by whiskey would be sent out by the government. Nearly every time, the treaty was made in accordance to the premeditation of the white man, and it was easy to see that Indian title would soon be extinguished to all of their land in the state of Ohio, their most choice hunting ground on this continent. To this, Tecumseh the warrior and his brother, the Prophet, objected, and they were at this time the two most powerful men amongst the Indians. They wielded the greatest influence at the time. More than any others, they were both fine speakers and could argue to the point, and could arouse the feelings of their hearer to war or to sympathy at any time, just as they wished.

These two powerful men were holding meetings over all the west and speaking to large crowds. Their object, as they declared, was not war, but peace, and to unite all the tribes into a kind of confederacy so that one tribe could not sell their right to the soil without a majority of all the chiefs of that confederacy. They declared that the white race was all united. State after state had their rights, but the general government and the Great Father at Washington was chief over all. His arguments were both sensible and logical. But those meetings roused up the national government as well as the inhabitants of Darby, where it created a great deal of talk up to the year of 1810. The Indians had nearly all left our settlement, assuring me that if any trouble or war should break out I should have timely notice of it beforehand so that I might get out of the way of danger. The Indians from Tecumseh's town[138] had kept up a steady communication with me, and so I had no fear of an uprising from the friendly Indians of Ohio.

In the latter part of the summer of 1811, there was but one Indian left in Madison County, and he was camped on my farm. There was much talk that he might be there as a spy and many were afraid that he was there to collect information about our settlement. Finally, some of the settlers came and said that if he did not leave, they would shoot him. I did not know but some of them might be foolish enough to do so, and I told him that the neighbors was dissatisfied about his being here, and that he had better fix his business and leave for a while. He said he would, and gathered up all his furs and skins and packed them beneath a cross pole with a large buckskin over it, so that it would shed rain. Then he cut two forks and run them up betwixt two saplings right in my front yard and told me that if he never came back, the furs and skins should be mine. Before he left, he told me that he would go from here to Upper Sandusky, and from there he would go directly to Tecumseh's town on the Tippecanoe River, and that if there should be any fighting or war, I should be the first to know it on Darby. The next morning he left.

There had been a council held between Governor Harrison and Tecumseh, and all kinds of runners went out with information of the meeting.[139] The news excited the frontiers with dread and fear, and on Darby, some were for leaving the country and others for forting.

My brother, brother-in-law Henry Smith, and their families became very much excited, so much so that they thought we had better all leave now together. I tried to assure them and my neighbors that there was no danger, but we all met and decided to fort and made our headquarters with Henry Smith.[140] We hadn't been there but a part of one day until they began to find fault with the place and thought it unsafe. I discovered after a little while that they were whispering among themselves and getting out to one side to talk in my absence. I saw that they had lost confidence in me, and that was too mortifying for me to stand. I spoke to my wife and told her we would go home.

The next morning, I told her to go over to the fort and see what they were doing. She came back and told me that they were loaded up, ready to move. They went on down Darby as far as Duere Mill, and there fell in with another company and came back up on Little Darby, opposite of where Hampton is, and there built a fort and all moved into that. The land on which the fort stood is now owned by Alex Wilson. I visited them several times whilst they were forted there. They appeared to be partially contented; still, I could see a good deal of uneasiness in their conversation. The news that they received remained frightening and runners kept it up to the highest pitch.

I was now entirely alone except for my wife and three children. Things remained in this condition for a short time until one night about two o'clock I heard a knock at the door. I got up and asked who was there, and was answered in the Indian tongue. I then opened the door and made a fire. My Indian visitors told me that they had come to tell me that there had been a hard fight between the Indians and the whites on the Tippecanoe at Tecumseh's town. I asked when, and they said the night before last. They then told me not to be alarmed, for they all said the thing was ended and there would be a treaty immediately. They told me that Governor Harrison had moved against Tecumseh's town, and that they had had a hard fight. The attack was made in the night, but the Indians were badly whipped. The Indians made the attack and had got a great many of their men killed, and was obliged to retreat. They said that as soon as the fight was over, they started two men on foot to Upper Sandusky, as they had been informed that there was a promise made to me that if there was any certainty of war or any fighting, I was to be notified of it before anyone else in my neighborhood so that I could get out of the way of it if necessary. They came to Sandusky last night and started immediately here. They were instructed to say to me to rest easy, for there would be no more fighting. They gave me the names of several Indians that was killed and wounded that I was well acquainted with. They told me they wanted something to eat and that they must get back out of the settlement before daylight, as they did not wish to be seen as it might have a bad consequence on me if the whites should see them, so I got them a bite and they started back. They were safe as soon as they passed a little beyond where Pleasant Valley is. Beyond there was a dense forest to Sandusky except for a few settlements here and there. These they could easily avoid by passing around, and they did so. They were able to come in and pass out without being seen by anyone except myself and my wife.

In the course of a week or more, runners began to come in telling that there had been a fight in the west with the Indians. I visited the fort and they had listened to some of the runners, but nothing was certain. I could have told them all about it, but I dared not. If I had told them what I knew and how I got the news I do not know but that my life would have been in danger.

In about ten days or two weeks, the news came officially, but it did not differ materially from what I had got from the two Indians. I still kept my information of the battle secret till after the War of 1812 with Great Britain, which followed soon after. My neighbors now abandoned their fort and all got back on their farms and to work.

(*On the outbreak of hostilities in 1812, the Indian chiefs held a council and sent a deputation to Alder to learn which side to espouse, saying that the British wished them to go and fight for them, holding out the promise that in such case, they would support their families. He advised them to remain at first neutral, and told them they need not be afraid of the Americans harming their women and children. They followed his advice, for a while remained neutral, and eventually became warm friends of the Americans.* Howe)

The next news of an exciting nature was in 1812 when we learned that our government had declared war against England. Return J. Maigs [Return Jonathan Meigs] was governor of Ohio at that time and he soon ordered a draft for a certain number of men and sent them up towards the lake. Then he ordered another draft for one company of men to go out north some twenty miles beyond the settlement on the Sandusky Indian trail and build a blockhouse. The draft was made and I happened to be one of the victims caught, along with a good share of my neighbors, for the two drafts had taken over half of the men living in our settlement. All things being ready, we marched out and followed the Indian trail. I was made a kind of leader, for I knew every part of the trail from the salt springs to Upper Sandusky. We passed just beyond Mill Creek so as to have the creek handy for water, and there halted and went to work.[141] In the course of four or five days, we had our blockhouse finished on the north bank of the creek, perhaps three or four hundred yards from the stream. There was about seventy of us in all. Davis Watson[142] was our colonel and Frederick Lloyd was first lieutenant.

I told several of the men of my neighborhood that this was a very unwise measure for the governor to send us off so far from the settlement. I told them that if there was any Indians who wished to do mischief, they would not come here but would go directly into the settlement and kill our women and children. I had to be very careful what I said for fear they might think me not altogether true. We had been at the blockhouse for about two weeks when one day the colonel sent me and John Johnson out three or four miles on the trail to see if we could discover any signs of the Indians. After we got off a couple of miles, Johnson asked me if I couldn't contrive some plan to break things up so that we could get to go home. He said that if we could only get them confused some way, he thought the camp might be broken up. I told him that I thought I could very easily confuse them. "Well," said he, "what is your plan?" Johnson and I both were wearing moccasins. Said I, "We will follow this trail out here about three miles where there is a long mud hole. You go carefully around it so as not to make any tracks until you get beyond it, and then come through it this way. Then go back on the outside so as not to make any tracks and then come back through the mud hole as before, and so on. Repeat it fifteen or twenty times and then come back to me and report that there is moccasin tracks on ahead." John was greatly tickled at the idea.

I told him to go on ahead and I would set down and wait until he came back. He did so, and was gone half an hour before he returned. I asked him what discovery he had made. He said plenty of moccasin tracks. I then went back with him to see if they were made in a manner so as not to be easily detected. I told him I thought they would do and so we turned and went back to the blockhouse. As soon as made our appearance, they began to gather around us, and about the first question was, "What discoveries have you made?" I told them nothing serious. "Well, did you see any Indian signs?" I told them I saw a good many moccasin tracks. "Moccasin tracks," they said. I told them that yes, they were moccasin tracks. I saw the whole crowd was excited. We had one man on the sick list and at the word "moccasin track," he turned pale at once. "Well, do you think they were Indian tracks?" I told them that I was not going to pass my opinion, but I would go with any of them and show them the tracks as they were not more than three miles off. I then insisted on some of them going with me to see for themselves, but not a man would volunteer to go. "Well, did the tracks look fresh, like they were made today?" "Yes," I told them, "they looked like they might have been made today, anyhow, not more than a day or two." I again insisted on a half-dozen or more going with me and see for themselves, but they said no, the Indians might be lying in ambush and would shoot them down.

The commanding officer thought it not best to divide the company if there were Indians about, but keep together and prepare for battle. I told John Johnson to get the sick man to one side and tell him the secret, that he had made the moccasin tracks himself, and that there was going to be a false alarm that night, and for him not to be scared, that the object was to break up the camp, and that we would all get to go home. After the sick man was informed of the prospect, his whole countenance and demeanor was changed. As night was approaching, the officers began to make their night arrangements. Heretofore, our guns had been stacked together. I told them if I was the commanding officer, I would make every man take his gun and lie upon his arms for if there would be an attack, half the guns would be broken. The colonel said that that was very sensible and ordered every man to take his gun and see that it was loaded, and to lie with his gun in his arms.

I was very sure that Johnson and I would be put on guard that night, and so we were, and also Andy Clarno. When we went out to take our stations, we let Clarno onto the secret which relieved and tickled him very much. This was our plan: as soon as they all got bedded down and the talk had ceased, I was to fire my gun first and then the other two to fire immediately and then run in. We got out at our stations and waited very impatiently for them to get quiet and silent, but it seemed as though they were bound to talk all night. At perhaps about eleven o'clock, it all got still. There had been a dog gnawing on a bone not far off all night. I called out three times "Who was there," and received no answer and then fired my gun at the dog, but missed him. Johnson and Clarno fired their guns and then we ran in as quick as we could to see the stampede.

Well, you never saw a lot of frightened cattle run worse than they did. There seemed very little difference betwixt officers and privates. I hurried in to see the fun. First, I saw a man rise out of his bed with his blanket wrapped around him. As he ran half bent, he became tangled in his blanket and fell on a log with his whole weight on the inset of his gun. I heard it snap, but he rose and ran half bent as far as I could see him. Presently, I heard Frederick Lloyd's voice hallooing "Halt! Halt! Halt!" The colonel had a fine voice, but I could not hear him as there was so much noise. I then ran to the blockhouse where most of my neighbors were quartered in. When I got there, every fellow was puffing and blowing, but not a word was spoken by anyone. As soon as they could find their guns and shot pouch, they would dart out the door and follow the crowd. I passed one Calhoun that was not very well and who had seen a little service in the Revolutionary War. He did not think it proper to run, and it was a little dark.

He could not see exactly who it was and as I was passing around rather slyly, he arose, cocked his gun, and cried out, "Who the Hell is there?" Says I, "Don't shoot," and as I walked up to him, he said, "What the Hell does all this mean?" I told him I could not tell. Our sick man that we had let onto the secret of the alarm was lying on his couch laughing till he was actually in misery, but it had a good effect on him, for he was better the next morning and mended right along.

The colonel and Lieutenant Lloyd got them stopped with a great deal of effort and pretty soon I saw them coming in carrying one man. That scared me, for I was afraid that some of them, in their fright, had shot him. I walked up and asked him what the matter was. They said he had run against a rough-barked oak tree. His forehead was very badly cut and bleeding. He was knocked senseless, but I saw directly that he was coming to.

Presently, a man came up to the captain and me and said he believed there was Indians nearby for he had heard a terrible splashing going across the creek. He said there must have been fifteen or twenty. I knew there was no Indians so I took a circle across the creek and saw a man lying on his belly before the fire, wet all over. I went back to the captain and told him I had found the man that crossed the creek. I took the captain with me and went and showed him the man. The captain hallooed out, "Hello my friend, what wet you." Said he, "I ran across the creek." "Well, did anyone cross with you?" "Yes," said he, naming the man, "he and I crossed together." "Well, did anyone else cross with you?" He said no, there was none but they two. It was said that another, on his great flight, pitched off the bank and lodged in the fork of a tree or bush. Some looked scared and others looked mad.

Because they had begun to suspect a false alarm, the next thing was to call the roll and see how many was lost, missing, or wounded. They were all found present with one wounded, two wet, and one with a broken gun. The next thing was to call up the guard to learn at what or why we fired. I told them that I had heard a noise in the bush and called out three times, "Who is there." Getting no answer, I fired at the noise. About the same time, Clarno said he fired in response to our fire.

By the time the officers got through with the preliminaries, it was so near daylight that they did not think it necessary to put out guards or to lie down and try to sleep. Instead, we got up our fires and spent the balance of the night with some laughing and talking, and some looking sullen and mad. But if there had been one dozen Indians there that night, they could have taken the camp and held it successfully. With a few shots in our rear and the Indians' war whoop, our officers couldn't have stopped our men short of their homes.

The next morning after daylight, it was nothing but disorder and confusion. On the first attempt to call roll, objections were made. Some threatened to desert. Others declared they would have a new election and elect a new colonel because the colonel had run, and Lloyd was the only soldier amongst the officers and he should be colonel.[143] Colonel Watson was a man with a fine voice and could not be heard in such uproars. Lloyd was a man of strong lungs and had a coarse voice. You could have heard him hallooing "Halt! Halt! Halt!" a mile off. The men began to make preparations for an election, but someone sprung the question of its legality. They saw that they could not elect a commissioned officer without an order from the governor, and this threw them into confusion again. We that were in the plot to break up the camp thought it a favorable time to try our scheme.

I talked to the colonel and told him I knew a little about Indian warfare, and that he was doing a very unwise thing staying here. If there was any Indians in the country wishing to do any mischief, they would not come here and attack us without an overwhelming force, and that they would be sure to ascertain our strength first. If they were weak, they would just pass round us and go into our neighborhood and destroy the women and children, and plunder and carry off anything they saw fit. That was their nature; that they would have no object at all in attacking us here unless they was sufficiently strong to overpower us, and if I was in his place, I shouldn't hesitate one minute to discharge the men and let them go home. He said the whole responsibility would rest on him if he disobeyed the governor's orders. I told him I would not be afraid to risk it. Moreover, because of the condition of the men, he couldn't control them. He called a council of his officers, and by ten o'clock we were all discharged and on our road home, and the larger portion of us was with our families that night.

Lloyd came home, but in few weeks went over to Franklinton where General Harrison was stationed and enlisted in the army. Eventually, he took sick and died while in the service, for he was truly a soldier.

The war lasted about two more years and there was a treaty made betwixt the United States and Great Britain, and we were again at peace.

There was two of the Frakes that I became acquainted with in an early day while I was yet living with my Indian woman. Nathan and William Frakes were both drafted in the War of 1812, and both proved to be Tories and deserters. They were both arrested and tried at Chillicothe.[144] Nathan was shot, but the evidence against William was not so strong. He remained under arrest until the war came to a close and he was released.

Among our greatest privations during the early settlement of this country was the want of mills and blacksmiths. The first mill was started at Springfield, and here the water was carried for a long distance in hollow logs or troughs. They cut large, hollow trees and split them or hewed them off on one side, and they fit together so nicely that there was but very little leak. In this manner they made an overshot mill.[145] Benjamin Springer and myself went to this mill together while I yet retained my Indian woman.

In quite an early day, a man named Dyer erected a mill on Darby near George's mill, and Samuel Sandusky started a blacksmith shop close by, which made things quite handy. Not many years afterwards, Frederick Sager started a grist mill, and shortly thereafter, a carding machine was started at Dyer's mill. Before that, our women had carded their wool by hand to make their cloth. Within a few years, Uriah and Ambrose Beach started a carding machine and fulling mill and began spinning and weaving near Amity.[146] We now thought we had a country that people could live in. The river and creek bottoms were very productive and the grazing lands on the Darby Plains was abundant for horses and cattle. As elk and buffalo receded, the cow and the ox took their place, and as the black bear and panther began to give way, swine and sheep took their place. The Indian war whoop had ceased and the sound of the voice of the ministers of the Gospel was now to be heard in its place.

My father-in-law, Adam Blont, was yet back in the state of Virginia, but we had occasionally exchanged letters. In the fall of 1815, who should step into my house one afternoon but Adam Blout. He, with his entire family except one daughter that was married, was all in Ohio with Joseph Belaho, a son-in-law. I was surrounded with my mother, brother, and sister, my father-in-law, mother-in-law, sister-in-law, and brothers-in-law. What a change had taken place in about twenty years! Twenty years before, I was not able to speak one word of English and ten years before, I had no knowledge that my mother or brother were alive. But by the kindness of John Moore, I found my relations, and while visiting them became acquainted with my wife and brought her away with me. This was the cause of a large number leaving a land that was hard to make a living in and emigrating to a land that did truly flow with milk and honey.

Madison County was gradually being divided up into townships, and Canaan Township was stricken off from Darby and other townships and named Felps Township after a man by the name of Felps. Felps was a man of more than ordinary talent and ability. He was generally foremost in anything that was going on that was at all exciting. But he was also very unfortunate about getting into trouble and getting others in as well. About this time, George Blaylock was also a citizen of this township. He was a married man and he and his wife had a woman of bad character with them by the name of Sarah Whitney. In the process of time, she gave birth to an illegitimate child, which she managed to do in the absence of anyone. She foully disposed of the child but was under the necessity of calling a physician, and the matter then came to light. When she was pressed to tell what had become of the child, she told them that it had been born dead out at the barn. Seeing it was dead, she threw it into the hog pen where Blaylock was feeding some fifteen or twenty head of hogs and that they had devoured it. This created a good deal of talk and sensation. After she recovered, she still stayed with Blaylock and his wife, and finally the neighbors, with Felps as their leader, took it into their head to mob them in order to separate them.

They gave Blaylock notice that if Mrs. Whitney was not gone within a certain time they would be taken in hand, but no attention was paid to their threats. Finally a crowd, all blacked so as not to be known, gathered, and by all accounts, used Blaylock and Whitney very rough. The crowd took them a half mile or more into the woods and tied their hands securely together and then went away, leaving them with a good many threats about what would be done the next time. But Blaylock's wife had followed behind the noise at a proper distance so as not to be detected and after the crowd was gone out of hearing, she went up and unloosed them.

Things remained quiet for a couple of weeks, but one evening about sunset, John Kilgore, a young man and neighbor of mine, called on me and told me that they was going that night again to mob Blaylock and that they had sent him down to get me to go along. "Now John," said I, "some of you will be killed, for there is no man that will put up with that kind of treatment, and I would advise you to have nothing to do with it." He said Blaylock was a coward, and he did not think there was any danger. "Well," said I, "Levi Francis is his brother-in-law, and he will protect Blaylock, and Francis is no coward."

After a good deal of talk, Kilgore insisted that I should go with him and try to stop the mob. I told him I would do that, and so I went with him and found all the men collected together about a mile from Blaylock's house. There was fifteen or twenty in all, all in fine spirits and fortified with plenty of whiskey. I commenced giving them my views of the lawless course they were taking. Felps spoke up and said he would give his boot to any man that would come there to discourage them and would take him to the highest deoc[147] they could find and hoist it up within two rails of the bottom, and put his head under it, and leave him there.

I soon saw that I was in danger, for they all were about half drunk and I did not know what they might do. I told Felps that if I was the men, I would not go one step without him in the lead. He then began to limp, and said it would not do for him to go up at all, for he was lame and would be known. I told him then, "Some of you will be shot." At that, Isaac Johnson came up to me and put his hands on my shoulders and said, "Uncle Jonathan, Blaylock is a coward and daren't to pull the trigger." "Well," said I, "if he is a coward, Levi Francis is not, and he will be there." At this, Caleb Strobridge came up with a black chunk and told them to black themselves and be off.

All that intended to blackened their faces except Felps, who did not black his. Then they all took a dram and started. There was three or four of us that remained behind to see what would be done. They went off very still and in the course of twenty or thirty minutes, we heard them commence battering on the door. Presently, it seemed as if Blaylock was not at home and Mrs. Blaylock had opened the door and let them in. I told Kilgore that Blaylock was not there, and soon all left. Not being satisfied, in a week they all collected again, but this time they failed to call on me. Blaylock was aware of their coming and had his door well barred and had prepared a crack opened by the side of the door.

The men moved up silently and cautiously until they got to the cabin and then commenced striking their clubs on the door. Very quick a gun fired and Isaac Johnson fell mortally wounded. A man named Cary was also injured. This struck the men with terror, and they picked up their wounded men and carried them off. They carried Johnson but a small distance into the orchard and placed him under an apple tree. He died that night. Cary was yet alive in the morning and in his right mind. They sent to Worthington for a doctor. I got up there a while before the doctor came and when I spoke to Cary, he told me I was in the right, but he saw it too late. The doctor came after a little while and probed the wound, but finally told Cary that he could not live. Cary died the next day about noon. Thus ended the lives of two as fine men as there was in the country, two noble-hearted men led on by one bad man.

Not long afterwards, Felps got into an assault and battery with one John Roberts and after a good deal of hard swearing, had to flee the country. This so exasperated the people that they applied to the legislature to change the name of the township from Felps to Canaan, which was done.

The account of the last moving affair I got from Levi Francis, who had been with Blaylock throughout the day arranging things, and on the other side from the men in the mob. Blaylock was furnished with four good rifles, well loaded, and the two women stood prepared to load the guns as fast as they were discharged. Francis told me that he was setting not more than two hundred yards from the house with his gun when the mob approached, and after the first gun was fired, there was a minute or so space before the second gun was fired. He thought that Blaylock's heart had failed him and that he would now be killed, and that was one reason why he had not stayed with Blaylock. "I knew that if they had courage enough to overpower the house, the men found inside would be either shot or hung," said he, "most probably the latter. But when the second gun was fired, I knew there would be desperate works if the mob held on. I was satisfied from the groans there was two men killed."

Blaylock and Francis were both arrested and lodged in jail and remained there a whole year before their trial came up. Blaylock was acquitted on the ground that he was acting in self-defense, though he admitted to killing both men, saying that he fired both guns. Francis was also acquitted for the want of proof. Blaylock sold his farm soon after and went west. Francis remained, but there was a great hatred towards him by the Johnsons and Carys.

Soon after both men were acquitted, I had a talk with Francis and he told me that he knew his life was in danger and that the Johnsons would kill him if they had an opportunity. He told me about being out hunting one afternoon and that as he was coming in late in the evening, it was raining a little. Not more than a half mile from his home, he saw a man coming directly towards him. Francis stopped and hid in the bush and when the man got within a few rods of him, he saw that it was Michael Johnson with his gun on his shoulder and his hat drawn down to keep the rain out of his face. "I could have picked his eye out with my rifle," said he, "and I knew his object. He was going that night to waylay my house to kill me, but I turned another way and did not go home that night." Not more than a year after this conversation with Francis, Michael Johnson called and stayed all night with me. Through the evening's talk it came up about his brother being killed. He still firmly believed that Francis had killed one of the men, and he told me that he had not seen him the night that Francis was in the woods, for if he had, he should have surely killed him. I now had both of their stories, but kept them to myself. The farm on which the men fell mortally wounded is now owned by Mathias Slyh.

Stephen Cary left a wife and three children. She was sister to Isaac Johnson that was also killed. Of all women, she was the most unfortunate. She had now lost her husband and her brother in a way much to be lamented. She was left with very small means for a living and was forced to put out her three children and then work from place to place for her own support.

Abraham Cary, one of her sons, was placed with John Taylor, a mighty good place. Isaac, his twin, was kept amongst the Johnsons, and Sarah Cary, her daughter, was placed with a family named Erwin. All seemed to be going well. Cary married again to Jacob Lappen, a very fine man. Sarah was now fourteen or fifteen years old, bordering on womanhood and a very handsome girl, much beloved by all her young acquaintances. It was in the summer time, and the birds were very bad on the apples. One of the twin boys took the gun out to shoot birds, but after snapping it a dozen times or more and not getting it to go off, he came back to the house with it. As he walked into the yard, Sarah happened to be out in the yard and he raised up the gun and says, "Sally, I am going to shoot you." She said, "Don't," but at that he snapped the gun and it went off. The load and the ramrod which was in the barrel passed through her head and she instantly dropped dead. So there was another sad fate by an unthoughtful and reckless boy.

In about 1830, Jacob Lappen and his wife lived on Big Darby near Amity when they decided to make an evening visit to one of their near neighbors. Their children had stayed home, gone to bed, and was asleep. There were four children, the oldest not more than ten years old. The house took fire and when the oldest woke, the house was just on the verge of tumbling in. He picked up the smallest child and ran out with it. The other two, he said, had gotten out of bed, but instead of running out crawled under the bed. He called to them and could hear them crying, but dared not venture in, and so they was burned to death. What a sad fate to the father and mother.

My mother enjoyed life in this new country very finely and became acquainted with many of the Indians, and on the most friendly terms. I took great delight in introducing them to her. Formerly, she had hated them intensely, but how wonderfully circumstances had changed things. They took great delight in making her little presents such as baskets that were finely woven, checkered, and painted, and moccasins ingeniously ornamented with beads and porcupine quills. In the fall of the year, or the spring, they would bring a few cranberries, which was quite an article of trade with them, and frequently a loaf of the finest maple sugar. All of these seemed to rivet the ties of friendship between them. She looked upon them as my guardians and protectors.

When my mother was about seventy-two years of age, she took sick and died and was buried in the Foster graveyard. My half-sister had died a few years before and was buried at the same place. And so one after another of my relations that followed me to this country began to pass off. My brother's wife, and my father-in-law, and mother-in-law, and some of their children have also passed away and are buried in the same graveyard upon the land that I expect to own, and where I expect my bones to he laid.

Simon Kenton

One day in the fall of 1818, I had been out hunting, for that was my daily business in the hunting season. It was raining that afternoon and I came into the house dripping with water. As I stepped in, a tall, bony man, six foot and an inch or two rose up before me and says, "How do you do, Jonathan Alder." I told him I was well. Said he, "I have been running you for more than twenty years and have never been able to overtake you till now. My name is Simon Kenton." I told him to be seated and that after supper, we would tell some hard stories to the children.

Following dinner, Kenton requested me to tell him about some of the fights and skirmishes that the Indians had had in the last ten years of my time with them, so I began to tell him of the fight at the Meockee towns [Mequashake] where the thirty-six men was all buried in one hole in a large quagmire. As soon as I got far enough along that he understood what fight it was, he said, "Now stop, and let me tell that story," and so I stopped and he began.

He told me where he and his men crossed the Ohio and how stealthily and cautiously they moved along up through the country until they got to the little town and made the attack. The Indians soon fled except for the six that had got surrounded. "The Indians took shelter in one of the houses," said he. "My men attempted to rush the house and take them by storm, but the Indians' fire was so deadly that they were forced to fall back. We then made several other attempts, but they were also unsuccessful. Every now and then, the Indians would pick off a man. We fell back, thinking that they would come out to make their escape, but they did not. Then we renewed the attack and lost another man or two. I decided that that would not do, so we contrived to shoot fire onto the roof of the house and when we did, they was then forced to come out. They broke and ran and my men shot down four of them directly. The other two got betwixt some logs and them two killed six more of my men before we got them killed. When I gathered the dead all up, I found I had thirty of my men killed and six dead Indians.

"I knew that it would not do to remain there long, for I had fewer than two hundred men and twenty or thirty of them were wounded, and I was poorly prepared with provisions. So we went to one of the quagmires and cut out the turf about five feet in diameter, and the dead was brought there. We would drop a man in the hole and he would go immediately out of sight. We dropped into that hole one-and-thirty white men and the six Indians. Then we gathered up and made a retreat back as fast as possible with what prisoners we had taken." "Now," said he, "is that a true statement?" I told him it was. "Well," said he, "I was head commander there."

When I would begin to tell of a fight, he would stop me and then go on and tell the balance of it, and I found that perhaps half of our fighting over the last ten years had been done with troops under his command. In several of the little skirmishes where the whites was drove and whipped, he would take up the story and tell all—how the attack was made and how many was lost, and how they had to run. I soon found that he had been running me for twenty years or more. Now the name of Simon Kenton was very familiar amongst the Indians and with myself. He then wanted me to give him a sketch of my captivity and life with the Indians. He had become very familiar with my name when he lived close to Zanesfield beside the Indians, and had a great deal of anxiety to see me and learn my history. I went on to give him a short history of my captivity, and adoption, and life as briefly as possible. He then gave me quite a lengthy history of his life from a boy of sixteen up to that time, which was very interesting.

He was born in the state of Virginia in the year 17—.[148] At the age of sixteen he said he had a difficulty with a rival lover by the name of Veck.[149] The young lady and his rival and himself were all schoolmates. Him and Veck met one day by themselves and soon got into a quarrel, and from that a fight. He threw Veck to the ground and kicked him several times in the breast, and he soon commenced vomiting blood and finally fainted away. "Then I became alarmed and ran to him, and picked him up and spoke as kind to him as I could, but received no answer," said he. "I laid him down and felt sure that I had killed him and like Moses, I fled the country. I left immediately without giving my folks any information. I crossed over the Allegheny Mountains without road or path, slept in the woods at night and finally landed at Fort Pitt, almost starved and naked. I joined the garrison there and was employed as a hunter and remained there awhile, but not feeling safe, I struck out down the Ohio River. After wandering around with one Williams, I got into Kentucky.[150]

"Whilst there in the glory of hunting, I had supposed that I and Williams were the only men in Kentucky, but one day we fell in company with one Stover who gave us to understand that one Colonel Boone was also in Kentucky, not more than one hundred miles off."¹⁵¹ Stover conducted Kenton to where Boone was stationed and there introduced him to the noble Daniel Boone. "I was introduced to him as Simon Butler, for I had changed my name from Kenton to Butler, supposing myself to be a fugitive from justice. But in fact, after many years I found that I had done Veck no serious injury. I remained a few days with Boone and on returning to my cabin, I found it in ashes. A little way off, I found a stake firmly drove in the ground and some charred wood lying round it, and charred bones which too plainly told the fate of my comrade Williams."¹⁵²

Kenton then hastened back and joined himself to Boone's settlement. He roamed there and hunted in all the glory of the sport of the chase until three of them took in mind to cross the Ohio and steal a few horses from the Indians.¹⁵³ They succeeded in crossing the river and got up the Scioto as far as Chillicothe. There they found the Indians camped, and nearby were some very valuable horses in a pound and they succeeded in taking out seven. "Our scout up the river had all been in the night, laying by in the daytime. It was now about midnight and we struck off down the river as fast as possible, knowing that the Indians would follow us. On the second day we reached the Ohio in safety, but there was a very high wind and the waves rolled so high that we could not induce the horses to take to the water. We waited until evening, hoping that the winds would fall and that we might be able to cross the next morning. But it was not to be so. The winds blew that night almost like a hurricane and the next morning, knowing that the Indians was after us, we concluded to strike down the river to the Falls where we could ferry across.¹⁵⁴ Each mounted a horse and started down the river, leaving the four horses. Then we concluded that we might as well take all the horses, as they were very valuable ones and so rode back to get the others.

"We all dismounted and hitched our horses and then separated to look for the others. Presently, I saw two Indians and a white man approaching me in rapid speed on horseback. I raised my gun and aimed at the front one and pulled the trigger, and the powder flashed in the pan.[155] I then attempted to escape by flight, but they soon over-took me and commenced handling me very rough. Just then, I saw my comrade Montgomery making to my assistance with all speed, but two of the Indians raised their rifles and he fell dead.[156] Then they immediately scalped him and then came up and slapped me several times in the face with the bloody scalp, calling me a horse thief.

"They cut switches and whipped me over the head and face se-verely and then threw me to the ground. They tied a buffalo tug around my neck and fastened that to a sapling then drove stakes in the ground and stretched out my arms and feet, and fastened them to the stakes. They also fastened a pole across my breast and then gave me a few kicks and left me in that condition until they gathered up all their horses."

The third member of Kenton's party, a man named Clarke, had in the meantime plunged into the thick woods unobserved by the Indi-ans and made his escape.[157] "After they had gathered up all their hors-es, they loosed me and placed me on the wildest one. They tied my feet under his belly and my hands behind my back and then turned the horse loose. He reared and plunged, and ran through the brush tearing my clothes and flesh at a horrible rate until he became wor-ried down. Then he followed along after the rest as tame as a dog. In this way, they got back to what is Old Chillicothe." Then they held a council, but in the meantime had him naked and tied to a stake where the squaws and children and men took great delight in buffet-ing him until midnight.

"I was then taken away and tied down and guarded till morning. The council had decided to burn me at the stake, but that I must also first run the gauntlet—a favorite amusement with them. When I was let out the next morning, the whole village, women and children to the number of perhaps three hundred, had formed into parallel lines six or eight feet apart and perhaps half a mile long. I was taken to the farthest end and there instructed that if I should be able to reach the council house without being overtaken by those behind, I would not be whipped. There was several behind me with whips, and I was not to break through the lines. The word was given to start and I done so, and as I would pass them some would strike me with sticks and some with their fists, but I saw one step out of line with his butcher knife in his hand. I broke through the lines and that gave them all the privilege to pursue me. They soon overtook me and threw me to the ground and kicked and beat me until the blood streamed from all parts of my body. They finally quit and left me there unable to rise, but as soon as I recovered enough, they took me to the cabin and there guarded me for the night.

"As soon as I had recovered enough strength sufficient to travel, they started with me to Wapatomika, the place decided upon for my execution.[158] We arrived there after a few days' travel, and the word was spread abroad that there was a white man to be burned. The day was set and all the necessary arrangements was made. There was a stake set firmly in the ground a few hundred yards outside of the village and the necessary quantity of dogwood was prepared. I was led out in a solemn manner and stripped and blackened, and seated on the ground not far from the stake. I could now see no possible escape from the fire fagot. The time seemed to be growing very short, and the people seemed to be gathering in a very fast time. I saw a stout-looking white man walking up in quite a hurry and to my surprise, it was Simon Girty. I knew him as soon as he got close to me, although I had not seen him for several years, and for the reputation he bore, I could expect no favor from him.

"He walked right up and commenced asking me questions. He asked me where I was from. I told him Kentucky. He then asked me how many white men there was there. I told him I could not tell him how many men there was there, but I could tell him the number of officers and their rank, so I named over a number of officers sufficient to command five times as many men as there was in Kentucky. He then asked me what my name was. I told him he needn't ask that. Says I, 'You know me.' He declared he did not. Says I, 'I know you. You are Simon Girty. You and I used to be schoolmates.' Well, he looked at me close and said he did not know me, and says he, 'What is your name?' I suppose my being naked and blackened, I was so disfigured that he could not recognize me. I told him my name was

Simon Kenton. When I gave him the name Simon, he recognized me and he sprang at me and caught me around the neck, and kissed me. He wept and cried aloud; he shook me by the hand and seemed loath to let go of me, but when he did let go, he turned to the Indians and began talking to them in great earnest, which he explained to me afterwards. He told them that this young man was one of his old playmates and schoolmates, and was his namesake, called after him. He was Simon Kenton and if they ever expected to do him a favor, to release to him this young man.[159]

"'Now,' said he, 'I have been with you several years, and have helped to fight your battles and have risked my life more than any of you, and have never even asked for a division of the spoils, but now release to me this young man and it is not likely that I will ever ask you for a favor of this kind again.' After he got through they gave one simultaneous grunt and I was untied and washed, and released and given up to Simon Girty. Well, my feelings cannot be described, for I expected before the sun went down to die at the stake—that horrible death of being roasted alive.

"There was a British trading post at that point and Girty took me to the store and dressed me from head to foot as well as I could wish, and gave me a horse and saddle and made me his companion. We roamed over the country from town to town. I was at perfect ease and there was but little inducement for me to wish to return again to the whites, for I considered myself like Moses—a fugitive from justice—for I had killed Veck and was anxious to keep as far away as possible. But how sudden things change. Girty and I had been over about Round Head and was on our way back to Wapatomika when we met a couple of Indians carrying a request from a council that Girty should come immediately to Wapatomika (now Zanesfield) and bring me with him. I saw at once that Girty was disturbed. When the Indians met us, they shook hands with Girty, but when I offered them mine, they refused it with a little scorn. We rode on to the town and when we got there, the council house was full. We walked in and the chiefs all rose up and shook hands with Girty, but when I offered them mine, they refused with a scowl. I then began to think that all was not right.

A History of Jonathan Alder

"After quiet was restored, they were all seated on the ground. A war chief that had been out about Wheeling with a party of men had been badly whipped. Several of his men had been killed and a good many wounded, and they had come back full of revenge, determined to seek their vengeance on any white man they could find. I was the only white man to be found and I saw while he spoke that every little bit, he would turn his eyes on me. I could see that they were all animated with his speech. Girty was the next to rise up as soon as he was done and he made quite a lengthy speech and seemed very eloquent. There was other chiefs who spoke afterwards and finally, when they all got through, the chiefs took a vote on it and decided by a large majority to put me to death. Girty then came to me and embraced me very tenderly and told me he had done all in his power to save me, but he could not and that it was now decided that I must die.

"As a last resort, Girty prevailed on the chiefs to convey me to Upper Sandusky to be executed, as that was the place where the British paid the Indians their annuity, and it was also the time of year that there would be Indians there from all the tribes to witness the solemn scene. They placed me in the hands of five Indians, the principal chief being one of them and they set out with me for Upper Sandusky. On their route they passed through a small village on the Scioto River where the great chief Logan then lived.[160] Prior to our getting there, Girty had been there and gave the chief a history of what was going on and had engaged him to intercede for me.

"We got there in the evening, and Logan kept us overnight and sent on two of his men to Sandusky to engage Captain Peter Druger to intercede for me the next morning.[161] He told me he would detain the party that day. That evening, the two young men returned. Logan shook hands with me and we set out, and when we arrived in sight of Upper Sandusky, they made a halt in order for all the Indians to come out, young and old, to view the prisoner and welcome them in.

"As I had run the gauntlet once, it was not required at this time. Hundreds came out to view me. I was then marched into the council house. A grand council was now called. This was the fourth council that was called to dispose of me and Captain Peter Druger, a Frenchman, was the first man to rise to speak. He said it was the wish of the

English government that every American that was caught would be killed, but still, he said, there must be a little cunning used in war. He thought that if this man was taken to Detroit to the head commander of the British, perhaps he could get some information out of him. That would be of more value than the life of twenty men. Said he, 'You have been to a heap of trouble with this man and have had no compensation. Notwithstanding you have got all your horses back, you ought to have some compensation. If you will let me have this man to take to Detroit to the head commander to be examined, I will give you one hundred dollars in rum and tobacco, or any other thing that you may mention.' After a little council, they agreed to take the rum and tobacco, which he paid down immediately, and him and I immediately left for Lower Sandusky.[162] On arriving there, we took water and went round to Detroit.

"This little Frenchman, Captain Druger, was naturally a very fine fellow and I got in with him on our way from Upper Sandusky to Detroit to try, if possible, to save my life. I would give him fifty cents a day as long as I lived, and he promised to do all he could for me. I was taken to Detroit and lodged in prison as a prisoner of war. I was now safe from the Indians, closely watched, but kindly treated. Through the friendly aid of our Mrs. Harvey, I, with two other fellow prisoners, made our escape.[163] Mrs. Harvey had stored dried beef, moccasins, and powder away in a hollow tree. It was on the third of June, 1779—a stormy night—that she met us in the garden with three good rifles and directed us where to find the hollow tree where she had stored away the powder, beef, and moccasins, all of which we found. We then made our long, tedious journey on foot down the Wabash River and crossed the Ohio at the Falls. After thirty days travel, we was again in Kentucky.

"After getting back in Kentucky, like the great chief Logan, I felt determined to avenge myself of the wrongs that had been inflicted on me. I joined myself to the garrison and went with almost every expedition that was sent out, and almost every fight that you mentioned, I was in. Several times we got whipped and had to run for life. I made several hairbreadth escapes of being taken prisoner again, but the next fall, whenever there was a party going out, I was ready to go with them and so continued till the close of the war.

"I had now become acquainted with the lands of Kentucky and got in with the early surveyors as a guide and hunter, and to show them the best lands. They gave me land for my services and so I made large entries of some of the best lands of Kentucky. I had them entered in the name of Simon Butler and cut the initials of my name on every corner tree.[164] I had lands enough to make me independently rich. After peace was made, men was coming into Kentucky from all parts. One day I fell in company with a man from Virginia, right from the county that I was from. I commenced very carefully to asking him questions about the Kentons and I found that he knew them. Then I inquired about the Vecks and found he also knew them. I then inquired about a difficulty of one of the Kenton boys and one of the Veck boys, and if he knew all about that. He said one of the Veck boys and Simon Kenton had had a fight, and that young Kenton had left. They supposed he had run off, and that they had never heard of him since. I inquired what had become of the Veck boy and he said he was living there and married. I made inquiries until I was satisfied that I had not killed the boy and then I made myself known to him, and told him that I was the same, identical Simon Kenton.

"I then arranged to do up my business and went back to Virginia after an absence of nearly thirty years. In my absence from Kentucky, I found that other men was taking possession of my land. It was not uncommon for two or three warrants to be laid on the same piece of land, and we commenced lawing. I had suit after suit and I lost every foot of my land. My titles were defective in consequence of the name. My real name had now become well known and I found myself reduced almost to poverty. To remain in Kentucky where I had lost a fortune was too much for me, and to go back to Virginia then was no inducement. Disheartened and discomfited, I gathered up what little I had and crossed the Ohio River, and made my way up through the country to Urbana. I remained there a few years and then selected me a piece of land on the Mad River close to Zanesfield, almost in sight of where I got blacked and viewed the stake and the wood that was to have terminated my life when Girty came to my rescue. I had set down by the side of the very people that treated me so inhumanly and that I so bitterly hated and fought for twenty years. They are now my neighbors and my friends. As my hate was then, so is my love now. Like the great chief Logan, I had fully glutted my ambition and now all I want is peace."[165]

Kenton called and stayed overnight with me once afterwards in 1828 when we put in a long evening's talk. He was then on his way to Chillicothe to draw his pension. The government had granted him a pension of twenty dollars a month. He told me that night that the Frenchman that he had promised the fifty cents per day to save his life had visited him twice after the war, and that he had paid him near a thousand dollars. The last time, he said the Frenchman told him he would never ask him for any more and that he had not seen him since.

In the fall of 1831, the Indians at Lewistown sent me special word that they wanted to see me and that I should come up immediately. I rode up and they told me that they were about to sell their reserve and if I wished, they thought they would give me a portion of their land, perhaps about a mile square. They had offered me that amount of land several times before, provided I would come and live on it, but I had lived a long time with them and thought I would rather live amongst the whites. I also did not wish to raise my family by the side of them, so I declined that offer. But as they were going to sell, they thought they would give me the land now, as they were going to leave. They always contended that I had a right to the reserve, and the government had failed to give me land. They told me they had set a time in two weeks for a meeting to transact the business. There would be a motion made to strike off a reserve to me and that it would be done by a vote of all the male citizens, and that I should come up any time after that. I stayed a few days with them visiting round and went up again in the course of a month or so, but they told me that the motion had failed and they held parlays about it for two weeks. They said there was so many young Indians that had grown up since I had left them that knew nothing about me, and they had all pretty much voted against the measure. But they also told me they had passed a resolution unanimously to give me land in their reserve where they were going beyond the Missouri River in Kansas if I would only go with them out there on their journey. They would not ask me to settle on it, or my children, until it suited me. I studied the matter over, and it was such a vast distance that I thought it would never do me or my children any good. Still, I told them that I could not give them an answer then but would study the matter over and let them know, so I came home and left them.

John M. Elvain of Columbus was Indian Agent at that time, and James B. Gardner was appointed commissioner to make the treaty or purchase. Elvain was a man that I was intimately acquainted with. The treaty was not ratified until April 1832.[166] After that, I visited Elvain at Columbus and stated the case to him, and he advised me by all means to accept their offer and move. He said that he wanted me to go along with him as an interpreter as he had the Indians moved and said he would bear all my expenses out there and back, and pay me good wages besides. I finally made the arrangement with him to go as an interpreter.

The Indians would not be removed until sometime that summer or in the fall, but he was to let me know. In the meantime, I was to fix for the trip. He was then spending the most of his time up there with the Indians in getting ready for the trip. When they had got all their arrangements made and the day set when to start, he came down home to arrange for the trip and to let me know. He happened to meet Thomas Kane in Columbus. Kane lived not far from me. Elvain wrote me a letter telling me about the arrangements and Kane promised to deliver it, which he could easily do. Kane put it into his pocket and thought no more of it till the day before the Indians was to start. The next morning, he brought me the letter. That very evening Elvain was to start—and what to do? I did not know, so I gave it up.

It was sometime the next summer before I saw Elvain. I met him in Columbus and he wanted to know why I disappointed him so. I told him how it was. He was very sorry. He said they had a fine and pleasant trip without any accident and he said that if I had only come on up when I got the letter, I would have been there on time. He said they were all ready when he got there with all their farming utensils gathered up for me to move. He said they even had wooden harrows and sleds and wagons. He told them he could not take all that plunder; they must sell it off. He said they parlayed for a week before they would consent to make a sale and sell it off, so finally they consented to make a sale and he said it was a solid month before they got started. He described their reserve in Kansas as being very fine. This ended my career with the Indians. We separated so far apart that I have never saw one of them since.

NOTES,
BIBLIOGRAPHY
& INDEX

Notes

1. David Hackett Fischer and James C. Kelly, *Bound and Away: Virginia and the Westward Movement* (Charlottesville and London: University Press of Virginia, 2000), pp. 74–134; Lyman Chalkley, "Before the Gates of the Wilderness Road: The Settlement of Southwestern Virginia," *Virginia Magazine of History and Biography* 30 (1922): 183–202; Jack M. Sosin, *The Revolutionary Frontier, 1763–1783* (Albuquerque: University of New Mexico Press, 1967), pp. 43–45, 176–79; and Robert D. Mitchell, *Commercialism and Frontier: Perspectives on the Early Shenandoah Valley* (Charlottesville: University Press of Virginia, 1977). See also Miles Sturdivant Malone, "The Distribution of Population on the Virginia Frontier in 1775" (Ph.D. diss., Princeton University, 1935). Alder family genealogical information has been extracted from the Church of Jesus Christ, Latter Day Saints Ancestral File 1QCZ-QVT.

2. J. Hector St. John de Crevecoeur, *Letters from an American Farmer and Sketches of Eighteenth Century America,* edited and with an introduction by Albert E. Stone (New York: Penguin Books, 1981), pp. 78–79, 84–86; Philip Vickers Fithian, *Journal, 1775–1776: Written on the Virginia-Pennsylvania Frontier and in the Army around New York,* edited by Robert Greenhalgh Albion and Leonidas Dodson (Princeton: Princeton University Press, 1934), pp. 150–51.

3. Parke Rouse, Jr., *The Great Wagon Road from Philadelphia to the South* (New York: McGraw-Hill Book Company, 1973); For Boone's efforts to bring settlers into Kentucky, see John Mack Faragher, *Daniel Boone: The Life and Legend of an American Pioneer* (New York: Henry Holt and Company, 1992), pp. 68–97. See also Thomas Speed, *The Wilderness Road: A Description of the Routes of Travel by which the Pioneers and Early Settlers First Came to Kentucky* (New York: Burt Franklin, 1886).

4. Fithian, *Journal,* pp. 54, 152–53, 164. For an overview of Indian depredations within the area, see Wills De Hass, *History of the Early Settlement and Indian Wars of West Virginia . . .* (Wheeling: H. Hoblitzell, 1851), pp. 201–330; Alexander Scott Withers, *Chronicles of Border Warfare . . . ,* edited and annotated by Reuben Gold Thwaites (Cincinnati: Robert Clarke Company, 1895), pp. 318–64; Joseph Doddridge, *Notes on the Settlement and Indian Wars of the Western Parts of Virginia and Pennsylvania, 1763–1783* (Pittsburgh: John S. Ritenour and William T. Lindsey, 1912).

5. There are few studies for the general reader that deal with Ohio's prehistoric Indians. Among the best are Martha A. Potter, *Ohio's Prehistoric Peoples* (Columbus:

Ohio Historical Society, 1968); Roger G. Kennedy, *Hidden Cities: The Discovery and Loss of Ancient North American Civilization* . . . (New York: Free Press, 1994); Robert Silverberg, *The Mound Builders* (Athens: Ohio University Press, 1970); David S. Brose et al., *Ancient Art of the American Woodland Indians* (New York: Harry N. Abrams and the Detroit Institute of Arts, 1986); and William F. Romain, *Mysteries of the Hopewell: Astronomers, Geometers, and Magicians of the Eastern Woodlands* (Akron, Ohio: University of Akron Press, 2000). See also James E. Fitting, "Prehistory—Introduction," in Bruce G. Trigger, ed., *Handbook of North American Indians,* vol. 15, *Northeast* (Washington, D. C.: Smithsonian Institution, 1978), pp. 14–15; Robert E. Funk, "Post-Pleistocene Adaptations," ibid., pp. 16–27; James B. Griffin, "Late Prehistory of the Ohio Valley," ibid., pp. 547–59; and William A. Hunter, "History of the Ohio Valley," ibid., pp. 588–93. Those willing to investigate the specialized archaeological literature should begin by consulting three recent volumes published by the Ohio Archaeological Council: William S. Dancey, ed., *The First Discovery of America: Archaeological Evidence of the Early Inhabitants of the Ohio Area* (Columbus: Ohio Archaeological Council, 1994); Paul J. Pacheco, ed., *A View from the Core: A Synthesis of Ohio Hopewell Archaeology* (Columbus: Ohio Archaeological Council, 1996); and Robert A. Genheimer, ed., *Cultures Before Contact: The Late Prehistory of Ohio and Surrounding Regions* (Columbus: Ohio Archaeological Council, 2000).

6. Reuben Gold Thwaites, ed., *The Jesuit Relations and Allied Documents: Travels and Explorations of the Jesuit Missionaries in New France, 1610–1791,* 73 vols. (New York: Pageant Book Co., 1959); George T. Hunt, *The Wars of the Iroquois: A Study in Inter-tribal Relations* (Madison: University of Wisconsin Press, 1940); Phillip R. Shriver, "The Beaver Wars and the Destruction of the Erie Nation," *Timeline Magazine* I (1984/1985): 29–41.

7. Richard White, *The Middle Ground: Indians, Empires, and Republics in the Great Lakes Region, 1650–1815* (Cambridge: Cambridge University Press, 1991); Michael N. McConnell, *A Country Between: The Upper Ohio Valley and Its Peoples, 1724–1774* (Lincoln: University of Nebraska Press, 1992); Helen Hornbeck Tanner, ed., *Atlas of Great Lakes Indian History* (Norman: University of Oklahoma Press, 1987); Helen Hornbeck Tanner and Erminie Wheeler-Voegelin, *Indians of Ohio and Indiana Prior to 1795,* 2 vols. (New York and London: Garland Publishing, 1974); Erminie Wheeler-Voegelin, *Indians of Northwest Ohio: An Ethnohistorical Report on the Wyandot, Potawatomi, Ottawa, and Chippewa of Northwest Ohio* (New York and London: Garland Publishing, 1974); Erminie Wheeler-Voegelin, *Indians of Northern Ohio and Southeastern Michigan: An Ethnological Report* (New York: Garland Publishing, 1974); Elisabeth Tooker, "Wyandot," in Trigger, *Handbook of North American Indians,* pp. 398–406.

8. Johanna E. Feest and Chirstian F. Feest, "Ottawa," in Trigger, *Handbook of North American Indians,* pp. 772–86.

9. Bert Anson, *The Miami Indians* (Norman: University of Oklahoma Press, 1970). Charles Callender, "Miami," in Trigger, *Handbook of North American Indians,* pp. 681–89.

10. Charles Callender, "Shawnee," Trigger, *Handbook of North American Indians,* pp. 622–35.

11. Richard Aquila, *The Iroquois Restoration: Iroquois Diplomacy on the Colonial Frontier,*

1701–1754 (Lincoln and London: University of Nebraska Press, 1997), pp. 102–03, 194–203.

12. C. A. Weslager, *The Delaware Indians: A History* (New Brunswick: Rutgers University Press, 1972), pp. 196–328.

13. Larry L. Nelson, *A Man of Distinction Among Them: Alexander McKee and the Ohio Frontier* (Kent and London: Kent State University Press, 1999), pp. 1–23; McConnell, *A Country Between*, pp. 207–32. See also A. Gwynn Henderson, "The Lower Shawnee Town on Ohio: Sustaining Native Autonomy in an Indian 'Republic'" in Craig Thompson Friend, ed., *The Buzzel about Kentucky: Settling the Promised Land* (Lexington: University of Kentucky Press, 1999), pp. 25–56.

14. Anthony F. C. Wallace, *The Death and Rebirth of the Seneca* (New York: Vintage Books, 1972), pp. 49–110; James H. Howard, *Shawnee! The Ceremonialism of a Native American Tribe and Its Cultural Background* (Athens: Ohio University Press, 1981), pp. 129–222. Archer B. Hulbert and William N. Schwarze, eds., "David Zeisberger's History of the Northern American Indians," *Ohio State Archaeological and Historical Society Publication* 19 (1910): 128–141.

15. W. Vernon Kinietz, *The Indians of the Western Great Lakes, 1615–1760* (Ann Arbor: University of Michigan Press, 1940), pp. 5–405, passim.

16. For an overview of military affairs during this period, see Larry L. Nelson and David C. Skaggs, "Introduction," and David C. Skaggs, "The Sixty Years' War for the Great Lakes, 1754–1814: An Overview," in David C. Skaggs and Larry L. Nelson, eds., *The Sixty Years' War for the Great Lakes: 1754–1814* (Lansing: Michigan State University Press, 2001). There is a deep trove of scholarship centering on the colonial era military history of Ohio and the Old Northwest. Standard works include Randolph C. Downes, *Council Fires on the Upper Ohio* (Pittsburgh: University of Pittsburgh Press, 1940); Wiley Sword, *President Washington's Indian War: The Struggle for the Old Northwest, 1790–1795* (Norman: University of Oklahoma Press, 1985); David C. Skaggs, ed., *The Old Northwest in the American Revolution: An Anthology* (Madison: State Historical Society of Wisconsin, 1976); Fred Anderson, *Crucible of War: The Seven Years' War and the Fate of Empire in British North America, 1754–1766* (New York; Alfred A. Knopf, 2000); and John Sugden, *Blue Jacket: Warrior of the Shawnees* (Lincoln and London: University of Nebraska Press, 2000).

17. James Smith, *An Account of the Remarkable Occurrences in the Life and Travels of Col. James Smith . . .* (Lexington: John Bradford, 1799), pp. 10–11; William Smith, *An Historical Account of the Expedition Against the Ohio Indians, in the Year 1764, Under the Command of Henry Bouquet, Esq. . . .* (Philadelphia: William Bradford, 1764), p. 78. For general works regarding Indian captives and captivity narratives, see James Axtell, "The White Indians," in James Axtell, *The Invasion Within: The Contest of Cultures in Colonial North America* (Oxford: Oxford University Press, 1985), pp. 302–28; Colin Calloway, "Neither White Nor Red, White Renegades on the American Frontier," *William and Mary Quarterly* 17 (1986): 43–66; June Namias, *White Captives: Gender and Ethnicity on the American Frontier* (Chapel Hill: University of North Carolina Press, 1993); Gary L. Ebersole, *Captured by Texts: Puritan to Postmodern Images of Indian Captivity* (Charlottesville: University

Press of Virginia, 1995); and Kathryn Zabelle Derounian-Stodola and James Arthur Levernier, *The Indian Captivity Narrative, 1550–1900* (New York: Maxwell Macmillan, International, 1997). For general studies examining the representation of Indians in literature and other media, see Gordon M. Sayre, *Les Sauvages Americains: Representations of Native Americans in French and English Colonial Literature* (Chapel Hill and London: University of North Carolina Press, 1997) and Robert F. Berkhofer, Jr., *The White Man's Indian: Images of the American Indian from Columbus to the Present* (New York: Alfred A. Knopf, 1978). Many captivity narratives survive from prisoners who were taken by Indians living in Ohio. Most of these can be found in Wilcomb E. Washburn, gen. ed., *The Garland Library of Narratives of North American Indian Captivities*, 111 vols. (New York and London; Garland Publishing, 1975–77).

18. Smith, *An Historical Account*, p. 80.

19. Eric Hinderaker, *Elusive Empires: Constructing Colonialism in the Ohio Valley, 1673–1800* (Cambridge and New York: Cambridge University Press, 1997); Colin G. Calloway, *The American Revolution in Indian Country: Crisis and Diversity in Native American Communities* (Cambridge and New York: Cambridge University Press, 1995), particularly pp. 158–81 and 272–91; Robert S. Allen, *His Majesty's Indian Allies: British Indian Policy in the Defence of Canada, 1774–1815* (Toronto and Oxford: Dundurn Press, 1992). See also Colin G. Calloway, "Suspicion and Self-Interest: The British Indian Alliance and the Peace of Paris," *Historian* 48 (1985): 41–60.

20. Sword, *President Washington's Indian War*; Sugden, *Blue Jacket*, particularly pp. 99–189; Harvey Lewis Carter, *The Life and Times of Little Turtle: First Sagamore of the Wabash* (Urbana and Chicago: University of Illinois Press, 1987), pp. 82–155; John Sugden, *Tecumseh: A Life* (New York: Henry Holt and Company, 1997); R. David Edmunds, *The Shawnee Prophet* (Lincoln and London: University of Nebraska Press, 1983). See also G. Michael Pratt, "The Battle of Fallen Timbers: An Eyewitness Perspective," *Northwest Ohio Quarterly* 67 (1995): 4–34; Dwight L. Smith, "Wayne's Peace with the Indians of the Old Northwest, 1795," *Ohio State Archaeological and Historical Quarterly* 59 (1950): 239–55.

21. R. David Edmunds, "'A Watchful Safeguard to Our Habitations': Black Hoof and the Loyal Shawnees," in Frederick E. Hoxie, Ronald Hoffman, and Peter J. Albert, eds., *Native Americans and the Early Republic* (Charlottesville and London: University Press of Virginia, 1999), pp. 162–99; R. David Edmunds, "Forgotten Allies: The Loyal Shawnees and the War of 1812," in Skaggs and Nelson, *The Sixty Years' War for the Great Lakes*, pp. 337–52.

22. Carl Grover Klopfenstein, "The Removal of the Indians from Ohio, 1820–1843" (Ph.D. diss., Western Reserve University, 1955).

23. Carl W. Albrecht, Jr., "The Peaceable Kingdom: Ohio on the Eve of Settlement," *Timeline Magazine* 2 (June/July 1985): 18–25; Hulbert and Schwarze, "Zeisberger's History," p. 66.

24. Timothy Flint, *Recollections of the Last Ten Years in the Valley of the Mississippi* (Carbondale: Southern Illinois University Press, 1968), pp. 13–14. For a general overview, see Douglas Hurt, *The Ohio Frontier: Crucible of the Old Northwest, 1720–1830* (Bloomington

and Indianapolis: Indiana University Press, 1996). The observations of early travelers to Ohio have been widely published. For representative collections, see Reuben Gold Thwaites, *Early Western Travels, 1748–1846* . . ., 32 vols. (Cleveland: A. H. Clark Co., 1904–7); Emily Foster, ed., *The Ohio Frontier: An Anthology of Early Writings* (Lexington: University Press of Kentucky, 1996); Robert A. Wheeler, ed., *Visions of the Western Reserve: Public and Private Documents of Northeastern Ohio, 1750–1860* (Columbus: Ohio State University Press, 2000). Numerous unpublished reminiscences are included in the collections of the Ohio Historical Society and in the Lyman C. Draper Collection of the State Historical Society of Wisconsin. See Andrea Lentz, ed., *A Guide to The Manuscripts at The Ohio Historical Society* (Columbus: Ohio Historical Society, 1972) and Josephine L. Harper, *Guide to the Draper Manuscripts* (Madison: State Historical Society of Wisconsin, 1983).

25. R. Carlyle Buley, *The Old Northwest Pioneer Period, 1815–1840*, 2 vols. (Bloomington: Indiana University Press, 1950), 1:444–48; for a general account, see also William T. Utter, *The Frontier State: 1803–1825* (Columbus: Ohio Historical Society 1942).

26. Hubert G. H. Wilhelm and Allen G. Noble, "Ohio's Settlement Landscape," and Richard T. Lewis, "The Development of the Economic Landscape," in Leonard Peacefull, ed., *A Geography of Ohio* (Kent, Ohio, and London: Kent State University Press, 1996), pp. 80–109 and 110–26; for a general overview, see Francis P. Weisenburger, *The Passing of the Frontier, 1825–1850* (Columbus: Ohio Historical Society, 1941).

27. Wilhelm and Noble, "Ohio's Settlement Landscape"; Lewis, "The Development of the Economic Landscape"; Weisenburger, *The Passing of the Frontier*, pp. 89–118. For general studies, see Roger Grant, *Ohio on the Move: Transportation in the Buckeye State* (Athens: Ohio University Press, 2000), particularly pp. 52–109; Harry N. Scheiber, *Ohio Canal Era: A Case Study of Government and the Economy, 1820–1861* (Athens: Ohio University Press, 1987); and Karl Raitz, ed., *The National Road* (Baltimore: Johns Hopkins University Press, 1996).

28. Weisenburger, *The Passing of the Frontier*, pp. 183–210; James M. Miller, *The Genesis of Western Culture: The Upper Ohio Valley, 1800–1825* (Columbus: Ohio State Archaeological and Historical Society, 1938); W. H. Venable, *Beginnings of Literary Culture in the Ohio Valley* (Cincinnati: R. Clarke and Co., 1891).

29. Mary Rowlandson, *The Soveraignty and Goodness of God* (Cambridge, 1682). For this and the following two paragraphs, see also Richard VanDerBeets, *The Indian Captivity Narrative: An American Genre* (Lanham, Md.: University Press of America, 1984), pp.1–37; and Derounian-Stodola and Levernier, *The Indian Captivity Narrative*, pp. 1–38.

30. Henry Howe, *Historical Collections of Ohio: Containing a Collection of the Most Interesting Facts, Traditions, Biographical Sketches, Anecdotes, etc., Relating to its General and Local History* . . . (Cincinnati: Bradley and Anthony, 1847), pp. 333–36, 263–64, 249.

31. Orley Brown, *The Captivity of Jonathan Alder and His Life with the Indians, As Dictated by Him and Transcribed by His Son Henry* (Alliance, Ohio: Orley E. Brown, 1965).

32. W. H. Beers, *The History of Madison County* . . . (Chicago: W. H. Beers and Co., 1883), pp. 271–88.

33. Doyle H. Davison, "A History of Jonathan Alder: His Captivity and Life with the Indians," typescript, Ohio Historical Society, 1935.

34. See Derounian-Stodola and Levernier, *The Indian Captivity Narrative,* pp. 10–13.

35. See also Jonathan Alder, *Captivity of Jonathan Alder by the Indians in 1782* (Chillicothe: D. K. Webb, 1944); William Curry, "Jonathan Alder," *Ohio Archaeological and Historical Publications* 15 (1906): 378–82; John Warfield Simpson, *Visions of Paradise: Glimpses of Our Landscape's Legacy* (Berkley, Los Angeles, London: University of California Press, 1999), pp. 11–14, 28, 55–56; Johnda T. Davis, ed., "The Journal of Jonathan Alder," typescript, State Library of Ohio, 1988; Walter High Walley, "The Saga of the Movable Alder Cabin," typescript, Ohio Historical Society, 1989.

36. Alder was born on September 17, 1773, in Gloucester, New Jersey, a short distance from Philadelphia. Ancestral file 1QCZ-QVT, Church of Jesus Christ, Latter Day Saints. Where variant versions of the Alder narrative materially differ from or add to the Henry Clay Alder account, I have added these details in italics and noted the source. These variant versions are found in Henry Howe, *Historical Collections of Ohio,* pp. 333–36, 663–64, 249; W. H. Beers, *The History of Madison County,* pp. 271–88; George W. Hill, "The Shawnees and the Capture of Jonathan Alder, from the Alder Manuscript," Ashland, Ohio *Press,* 26 January-6 April 1882.

37. The subsequent narrative shows that Alder was captured in early spring, 1782.

38. Probably *Lyonia mariana* or "staggerbush," a relative of rhododendron. The plant is found throughout the Atlantic coast states where it grows in sandy pine thickets. See Steven Foster and Roger A. Caras, eds. *A Field Guide to Venomous Animals and Poisonous Plants: North America North of Mexico* (Boston and New York: Houghton Mifflin Company, 1994), s.v. "staggerbush."

39. To "halloo" is to yell, or call out.

40. During the Revolutionary War era, employees of the British Indian Department would frequently accompany Indian war parties on their raids into Kentucky and Virginia. Often, these employees were themselves captives who had been adopted and raised by the Indians. The British Indian Department was the Crown agency charged with the responsibility of maintaining the British government's alliance with the Ohio Country Indian nations. Agents accompanied war parties to interrogate prisoners, evaluate intelligence, and, if possible, see that captives were treated humanely. In February 1791, a Delaware war party captured nine-year-old John Brickell near present-day Uniontown, Pennsylvania. George Girty, Simon Girty's brother, traveled with the party. When Brickell was captured, Girty explained to him that "now there is war, and you are a prisoner, and we will take you to our town and make an Indian of you; and you will not be killed if you go peaceably, but if you try to get away, we won't be troubled with you, but we will kill you and take your scalp to our town." Brickell replied that he would go peaceably and give them no trouble. Likewise, Thomas Ridout was captured by a Shawnee raiding party along the Ohio River in 1787. Just as he was made a prisoner, a white man "about twenty-two years of age, who had been taken prisoner when a lad and had been adopted, and was now a chief among the Shawanese," came up to Ridout and "stood up and said to me in English,

Don't be afraid, sir, you are in no danger, but are given to a good man, a chief of the Shawanese, who will not hurt you but, after some time, will take you to Detroit where you may ransom yourself. Come and take your breakfast." John Brickell, "Narrative of John Brickell's Captivity Among the Delaware Indians," *American Pioneer* 1 (1842): 43–59; Thomas Ridout, "An Account of My Capture by the Shawanese Indians," *Western Pennsylvania Historical Magazine* 12 (1929): 3–31.

41. Indian attacks could be almost unimaginably violent and brutal. But the act of capture, particularly for those prisoners who, like Alder, were later to be adopted, was extraordinarily gentle, usually consisting of laying a hand on the shoulder of the captive or taking his hand. Compare Alder's capture with Simon Kenton's, described later in this narrative, who was apprehended by a Shawnee party after stealing their horses.

42. George Hill identified this fort as Fort Chiswell, located in Wythe County, just outside of Max Meadows, Virginia. The post had been constructed in 1758 by Colonel William Byrd. During the Revolution, the fort guarded strategically important lead mines located nearby. Reuben Gold Thwaites and Louise Phelps Kellogg, eds., *Documentary History of Dunmore's War, 1774* (Madison, State Historical Society of Wisconsin, 1905), p. 52.

43. A leather thong made of buffalo hide specially constructed to restrain prisoners.

44. Indian war parties and their prisoners traveled in single file with each member placing their feet in the footprints of the person in front of them. This concealed the number of people in the party and made their trail more difficult to follow. Captives frequently referred to this style of travel as "marching."

45. Probably near present-day Fort Gay, West Virginia. The Big Sandy forms the boundary between Kentucky and West Virginia.

46. Opposite South Point, Ohio.

47. A temporary or semipermanent dome-shaped dwelling constructed of bent saplings covered with either tree bark or animal hides. See Peter Nabokov and Robert Easton, *Native American Architecture* (New York and Oxford: Oxford University Press, 1989), pp. 52–75.

48. Alder is referring to the Scioto Salt Licks, or Scioto Saline, located along Salt Lick Creek in Jackson and Ross Counties. Originating in Jackson, Salt Lick Creek enters the Scioto River about twelve miles south of Chillicothe. Naturally occurring saltwater springs are found throughout the area. Archaeological evidence suggests that these springs have been used for salt production for at least 8,000 years. Their existence was noted by Christopher Gist in 1750 and their general whereabouts was indicated on a map showing the Ohio Country frontier produced by Lewis Evans in 1755. Daniel Boone spent ten days at this site in June 1778 while a captive of the Shawnees. White settlers discovered the licks following the Revolutionary War in the mid-1780s. Salt production became one of the most important industries in early Jackson County. By 1808, salt makers in Jackson, who boiled approximately 600 gallons of brine to produce one bushel of salt, were generating between fifty and seventy

bushels of salt per week. Production declined dramatically after 1810 when a more concentrated salt-bearing brine was discovered along the Kanawa River in West Virginia. See John Filson, *The Discovery, Settlement and Present State of Kentucke* . . . (Wilmington, Del.: James Adams, 1784), pp. 65–66; M. C. Hansen, "The Scioto Saline: Ohio's Early Salt Industry," *Ohio Geology* 6 (1995): 1–4; William M. Darlington, ed., *Christopher Gist's Journals* (Pittsburgh: J. R. Weldin and Co., 1893), p. 42; S. P. Hildreth, *Pioneer History: Being an Account of the First Examinations of the Ohio Valley and the Early Settlement of the Northwest Territory* . . . (Cincinnati: H. W. Derby and Co., 1848), pp. 475–77.

49. The Pickaway Plains lay on the east bank of the Scioto River bounded by Scipio Creek to the south and present-day Circleville to the north.

50. Big Darby originates in southeastern Logan County and then follows a generally southeasterly course until it enters the Scioto River opposite Circleville. The North Fork of Paint Creek originates in southern Madison County and then flows in a southeasterly direction until it meets Paint Creek a few miles from its confluence with the Scioto River at present-day Chillicothe.

51. Howe included this anecdote in the Franklin County section of his 1847 *Historical Collections* with the notation that it had come from the Alder narrative. He retained the story, but not its attribution, in subsequent editions. Howe, *Historical Collections of Ohio,* p. 167; Henry Howe, *Historical Collections of Ohio in Three Volumes, An Encyclopedia of the State* . . . (Columbus: Henry Howe and Son, 1889), 1:608.

52. "Mingo" was a general term referring to members of the Iroquois Confederacy (Six Nations) who had moved from their traditional lands in upstate New York into Ohio. Most Ohio Mingos were Seneca, Caughnawaga (French Catholic Mohawks), Oneida, and Cayuga. During the Revolutionary War era, many Mingos made their home within Wyandot villages. The Mingo village that Alder refers to may be Zanes Town, built along the upper reaches of the Mad River in 1778. The village was the home of Isaac Zane. Tanner, *Atlas of Great Lakes Indian History,* pp. 84–85.

53. We do not normally enter another person's home without permission or announcing our arrival. Likewise, Indian etiquette demanded that they follow a clearly defined protocol when they entered one another's villages. The traveling party would generally halt a few miles from the village and send runners into the settlement to announce their presence. The village would respond by sending a delegation, sometimes with gifts, to the travelers to welcome them and to provide an escort into the town. While this delegation led their guests to the village, others in the town would prepare a feast for the travelers, provide for their lodging, and begin any arrangements necessary to receive prisoners or dignitaries that might be accompanying the traveling party. For a discussion of Indian protocol, see William N. Fenton, "Structure, Continuity, and Change in the Process of Iroquois Treaty Making," in Francis Jennings, ed., *The History and Culture of Iroquois Diplomacy: An Interdisciplinary Guide to the Treaties of the Six Nations and Their League* (Syracuse: Syracuse University Press, 1985), pp. 3–36.

54. Prisoners were often required to run a gauntlet when they entered their captors' village. The gauntlet consisted of two parallel lines of Indians armed with sticks, switches, clubs, and sometimes more lethal weapons. Captives had to run between the lines to a place of safety while either avoiding or enduring the blows that were

given. Captives who were to be tortured could receive a staggering degree of punishment at this time. But prisoners, like Alder, who were to be adopted, frequently encountered only minimal abuse. Note that Alder seems to suggest that his gauntlet consisted only of women and a few children. John J. Barsotti, ed., *Scoouwa: James Smith's Indian Captivity Narrative* (Columbus: Ohio Historical Society, 1978), pp. 22.

55. Indians used distinctive "whoops" or "halloos" to communicate with one another. The Moravian missionary John Heckewelder described two of these calls, the "scalp yell" or "death halloo," and the "alarm whoop." According to Heckewelder, when the scalp yell was given, it conveyed a sense of both triumph and terror. "Its elements," he claimed, "seem to be glory and fear, so as to express at once the feelings of the shouting warriors, and those with which they have inspired their enemies.

"Different from this yell is the alarm whoop, which is never sounded but when danger is at hand. It is performed in quick succession, much as with us the repeated cry of 'Fire! Fire!' when the alarm is very great and lives are known or believed to be in danger. Both this and the scalp yell consist of the sound 'aw' and 'oh,' successively uttered, the last more accented, and sounded higher than the first; but in the scalp yell, this last sound is drawn out at great length, as long indeed as the breath will hold it, and is raised about an octave higher than the former; while in the alarm whoop, it is rapidly struck on as it were, and only a few notes above the other. These yells or whoops are dreadful indeed, and well calculated to strike with terror those whom long habit has not accustomed to them. It is difficult to describe the impression which the scalp yell, particularly, makes on a person who hears it for the first time." John Heckewelder, *History, Manners, and Customs of the Indian Nations Who Once Inhabited Pennsylvania and the Neighbouring States* (Philadelphia: Historical Society of Pennsylvania, 1876), pp. 216–17.

56. Council houses were large, permanent buildings reserved for public meetings and rituals. In 1751, Christopher Gist described the council house that he observed at a Shawnee village on the Ohio River as "a kind of state house, about ninety feet long, with a tight cover of bark, in which they hold their councils." In 1766, the Presbyterian missionary Charles Beatty was asked to preach at the Delaware village New Comers Town on the Muskingum River. Beatty claimed that the council house there was a "long building, with two fires in it, at a proper distance from each other, without any chimney or partition. The entry into it is by two doors, one at each end. Over the door a turtle was drawn, which is the ensign of their particular tribe. On each doorpost was cut out the face of a grave old man, an emblem, I suppose, of that gravity and wisdom that every senator there ought to be possessed of. On each side, the whole length of the house within, is a platform, or bed, five feet wide, raised above the floor one foot and a half, made of broad split pieces of wood, which serves equally for a bed on which to sleep, and a place on which to sit down. It is covered with a handsome matt, made of rushes." Darlington, *Christopher Gist's Journals*, pp. 44–45; Charles Beatty, *The Journal of a Two Months Tour, with a View of Promoting Religion Among the Frontier Inhabitants of Pensylvania [sic]* . . . (London: Davenhill and Pearch, 1768), p. 44; Guy Soulliard Klett, ed., *Journals of Charles Beatty, 1762–1769* (University Park: Pennsylvania State University Press, 1962), pp. 60–61.

57. Captives were frequently adopted to replace specific individuals. When James Smith was adopted by the Ohio Caughnawaga in 1755, he was told by a tribal elder, "My son, you are now flesh of our flesh and bone of our bone. By the ceremony which was performed this day . . . you are taken into the Caughnewaga nation and initiated into a warlike tribe; you are adopted into a great family, and received with great seriousness and solemnity in the room and place of a great man; after what has passed this day, you are now one of us by an old strong law and custom. My son, you have now nothing to fear, we are now under the same obligations to love, support, and defend you that we are to love and defend one another. Therefore, you are to consider yourself as one of our people." Barsotti, *Scoouwa*, p. 31.

58. Adoption ceremonies often included both bathing the prisoner and then presenting them with a new set of Indian clothes. Bathing was a ritual of purification in which the captive's "white" blood was washed away. The new clothes were the outward sign of this inward transformation. Ibid., pp. 29–31.

59. Chief (or Captain, or Colonel) John Lewis was a well-known Shawnee headman for whom the village of Lewistown was named. Most sources claim that he lived with a white woman named either Molly or Polly Kizer who had been taken prisoner when an infant and raised with the Indians. During the War of 1812, Chief Lewis was a strong supporter of the Americans and urged the tribes within the region to remain neutral. Thomas L. McKenney and James Hall, *History of the Indian Tribes of North America*, 2 vols. (Kent: Volair, 1978) 1:379–81; James B. Finley, *Life Among The Indians; or, Personal Reminiscences and Historical Incidents* . . . (Cincinnati: Cranston and Curts, 1857), p. 512.

60. Isaac Zane was born in Berkley County, Virginia, in 1753. In 1763, he and his brother Ebenezer were captured by the Wyandots and taken to Detroit. Later, he lived on the Sandusky River. Most sources list his wife as Myerrah (White Crane), the daughter of the Wyandot headman Tarhe. His marriage produced five children— a son, Isaac Zane, and four daughters. Greatly respected by the Wyandots, he acted as their translator during the negotiations preceding the Treaty of Greenville. Following the treaty, he acquired 1,800 acres in Logan County near present-day Zanesfield. He died there in 1816. Howe, *Historical Collections of Ohio* (1891), 2:357; O. K. Reames, *History of Zanesfield and Sketches of the Interesting and Historical Places of Logan County, Ohio* (Zanesfield: O. K. Reames, 1929).

61. Colonel William Crawford. In May 1782, Crawford had led an expedition of 400 Washington and Westmoreland County troops against the Indian villages located at Upper Sandusky. The Indians defeated the Americans on June 4 and 5 and captured Crawford on June 7. Crawford was burned in retaliation for the unprovoked murder of ninety-seven Christian Delawares at Gnadenhutten the previous March. The crime had been perpetrated by Crawford's second-in-command, David Williamson. Consul W. Butterfield, *An Historical Account of the Expedition Against Sandusky Under Colonel William Crawford in 1782* (Cincinnati: R. Clarke and Co., 1873), pp. 327–61; Dr. Knight and John Slover, *Indian Atrocities: Narratives of the Perils and Sufferings of Dr. Knight and John Slover Among the Indians* . . . (Cincinnati: U. P. James, 1867).

62. Crawford was executed at Tymochtee, a Delaware town at the site of present-day Crawford, Ohio, in northwest Wyandot County. Tanner, *Atlas of Great Lakes Indian History*, p. 85.

63. Present-day Oldtown, Ohio. Tanner, *Atlas of Great Lakes Indian History*, p. 85. See also William Albert Galloway, *Old Chillicothe: Shawnee and Pioneer History* (Xenia, Ohio: Buckeye Press, 1934), pp. 10–18.

64. Alder was suffering from malaria, a common frontier ailment. See Buley, *The Old Northwest*, 1:240–47.

65. Many frontier settlers considered Simon Girty the most notorious renegade active on the Ohio frontier during the colonial era. Girty had been born in western Pennsylvania in 1741. He, his mother and step-father, and three of his brothers were captured by the Indians in 1755, and Girty spent the next three years with the Senecas. After returning to white society, he lived near Fort Pitt (Pittsburgh). When the Revolution began, he remained loyal to the British government and joined the British Indian Department in 1778. Consul W. Butterfield, *History of the Girtys: Being a Concise Account of the Girty Brothers . . .* (Cincinnati: R. Clarke and Co., 1890); Colin Calloway, "Simon Girty: Interpreter and Intermediary," in James A. Clifton, ed., *Being and Becoming Indian: Biographical Studies of North American Frontiers* (Chicago: Dorsey Press, 1989), pp. 38–58.

66. Despite his fearsome reputation, Girty often interceded on behalf of captives, trying to secure their release or at least see to their comfort. Girty visited another captive, Oliver Spencer, when Spencer was being held along the Maumee River near present-day Defiance in 1790. Although Girty was probably at the village to secure Spencer's release, he told the captive that he would never see home again, but if he should turn out to be a good hunter and a brave warrior, he might one day be an Indian chief. According to Spencer, "his dark shaggy hair, his low forehead; his brows contracted and meeting above his short, flat nose; his gray sunken eyes, averting the ingenuous gaze; his lips thin and compressed, and the dark and sinister expression of his countenance, to me seemed the very picture of a villain." O. M. Spencer, *Indian Captivity: A True Narrative of the Capture of the Rev. O. M. Spencer by the Indians . . .* (New York: Waugh and Mason, 1835), pp. 87–88.

67. According to an early account, Girty laughed at Crawford, a personal friend from his days in Pittsburgh, as the American officer was being tortured and burnt. Knight and Slover, *Indian Atrocities*, pp. 21–24.

68. Girty saved Kenton in the fall of 1778. Kenton related the episode to Alder in 1818. See below. Butterfield, *History of the Girtys*, pp. 76–81; Edna Kenton, *Simon Kenton: His Life and Period, 1755–1836* (Garden City, N. J.: Country Life Press, 1930), pp. 121–23.

69. Alexander McKee and Matthew Elliott. McKee and Elliott were both Pittsburgh loyalists who, with Girty, fled to Detroit in 1778 and joined the British Indian Department. Both men enjoyed long careers with the agency. At his death in 1799, McKee was assistant superintendent and inspector general for Indian affairs in Upper and Lower Canada, the second highest position dealing with Indian policy in British North America. Elliott served as the superintendent of Indian affairs at Fort

Malden (in Ontario, opposite Detroit) during the War of 1812. Reginald Horsman, *Matthew Elliott, British Indian Agent* (Detroit: Wayne State University Press, 1964); Nelson, *A Man of Distinction*.

70. The mutual exchange of prisoners was one of the provisions of the Treaty of Fort McIntosh, concluded on January 21, 1785. See "Treaty with the Wyandots, etc., 1785," in Charles J. Kappler, ed., *Indian Treaties: 1778–1883* (New York: Interland Publishing, 1972), pp. 6–8.

71. Many Indians regarded dreams, both those occurring naturally during sleep and those brought on by fasting or other physical exertion, to be omens of extraordinary power. Although Alder (or more probably George Hill's informant in the 1880s) ends the anecdote in a way that seems to dismiss Succohanes's concern as silly or unwarranted, it is important to note that the actions that Alder's father directed him to do in order to remove himself from danger were uncomfortable and, to a certain degree, dangerous. Furthermore, despite the inconvenience, Alder went about his tasks without raising any objections. These facts testify to the faith that Succohanes placed in the accuracy of his vision and to the lengths that he was willing to go to see that the foretold events did not take place. Hulbert and Schwarze, "Zeisberger's History," p. 101, 120; Wallace, *The Death and Rebirth of the Seneca,* (New York: Vintage Books, 1972), pp. 59–75.

72. Few people bathed regularly, if at all, in the 1840s, when Alder created his narrative. Only a small portion of homes had indoor plumbing, and most people washed from a basin or from a tub kept outside for the purpose. Jack Larkin, *The Reshaping of Everyday Life, 1790–1840* (New York: Harper and Row, 1988), pp. 163–66.

73. The Sandusky Plains are bounded by the Sandusky River, the Little Scioto River, and Tymochtee Creek in Wyandot and Crawford Counties.

74. The British government continued to give the Ohio nations outright gifts and annuities throughout the Indian Wars fought during the early 1790s. Annuities were dispensed with great solemnity and while observing a formal protocol. Isaac Weld, an Irishman traveling in Upper Canada (present-day Ontario) was in Malden (present-day Amherstberg, opposite Detroit) in October 1796 on the day that the region's Indians were on hand to receive their annuities. These gifts were distributed by the British Indian agent Matthew Elliott and his staff.

According to Weld, "A number of chiefs of the different tribes had previously come to our friend [Elliott], who is at the head of the department in this quarter, and he had given to them, each, a bundle of little bits of cedar wood, about the thickness of a small pocketbook pencil, to remind him of the exact number of individuals in each tribe that expected to share the bounty of their great father. The sticks in these bundles were of different lengths, the longest denoted the number of warriors in the tribe, the next in size the number of women, and smallest, the number of children. Our friend, on receiving them, handed them over to his clerks, who made a memorandum in their books of the contents of each bundle, and of the persons that gave them, in order to prepare the presents accordingly.

"A number of large stakes were first fixed down in different parts of the lawn, to each of which was attached a label with the name of the tribe, and the number of persons in it, who were to be provided for; then were brought out from the stores several bales of thick blankets, of blue, scarlet, and brown cloth, and of coarse figured cottons, together with large rolls of tobacco, guns, flints, powder, balls, shot, case-knives, ivory and horn combs, looking-glasses, pipe-tomahawks, hatchets, scissors, needles, vermilion in bags, copper and iron pots and kettles, the whole valued at about 500 pounds sterling. The bales of goods being opened, the blankets, cloths, and cottons were cut up into small pieces, each sufficient to make for one person a wrapper, a shirt, a pair of leggings, or whatever else it was intended for; and the portions of the different articles intended for each tribes were thrown together in a heap at the bottom of the stake which bore its name.

"This business took up several hours, as there were no less than 420 Indians to be served. No liquor, nor any silver ornaments, except to favorite chiefs in private, are ever given on the part of the government to the Indians, notwithstanding they are so fond of both; and a trader who attempts to give these articles to them in exchange for the presents they have received from the government, or indeed, who takes from them on any conditions, their presents, is liable to a very heavy penalty for every such act by the laws of the province.

"The presents having been all prepared, the chiefs were ordered to assemble their warriors who were loitering about the grounds at the outside of the lawn. In a few minutes, they all came and, having been drawn up in a large circle, our friend delivered a speech on the occasion, without which ceremony, no business, according to Indian custom, is ever transacted. In this, they were told that their great and good Father, who lived on the opposite side of the big lake (meaning thereby the king) was ever attentive to the happiness of all his faithful people; and that with his accustomed bounty, he had sent the presents which now lay before them to his good children, the Indians; that he had sent the guns, the hatchets, and the ammunition for the young men, and the clothing for the aged, women, and children; that he hoped the young men would have no occasion to employ their weapons in fighting against enemies, but merely in hunting; and that he recommended it to them to be attentive to the old, and to share bountifully with them what they gained by the chase; that he trusted the great spirit would give them bright suns and clear skies, and a favorable season for hunting; and that when another year should pass over, if he still continued to find them good children, he would not fail to renew his bounties, by sending them more presents from across the big lake.

"This speech was delivered in English, but interpreters attended, who repeated it to the different tribes in their respective languages, paragraph by paragraph, at the end of every one of which the Indians signified their satisfaction by a loud coarse exclamation of 'Hoah! Hoah!' The speech ended, the chiefs were called forward, and their several heaps were shown to them, and committed to their care. They received them with thanks; and beckoning to their warriors, a number of young men quickly started from the crowd, and in less than three minutes, the presents were conveyed from the lawn and laden on board the canoes, in waiting to convey them to the island and adjacent villages.

"The utmost regularity and propriety was manifested on this occasion in the behavior of every Indian. There was not the smallest wrangling amongst them about their presents, nor was the least spark of jealousy observable in any one tribe about what the other had received; each one took up the heap allotted to it and departed without speaking a word." Isaac Weld, *Travels Through the States of North America and the Provinces of Upper and Lower Canada during the Years 1795, 1796, and 1797,* 2 vols. (London: J. Stockdale, 1799) 2:192–96.

75. A musket is a smooth-bored (i.e., unrifled) military weapon. Joseph M. Thatcher, Jr., *Infantry Small Arms, 1795–1815* (Columbus: Anthony Wayne Parkway Board and The Ohio State Museum, 1962), p. 1.

76. Ottawa and Chippewa (Ojibwa), Indian nations who lived along the upper Great Lakes and who were occasional enemies of the Ohio nations. Tanner, *Atlas of Great Lakes Indian History,* pp. 58–59, 98–99.

77. Alder's adversary had pulled his weapon's trigger. Although the rifle was "well loaded and primed," it had not gone off.

78. The ramrod was used in loading the weapon to push the ball from the barrel's muzzle to the powder charge in the breech. Thatcher, *Infantry Small Arms,* p. 1.

79. "Green corn" refers to corn that is not fully matured. Corn on the cob is green corn. The green corn festival was one of the major observances during the Eastern Woodland Indian year. It marked the first harvest and provided an opportunity to give thanks and to celebrate nature's bounty. Captive Oliver Spencer also attended a green corn festival along the Maumee River and, like Alder, noted that the occasion was marked by orations, dancing, athletic contests, and feasts. Spencer, *Indian Captivity,* pp. 94–100; Hulbert and Schwarze, "Zeisberger's History," pp. 137–40; Heckewelder, *History, Manners, and Customs of the Indian Nations,* pp. 208–14; Wallace, *The Death and Rebirth of the Seneca,* pp. 50–59.

80. Finely woven, thin cotton cloth.

81. Mast is the naturally occurring supply of beechnuts, acorns, chestnuts, and the like found on a forest floor. Mast was an important food source both for wild animals and domesticated livestock.

82. James Finley, a Methodist missionary with the Upper Sandusky Wyandots, claimed that "in hunting bears, the Indians search for them in the hollow trees and rocks. If it is ascertained that there is one inside, then in order to get him out, one climbs up a tree that is convenient; or, if there is not such a one, they cut one so as to lodge it near the hole. Then he fastens a bunch of rotten wood to the end of a pole, sets it on fire, and slips it off the end of his pole into the hollow of the tree, where it soon sets fire to the rotten wood. At first, the bear begins to snuff and growl, and strike with his fore feet as if he would put it out. But the fire, steady in its progress, soon routs him and he comes out in great wrath. By this time, the Indian is down and has taken the most advantageous position with his rifle, and when the bear is fairly out, he fires at him. If he does not succeed the first shot, his comrade fires whilst he reloads; and so they keep up the fire until bruin yields up his life." Finley, *Life Among the Indians,* pp. 297–98.

83. In early October 1786, the Kentucky backwoodsman Benjamin Logan led a

party of 790 mounted troops including Daniel Boone, Simon Kenton, and James Trotter against a cluster of Indian villages along the upper Mad River. The combined village settlement, located in southern Logan and northern Champaign Counties, was comprised of Mequashake (Mack-a-chack), Wapakoneta, Piqua, Blue Jacket's Town, Wakatomica, Kispoko or McKee's Town, and Zane's Town. Logan's men destroyed the entire settlement on October 6 and 7. Tanner, *Atlas of Great Lakes Indian History*, pp. 84–86.

84. Hog Creek is a tributary of the Ottawa River. This settlement was just north of present-day Wapakoneta. Tanner, *Atlas of Great Lakes Indian History*, p. 88.

85. In southeast Hancock County near Mt. Blanchard. Blanchard's Fork is a tributary of the Auglaize River. Ibid.

86. Probably *Ipomoea pandurata,* a relative of the morning glory. David Zeisberger claimed the Indians used the plant "when famine threatens and the supply of corn runs low, sometimes sustaining life with [it] for a considerable period." Hulbert and Schwarze, "Zeisberger's History," p. 47.

87. In 1755–56, captive James Smith noted that the Indians with whom he was living lived in buildings similar to European-style log cabins. According to Smith, "The holes or open places that appeared, the squaws stopped with moss, which they collected from old logs . . . and notwithstanding the winters are hard here, our lodging was much better than what I expected." Barsotti, *Scoouwa,* pp. 45–46. See also Finley, *Life Among the Indians,* pp. 295–96.

88. According to David Zeisberger, "if an Indian hunter hears an owl screech in the night, he immediately throws some tobacco into the fire, muttering a few words at the same time. Then, they promise themselves success for the next day, for the owl is said to be a powerful spirit. In dreams, they claim, it has been made known to them what creatures to regard as their *Manitou,* and what offering to bring to them. Such offerings are then regarded by God as rendered to him." Hulbert and Schwarze, "Zeisberger's History," p. 139.

89. Probably John Brickell. Brickell was captured in 1791 and adopted by Whingwy Pooshies, or Big Cat. Brickell lived with Big Cat on the Auglaize River a short distance from its confluence with the Maumee from May 1791 until June 1795. Brickell, "Narrative of John Brickell's Captivity," pp. 43–59.

90. The 1795 Treaty of Greenville.

91. Franklinton, present-day Columbus, was located on the west side of the Scioto River, near its confluence with the Olentangy. Plotted in 1797, it was the first town in the Scioto Valley north of Chillicothe to be settled. It served as the county seat for Franklin County until replaced by Columbus in 1824. Howe, *Historical Collections* (1847), pp. 168–69.

92. Eight-year-old Jeremiah Armstrong, his ten-year-old brother John, and their fourteen-year-old sister Elizabeth were captured from their home near Blennerhassett's Island on April 24, 1794. William T. Martin, *History of Franklin County: A Collection of Reminiscences of the Early Settlement of the County . . .* (Columbus: Follett, Foster, and Co., 1858), pp. 122–35.

93. Robert Armstrong was captured by the Wyandots and lived at a village located at the site of the former Ohio Penitentiary in Columbus (possibly a Mingo village known as Salt Lick, destroyed by Virginia troops in 1774). Following his release after the Treaty of Greenville, he traveled to Chillicothe but returned to Franklinton (Columbus) shortly thereafter. Active in local affairs, he was elected to the Franklin County Board of Commissioners in 1810, 1813, 1816, 1821, and 1824. When the "Borough of Columbus" was incorporated in February 1816, Armstrong was also elected to its first Board of Councilmen. In 1813, he opened a well-known inn and hotel, the Sign of the Red Lion, on High Street. Ibid., 122–35, 144–45, 288, 439, 441. See also James B. Finley, *History of the Wyandott Mission at Upper Sandusky, Ohio* . . . (Cincinnati: J. F. Wright and L. Swormstedt, 1840), pp. 320–23.

94. James McPherson was born in Cumberland County, Pennsylvania, near Carlisle. On August 24, 1781, McPherson was on an expedition headed by George Rogers Clark to the Falls of the Ohio (Louisville) when his detachment, led by Captain Archibald Lochry, was attacked and overwhelmed at the mouth of the Miami River. McPherson and thirty-six others were taken prisoner. He was adopted by the Indians, eventually took an Indian wife, and, according to some reports, worked for the British Indian Department under Alexander McKee. Following the Treaty of Greenville in 1795, McPherson offered his services to the United States and was appointed an agent to the Shawnees and Wyandots still living in Ohio. During the War of 1812, he worked energetically to secure the allegiance of these tribes to the United States. At the war's end, he lived with the Lewistown Shawnees on the Logan County reservation until his death in 1830. Robert P. Kennedy, *The Historical Review of Logan County, Ohio* . . . (Chicago: S. G. Clarke Publishing Co. 1903), pp. 28–29.

95. Present-day Lewistown, Ohio. The 1818 Treaty of St. Mary's created the Lewistown Reservation, a tract of 40,300 acres surrounding Lewistown in Washington Township, Logan County. "Treaty with the Wyandots, etc. concluded at St. Marys September 17, 1818," Kappler, *Indian Treaties,* pp. 162–63.

96. Tecumseh was the great war chief of the Shawnees during the early nineteenth century. He led the Indian confederacy opposing the United States during the War of 1812 and died fighting troops commanded by William Henry Harrison at the Battle of the Thames near Moraviantown, Ontario, in October 1813. See Sugden, *Tecumseh*, and R. David Edmunds, *Tecumseh and the Quest for Indian Leadership* (New York: Harper Collins, 1984).

97. John Heckewelder told of the time that William Wells, a white captive who became the Miami chief Little Turtle's son-in-law, wounded a bear while out on a hunt. The bear would not move and "cried piteously." According to Heckewelder, Wells went up to the bear "and with seemingly great earnestness, addressed him in the Wabash language, now and then giving him a slight stroke on the nose with his ram-rod. I asked him, when he had done, what he had been saying to this bear? 'I have,' said he, 'upbraided him for acting the part of a coward; I told him that he knew the fortune of war, that one or the other of us must have fallen; that it was his fate to be conquered, and he ought to die like a man, like a hero, and not like an old woman;

that if the case had been reversed, and I had fallen into the power of *my enemy,* I would not have disgraced my nation as he did, but would have died with firmness and courage, as becomes a true warrior.'" Heckewelder, *History, Manners, and Customs,* p. 256.

98. A deer blate is a deer call.

99. See Kinietz, *The Indians of the Western Great Lakes,* pp. 109–20.

100. To spangle a horse was to hobble it by tying two of its legs together.

101. In 1772 and 1773, David Jones, a Presbyterian missionary who traveled through Ohio, noted that traders had set up establishments in many of the Indian villages that he visited and that Indians would pay for their purchases with cash. Further, Jones claimed that Indians expected cash in return for goods or services that they provided. David Jones, *A Journal of Two Visits Made to Some Nations of Indians on the West Side of the River Ohio, in the Years 1772 and 1773* (Burlington: Isaac Collins, 1774), pp. 33, 87, 99–101, 104, 108–09.

102. John Tanner, who was captured along the Great Miami River in 1789 and who spent the remainder of his life with the Chippewa (Ojibwa) residing in northern Michigan, Minnesota, and western Ontario, described a variant of this game. According to Tanner, the game was called "moccasin" and was "played by any number of persons, but usually in small parties. Four moccasins are used, and in one of them some small object, such as a little stick, or a small piece of cloth, is hidden by one of the betting parties. The moccasins are laid down beside each other, and one of the adverse party is then to touch two of the moccasins with his finger or a stick. If the one he first touches has the hidden thing in it, the player loses eight to the opposite party; if it is not in the second he touches, but in one of the two passed over, he loses two. If it is not in the one he touches first, and is in the last, he wins eight. The Crees play this game differently, putting the hand successively into all the moccasins, endeavoring to come last to that which contains the article; but if the hand is thrust first into the one containing it, he loses eight. They fix the value of the articles staked by agreement. For instance, they sometimes call a beaver skin, or a blanket, ten; sometimes a horse is one hundred. With strangers, they are apt to play high. In such cases, a horse is sometimes valued at ten." John Tanner, *The Falcon: A Narrative of the Captivity and Adventures of John Tanner During Thirty Years' Residence Among the Indians in the Interior of North America,* with an introduction by Louise Erdrich (New York: Penguin Books, 1994), p. 99.

103. Alder is referring to the practice of "bundling," in which parents allowed courting couples to sleep in the same bed with their clothes on, with the understanding that sexual relations would not take place. Common in the eighteenth century, the practice had nearly died out by 1800. Larkin, *The Reshaping of Everyday Life,* pp. 194–95.

104. The Moravian missionary John Heckewelder claimed that when Indians entered into marriage, it was understood by both partners that they would not live together any longer "than suites their pleasure or convenience. The husband may put away his wife whenever he pleases, and the woman may, in a like manner, abandon her husband." Heckewelder, *History, Manners, and Customs of the Indian Nations,* pp. 154–62.

105. Alder is referring to Anthony Wayne's victory at the Battle of Fallen Tim-

bers, fought in August 1794. For a general account, see Sword, *President Washington's Indian War,* particularly pp. 299–311.

106. Captives James Smith and John Brickell both hunted deer in this manner. According to Brickell, the Indians often practiced "candle hunting, and for this, they sometimes make candles, or tapers, when they cannot buy them. Deer come to the rivers to eat a kind of water grass, to get which they frequently immerse their whole head and horns. They seem to be blinded by light at night, and will suffer a canoe to float close to them. I have practiced that kind of hunting much since I came to live where Columbus now is and, on one occasion, killed twelve deer in one night." Barsotti, *Scoouwa,* p. 63; Brickell, "Narrative of John Brickell's Captivity," p. 47.

107. According to the Methodist missionary James Finley, when the Indians trapped raccoons, "one man will have perhaps three hundred racoon traps scattered over a country ten miles in extent. These traps are 'dead falls,' made of two saplings, and set over a log which lies across some branch or creek, or that is by the edge of some pond or marshy place. In the months of February and March, the racoons [*sic*] travel much and frequent the ponds for the purpose of catching frogs. The hunter generally gets round all his traps twice a week, and hunts from one to the other. I have known a hunter to take from his traps thirty racoons [*sic*] in two days, and sometimes they take more. From three to six hundred is counted a good hunt for one spring, beside the deer, turkeys, and bears." Finley, *Life Among the Indians,* pp. 296–97.

108. John Johnston, the United States Indian agent at Piqua during the early nineteenth century, noted that Scioto was a Wyandot word, but that he did not know the significance of the name. David Jones claimed that to the Shawnees, the river's name meant "hairy river" because at one time, deer were so plentiful along its banks that during the fall, the stream would be thick with hair. Howe, *Historical Collections* (1847), p. 594; Jones, *Journal of Two Visits,* p. 46.

109. Probably in the spring of 1794. Violence continued to escalate along the frontier throughout the late 1780s. Seeking to put an end to Indian raids along the Ohio River Valley, Congress authorized Josiah Harmar to lead an expedition against the Maumee Valley tribes in the fall of 1790. Harmar's troops were defeated in October by Indians led by the Miami chief Mishikinakwa, the Little Turtle. Little Turtle also defeated a second American expedition led by Arthur St. Clair in November 1791. In 1793, a third American force, led by Anthony Wayne, began to move against the confederated tribes living along the Maumee River. Wayne began his final advance to the Maumee on July 28, 1794. Sword, *President Washington's Indian War.*

110. Wayne had built Fort Recovery as a forward base in late 1793 and early 1794 on the site of St. Clair's defeat. The site is on the headwaters of the Wabash River at present-day Fort Recovery, Ohio, in Mercer County. Ibid., 258–71.

111. A Shawnee warrior who was known as Waweyapiersenwa (Whirlpool) before 1778, Blue Jacket was one of the most influential leaders of the Maumee Valley confederacy after 1794. Sugden, *Blue Jacket.*

112. The Battle of Fort Recovery began on the morning of June 30, 1794, when a column of packhorses and their dragoon escorts were attacked about one-half mile

from the post. Sword, *President Washington's Indian War*, pp. 272–86; Larry L. Nelson, "'Never Have They Done So Little': The Battle of Fort Recovery and the Collapse of the Miami Confederacy," *Northwest Ohio Quarterly* 64 (1992): 43–55.

113. Pistols that were carried in holsters draped over a horse in front of the saddle. Thatcher, *Infantry Small Arms*, p. 2.

114. Alexander McKee's son Thomas was also an officer in the British Indian Department. Captain Asa Hartshorne commanded a company of riflemen accompanying the ambushed packtrain. George Brown et al., gen. eds, *Dictionary of Canadian Biography*, 12 vols, (Toronto, Buffalo, London: University of Toronto Press, 1966–90), 5: s.v. "Thomas McKee." See also Sword, *President Washington's Indian War*, pp. 272–86; Nelson, *A Man of Distinction*, p. 180.

115. Fort Recovery was defended with small-caliber howitzers, artillery pieces capable of firing both solid shot and exploding shells. When Alder thought that he had heard a cannon go off behind him, it was actually the sound of an exploding round detonating to his rear. Sword, *President Washington's Indian War*, pp. 272–86.

116. In November 1778, Henry Hamilton, the British commander at Detroit, described a war party accompanying him along the Maumee River. "Their camp is formed in this manner—Large fires are kindled before which they lie in rows, on each side, with their feet towards the fire—At their heads are placed their arms leaning against a rock—In this position they go to sleep, and if any noise is made or alarm given, the first who hears it touches his neighbor, and the whole are presently roused, tho in silence, and take to their arms without bustle or confusion." John D. Barnhart, *Henry Hamilton and George Rogers Clark in the American Revolution, with the Unpublished Journal of Lieut. Gov. Henry Hamilton* (Crawfordsville, Ind: R. E. Banta, 1951), p. 122.

117. Alder is referring to a large Indian settlement known as the Glaize, or Grand Glaize, located at the confluence of the Auglaize and Maumee Rivers, the site of present-day Defiance, Ohio. Wayne and his army arrived at this site in early August and began at once to fortify the site. However, the post was not completed until after the Battle of Fallen Timbers was fought later in the month. Tanner, *Atlas of Great Lakes Indian History*, pp. 87–91; Helen Hornbeck Tanner, "The Glaize in 1792: A Composite Indian Community," *Ethnohistory* 25 (1978): 15–39; Randall L. Buchman, *The Confluence: The Site of Fort Defiance* (Defiance, Ohio: Defiance College Press, 1994), pp. 17–69.

118. Fort Miamis, built in 1794 at present-day Maumee, Ohio. The Indians were preparing to meet Wayne in what would be the Battle of Fallen Timbers, fought on August 20, 1794. F. Clever Bald, "Fort Miamis, Outpost Of Empire," *Northwest Ohio Quarterly* 16 (1944): 75–111.

119. Members of the Iroquois Confederacy, who lived in upstate New York, generally opposed the war being fought by the Maumee Valley nations against the United States. Their spokesman, the Mohawk leader Joseph Brant, spent a considerable time between 1791 and 1794 attempting to find a negotiated settlement to the conflict. Not all Iroquois, however, agreed with Brant. In August 1794, only a few days before the Battle of Fallen Timbers, John Adlum, a Pennsylvania surveyor, attended an Indian council at which a Seneca named Duquania "informed them that the British Agent

Col. McKee had told them that there was a great probability that there would soon be a war between them and the Americans, and as they had heard that their friends, the Six Nations had demanded a part of their country to be restored, that they were sending a deputation from seven different tribes who would join them in case of necessity, and that they themselves were ready to join their friends whenever required, and that a great portion of the warriors of the tribes they represented would also join them." Donald H. Kent and Merle Deardorff, eds., "John Adlum on the Allegheny: Memoirs for the Year 1794," *Pennsylvania Magazine of History and Biography* 84 (1960): 265–324, 435–80.

120. When Isaac Weld visited Malden two years after the battle, he was informed that "preparatory to the day on which they expected a general engagement, the Indians, contrary to the usages of most nations, observe a strict fast; nor does this abstinence from all sorts of food diminish their exertions in the field. . . . The day before General Wayne was expected, this ceremony was strictly attended to, and afterwards, having placed themselves in ambush in the woods, they waited for his arrival. He did not, however, come to the ground on the day that they had imagined, . . . but having reason to think he would come on subsequent day, they did not move from their ambush. The second day passed over without his drawing nearer to them; but fully persuaded that he would come up with them on the next, they still lay concealed in the same place. The third day proved to be extremely rainy and tempestuous; and the scouts having brought word that from the movements General Wayne had made, there was no likelihood of his marching towards them that day, the Indians, now hungry after having fasted for three entire days, determined to rise from their ambush in order to take some refreshment. They accordingly did so, and having no suspicion of an attack, began to eat their food in security. . . . In this situation, they were themselves surprised by General Wayne."

In 1816, John Norton, a British Indian Department employee who was aware of the Indians' deployment in 1794, remembered that "the warriors of the confederate bands suffered much from thirst and hunger, some of them having taken their stations fasting. The enemy also failed to advance this day. The succeeding day, many of the warriors, to alleviate the sufferings of the former, did not hasten to take their stations, but remained in the encampment." Weld, *Travels Through the States of North America*, 2: 211–13; Carl F. Klinck and James J. Talman, eds. *The Journals of Major John Norton, 1816* (Toronto: Champlain Society, 1970), pp. 184–86.

121. There is no such provision in the Treaty of Greenville, nor do the records of the negotiations leading to the treaty indicate that such a provision was discussed. Alder may be confusing the Treaty of Greenville with the treaty signed at the foot of the rapids of the Miami of Lake Erie (Maumee River) on September 29, 1817. The agreement, signed between the United States and the Ohio Wyandots, Senecas, Delawares, Shawnees, Potawatomis, Ottawas, and Chippewas, created the Upper Sandusky reserve and also granted substantial holdings to over twenty persons "connected with the said Indians, by blood or adoption." See "Treaty with the Wyandots, etc., Concluded at the foot of the Rapids of the Miami of Lake Erie, September 29,

1817," in Kappler, *Indian Treaties*, pp. 145–55. The Treaty of Greenville and the negotiations leading to it are found in *American State Papers: Documents, Legislative and Executive, the Congress of the United States—Indian Affairs*, 2 vols. (Washington: Gales and Seaton, 1832), 1:562–82.

122. The Treaty of Greenville was signed on August 3, 1795. *American State Papers*, pp. 562–82.

123. Indian hospitality was based upon unstinting generosity to guests. But hospitality was also understood to be reciprocal in nature. Alder was upset because his guests had violated Indian etiquette by trying to leave without eating, or even acknowledging, the food they had been offered. According to James Smith, the Indians "invite every one that comes to their house, or camp to eat, while they have any thing to give; and it is accounted bad manners to refuse eating, when invited." Barsotti, *Scoouwa*, p. 60.

124. John Taylor, a native of Kentucky, moved to Pleasant Valley in 1800. His brothers, Daniel and Richard, joined him along Big Darby Creek in 1803. According to one tradition, Alder loaned his cabin to Daniel Taylor and his wife, who were virtually destitute at the time, shortly after their arrival in central Ohio. Joshua Ewing and his brother James migrated from Kentucky to Big Darby in 1798. Chester E. Bryan, *History of Madison County, Ohio: Its People, Industries and Institutions* (Indianapolis: B. F. Bowen and Co., 1915), p. 97.

125. In 1804, the French traveler Constantin François Volney reported that Little Turtle kept a cow and made butter at his home near Fort Wayne, but that he did not "indulge himself in these things, but reserves them for the whites." C. F. Volney, *A View of the Soil and Climate of the Unite States of America: With Supplementary Remarks upon Florida; on the French Colonies on the Mississippi; and Ohio, and in Canada; and on the Aboriginal Tribes of America* (Philadelphia: Conrad and Co., 1804), p. 378.

126. Probably Crane Town, the home of Tarhe, the Crane. The settlement was located in Crane Township, Wyandot County, about four miles northeast of present-day Upper Sandusky. The area was designated an Indian reservation in September 1817. "Treaty with the Wyandots, etc.," Kappler, *Indian Treaties*, pp. 145–55.

127. An edged disk used for plowing.

128. Lucas Sullivant. Sullivant was born in 1765. A surveyor by trade, he began surveying the Virginia Military District in 1787. In August 1797, he plotted the town of Franklinton (later Columbus), Ohio. He permanently moved to the town in 1801. Active in civic and political affairs, he was one of Columbus's most prominent citizens at his death in 1823. John Beatty, "Franklinton, An Historical Address," *Ohio Archaeological and Historical Society Publications* 6 (1898): 59–71.

129. Davis and a companion, William Campbell, were taken prisoner in the fall of 1792. Howe, *Historical Collections* (1847), pp. 260–62; David Hartman, "Leaping Buck: The Story of Samuel Davis," typescript, Ohio Historical Society, 1976.

130. The boat's pilot and passengers were wary because Indians would often use adopted prisoners to lure unsuspecting river travelers into an ambush.

131. Tenskwatawa, The Prophet (or Open Door), was Tecumseh's younger broth-

er and a spiritual leader of great influence among the Shawnees and other Old Northwest Indian nations. He had told his followers that his powers would protect them from harm during the Battle of Tippecanoe, fought on November 7, 1811. See Edmunds, *The Shawnee Prophet*, particularly pp. 67–116.

132. Leather Lips, or Shateyarnyah (Two Equal Clouds) was a Sandusky Wyandot and signatory to the Treaty of Greenville. At the time of his death on June 1, 1810, he was estimated to be near seventy-eight years old. Bruce E. Johnson and Donald A. Grinde, Jr., eds., *The Encyclopedia of Native American Biography* (New York: Henry Holt and Co., 1997), s.v. "Leather Lips." See also William Curry, "The Wyandotte Chief Leather Lips: His Trial and Execution," *Ohio Archaeological and Historical Publications* 12 (1903): 378–82.

133. Round Head, or Stayeghtha, was a Wyandot war chief who had become an ardent follower of The Prophet. Leather Lips, an open supporter of the United States, was one of several people executed for witchcraft during the years leading up the War of 1812. Round Head fought with British forces during the War of 1812, accompanying Major Adam Muir's expedition against Fort Wayne in 1812 and participating in the siege against Fort Meigs in April-May 1813. He died of unknown causes in September 1813. Alder's account of Leather Lips's death closely parallels that told by James Finley, a Methodist missionary who lived with the Sandusky Wyandots from 1819 through 1827. However, the usually reliable John Heckewelder claimed that the murder was perpetrated by Tarhe, The Crane. Brown, *Dictionary of Canadian Biography*, vol. 5, s.v. "Stayeghtha." For Leather Lips's execution, see James B. Finley, *Autobiography of Rev. James B. Finley, or Pioneer Life in the West*, ed. by W. P. Strickland (Cincinnati: Cranston and Curts, 1853), pp. 212–18; Heckewelder, *History, Manners, and Customs of The Indian Nations*, pp. 295–99. See also Sugden, *Tecumseh*, p. 209.

134. Either John or Benjamin Sells. Ludwick Sells moved to the location of present-day Dublin, Ohio, with four of his sons, including Benjamin, in 1801. John, Benjamin's older brother, joined his family in 1809. John laid out the town of Dublin near their home in 1818. Martin, *History of Franklin County*, pp. 202–3.

135. A capote was a hooded overcoat frequently cut and sewn from a single woolen blanket.

136. Captain John was a well-known Shawnee headman who lived along the Scioto Valley. Henry Howe described him as "over six feet in height, strong and active, full of spirit, and fond of frolic." Howe, *Historical Collections* (1847), pp. 165–66; Finley, *Life Among the Indians*, pp. 508–12.

137. This incident took place during the autumn of 1779. The trader's name was Fallenash. Howe, *Historical Collections* (1847), p. 165.

138. Probably Prophet's Town, located near the confluence of the Tippecanoe and Wabash Rivers in Indiana. The Prophet and Tecumseh, along with many of their followers, had relocated there in the spring of 1808. Edmunds, *The Shawnee Prophet*, pp. 67–93.

139. Tecumseh and Harrison met in Vincennes, Indiana, in August 1810. Sugden, *Tecumseh*, pp. 180–90.

140. When Indian raids seemed likely, settlers would "fort up," that is, they would come together and construct temporary dwellings protected by a crude stockade. These temporary settlements were known as stations. For general studies, see Nancy O'Malley, "Stockading Up": A Study of Pioneer Stations in the Inner Bluegrass Region of Kentucky (Frankfort: Kentucky Heritage Council, 1987), and Richard Scamyhorn and John Steinle, Stockades in the Wilderness: The Frontier Defenses and Settlements of Southwestern Ohio, 1788–1795 (Dayton, Ohio: Landfall Press, 1987).

141. Mill Creek is a tributary of the Scioto running in a generally southeasterly course through the center of Union County.

142. Possibly David Watson, an early settler in London, Ohio. See J[oseph] A. Caldwell, Caldwell's Atlas of Madison County, Ohio . . . (Condit, Ohio, 1875), pp. 6–7, 12, 37, 62.

143. Militia companies elected their own officers. James T. Doyle, The Organization and Operational Administration of the Ohio Militia in the War of 1812 (Columbus: Anthony Wayne Parkway Board and The Ohio State Museum, 1958), pp. 13–14.

144. Chillicothe was the site of Camp Bull. The post was used to house British prisoners of war and American soldiers who had been convicted of serious violations of military law. See Patricia Fife Medert, Raw Recruits and Bullish Prisoners: Ohio's Capital in the War of 1812 (Chillicothe, Ohio: Ross County Historical Society, 1992).

145. A mill whose vertical wheel was powered by water flowing into it from above. D. W. Garber, Waterwheels and Millstones: A History of Ohio Gristmills and Milling (Columbus: Ohio Historical Society, 1970), pp. 9–23.

146. Alder is describing several types of mills, each with its own distinctive machinery and purpose. Grist mills ground grain. Carding mills cleaned and straightened wool fibers prior to their being spun into thread, while fulling mills cleaned and thickened woolen cloth by running wet fabric through rollers. See Andrew Gray, The Experienced Millwright: Or, A Treatise on the Construction of Some of the Most Useful Machines, with the Latest Improvements . . . (Edinburgh: Brown and Constable, 1804), pp. 24–26, 43–56, 69; David Craik, The Practical American Millwright and Miller . . . (Philadelphia: H. C. Baird, 1871), pp. 251–353, 396–402.

147. The meaning of this term in unclear.

148. Most sources claim that Kenton was born in Fauquier County, Virginia, in March 1755. See Kenton, Simon Kenton, pp. 13–31.

149. Most sources give the name of Kenton's rival as William Leachman, but John McDonald, in a biographical sketch of Kenton written in 1852, claims that the name was William Veach. Kenton, Simon Kenton, 22; John McDonald, Biographical Sketches of General Nathaniel Massie, General Duncan McArthur, Captain William Wells, and General Simon Kenton . . . (Dayton: D. Osborn and Son, 1852), pp. 198–99.

150. Thomas Williams. Kenton, Simon Kenton, p. 59.

151. Michael Stoner. Kenton had difficulty understanding because Stoner, a Dutchman, pronounced Boone's name with a thick accent, "Schpoon." Ibid., p. 70.

152. Kenton was mistaken about Williams's fate. Williams survived, although Kenton did not realize it until the two met accidentally in 1820. Ibid., p. 301.

153. Other sources, including many early Kenton biographers, claim that Kenton and his friends were sent to Ohio on a spying expedition by Colonel John Bowman. Whatever its purpose, the party set out from Kentucky on September 7, 1778. Ibid., pp. 97–98, 102–44.

154. The Falls of the Ohio, located at present-day Louisville, Kentucky.

155. Kenton's priming charge, located in a small pan along side the gun's lock, had ignited, but failed to detonate the main charge inside the barrel. A flash in the pan was characterized by a smoky, noisy demonstration that produced no results. For a discussion of lock construction and use, see Henry J. Kauffman, *The Pennsylvania-Kentucky Rifle* (Harrisburg: Stockpole Company, 1960), pp. 107–18.

156. Alexander Montgomery. Kenton, *Simon Kenton,* p. 106.

157. George Clark. Ibid., p. 107.

158. In Logan County near West Liberty, Ohio. Tanner, *Atlas of Great Lakes Indian History,* p. 80.

159. Kenton and Girty had probably met in the spring of 1774 when both were at Fort Pitt. During Dunmore's War later the same year, both men served as scouts for the Virginian army. Kenton, *Simon Kenton,* pp. 46–58.

160. Logan was a Mingo whose family was murdered in 1774. This village was located about six miles south of Kenton, Ohio. Tanner, *Atlas of Great Lakes Indian History,* pp. 79–80. "Logan, The Mingo Chief, 1710–1780," *Ohio Archaeological and Historical Society Publications* 20 (1911): 137–75.

161. Pierre Drouilliard, a fur trader and interpreter with the British Indian Department. Milo M. Quaife, ed., *The John Askin Papers,* 2 vols. (Detroit: Detroit Library Commission, 1928–31) 1:183.

162. Present-day Fremont, Ohio. Tanner, *Atlas of Great Lakes Indian History,* p. 80.

163. Other sources identify this woman as Rachel Edgar, the wife of Detroit trader John Edgar. Kenton, *Simon Kenton,* pp. 133–44.

164. Kenton had made a "tomahawk claim" to these lands. As he later learned to his sorrow, these claims were often denied in subsequent land disputes. Kenton, *Simon Kenton,* pp. 288–94; Doddridge, *Notes on the Settlement,* p. 81.

165. Kenton is paraphrasing "Logan's Oration," or "Logan's Lament." When Logan's family was killed in 1774, Logan undertook a series of retaliatory raids along the Ohio River Valley settlements in western Pennsylvania, Kentucky, and Virginia. These raids, in part, precipitated Dunmore's War in the fall of that year, which resulted in the defeat of the Ohio Country Indian nations. At his surrender, Logan delivered an impassioned speech in which he claimed, "there runs not a drop of my blood in the veins of any living creature. This called upon me for revenge. I have sought it; I have killed many; I have fully glutted my vengeance; for my country I rejoice at the beams of peace. But do not harbor a thought that mine is the joy of fear. Logan never felt fear. He will not turn on his heel to save his life. Who is there to mourn for Logan? Not one." Thomas Jefferson, *Notes on the State of Virginia* (Chapel Hill and London: Institute of Early American History and Culture at Williamsburg, Virginia, 1982), p. 63; Ray H. Sandefur, "Logan's Oration—How Authentic?" *Quarterly Journal of Speech* 46

(1960): 289- 96; James H. O'Donnell, III, "Logan's Oration: A Case Study in Ethnographic Authentication," *Quarterly Journal of Speech* 65 (1979): 150–56.

166. The treaty by which the Lewistown Indians gave up their reserve was signed on July 20, 1831, and ratified April 6, 1832. In exchange for their Ohio holdings, the Indians received sixty thousand acres west of the Mississippi upon which the government agreed to build a sawmill and blacksmith shop. Further, the Indians were to receive the proceeds from the sale of their Ohio land (with six thousand dollars given in advance) and "100 blankets, twenty ploughs, 100 hoes, fifty axes, ten rifles, twenty sets of horse gear, and Russia sheeting sufficient to make forty tents." Although Alder did not receive any land, the treaty, "at the request of the chiefs of the Senecas and Shawnees," granted 320 acres to James McPherson, "who has lived among them and near them for forty years, and from whom they have received numerous and valuable services," 320 acres to Henry McPherson, "an adopted son of their nation," and 160 acres to Martin Lane, an interpreter "who has lived a long time among the Senecas." "Treaty with the Seneca, etc., 1831," Kappler, *Indian Treaties,* pp. 327–31. See also "Removal of Indians from Ohio: Dunhue Correspondence of 1832," *Indiana Magazine of History* 35 (1939): 408–26.

Bibliography

Albrecht, Carl W., Jr. "The Peaceable Kingdom: Ohio on the Eve of Settlement."
Timeline Magazine 2 (June/July 1985): 18–25.

Alder, Jonathan. *Captivity of Jonathan Alder by the Indians in 1782.* Chillicothe, Ohio: D. K.
Webb, 1944.

Allen, Robert S. *His Majesty's Indian Allies: British Indian Policy in the Defence of Canada,
1774–1815.* Toronto and Oxford: Dundurn Press, 1992.

*American State Papers: Documents Legislative and Executive, the Congress of the United States—Indian
Affairs.* 2 vols. Washington: Gales and Seaton, 1832.

Anderson, Fred. *Crucible of War: The Seven Years' War and the Fate of Empire in British North
America, 1754–1766.* New York: Alfred A. Knopf, 2000.

Anson, Bert. *The Miami Indians.* Norman: University of Oklahoma Press, 1970.

Aquila, Richard. *The Iroquois Restoration: Iroquois Diplomacy on the Colonial Frontier, 1701–1754.*
Lincoln and London: University of Nebraska Press, 1997.

Axtell, James. "The White Indians." In *The Invasion Within: The Contest of Cultures in Colonial North America.* Oxford: Oxford University Press, 1985.

Bald, F. Clever. "Fort Miamis, Outpost of Empire." *Northwest Ohio Quarterly* 16 (1944):
75–III.

Barnhart, John D. *Henry Hamilton and George Rogers Clark in the American Revolution, with the
Unpublished Journal of Lieut. Gov. Henry Hamilton.* Crawfordsville, Ind.: R. E. Banta,
1951.

Barsotti, John J., ed. *Scoouwa: James Smith's Indian Captivity Narrative.* Columbus: Ohio
Historical Society, 1978.

Beatty, Charles. *The Journal of a Two Months Tour, with a View of Promoting Religion among the
Frontier Inhabitants of Pensylvania. . . .* London: Davenhill and Pearch, 1768.

Beatty, John. "Franklinton, an Historical Address." *Ohio Archaeological and Historical Society Publications* 6 (1898): 59–71.

Beers, W. H. *The History of Madison County. . . .* Chicago: W. H. Beers and Co., 1883.

Berkhofer, Robert F., Jr. *The White Man's Indian: Images of the American Indian from Columbus
to the Present.* New York: Alfred A. Knopf, 1978.

Brickell, John. "Narrative of John Brickell's Captivity Among the Delaware Indians."
American Pioneer I (1842): 43–59.

Brose, David S., et al. *Ancient Art of the American Woodland Indians*. New York: Harry N. Abrams and the Detroit Institute of Arts, 1986.

Brown, George, et al., gen. eds. *Dictionary of Canadian Biography*. 12 vols. Toronto, Buffalo, London: University of Toronto Press, 1966–90.

Brown, Orley. *The Captivity of Jonathan Alder and His Life with the Indians, as Dictated by Him and Transcribed by His Son Henry*. Alliance, Ohio: Orley E. Brown, 1965.

Bryan, Chester E. *History of Madison County, Ohio: Its People, Industries, and Institutions*. Indianapolis: B. F. Bowen and Co., 1915.

Buchman, Randall L. *The Confluence: The Site of Fort Defiance*. Defiance, Ohio: Defiance College Press, 1994.

Buley, R. Carlyle. *The Old Northwest Pioneer Period, 1815–1840*. 2 vols. Bloomington: Indiana University Press, 1950.

Butterfield, Consul W. *An Historical Account of the Expedition Against Sandusky Under Colonel William Crawford in 1782*. Cincinnati: R. Clarke and Co., 1873.

———. *History of the Girtys: Being a Concise Account of the Girty Brothers*. . . . Cincinnati: R. Clarke and Co., 1890.

Caldwell, J[oseph] A. *Caldwell's Atlas of Madison County, Ohio*. . . . Condit, Ohio, 1875.

Callender, Charles. "Miami." In Bruce G. Trigger, ed., *Handbook of North American Indians*, vol. 15, *Northeast*. Washington, D.C.: Smithsonian Institution, 1978.

———. "Shawnee." In Bruce G. Trigger, ed., *Handbook of North American Indians*, vol. 15, *Northeast*. Washington, D.C.: Smithsonian Institution, 1978.

Calloway: Colin. "Suspicion and Self-Interest: The British Indian Alliance and the peace of Paris." *Historian* 48 (1985): 41–60.

———. "Neither White Nor Red, White Renegades on the American Frontier." *William and Mary Quarterly* 17 (1986): 43–66.

———. "Simon Girty: Interpreter and Intermediary." In James A. Clifton, ed., *Being and Becoming Indian: Biographical Studies of North American Frontiers*. Chicago: Dorsey Press, 1989.

———. *The American Revolution in Indian Country: Crisis and Diversity in Native American Communities*. Cambridge and New York; Cambridge University Press, 1995.

Carter, Harvey Lewis. *The Life and Times of Little Turtle: First Sagamore of the Wabash*. Urbana and Chicago: University of Illinois Press, 1987.

Chalkley, Lyman. "Before the Gates of the Wilderness Road: The Settlement of Southwestern Virginia." *Virginia Magazine of History and Biography* 30 (1922): 183–202.

Craik, David. *The Practical American Millwright and Miller*. . . . Philadelphia: H. C. Baird, 1871.

Curry, William. "The Wyandotte Chief Leather Lips: His Trial and Execution." *Ohio Archaeological and Historical Publications* 12 (1903): 30–36.

———. "Jonathan Alder." *Ohio Archaeological and Historical Publications* 15 (1906): 378–82.

Dancey, William S., ed. *The First Discovery of America: Archaeological Evidence of the Early Inhabitants of the Ohio Area*. Columbus: Ohio Archaeological Council, 1994.

Darlington, William M., ed. *Christopher Gist's Journals*. Pittsburgh: J. R. Weldin and Co., 1893.

Davis, Johnda T., ed. "The Journal of Jonathan Alder." Typescript, State Library of Ohio, 1988.

Davison, Doyle H. "A History of Jonathan Alder: His Captivity and Life with the Indians." Typescript, Ohio Historical Society, 1935.

de Crevecoeur, J. Hector St. John. *Letters from an American Farmer and Sketches of Eighteenth Century America.* Edited and with an introduction by Albert E. Stone. New York: Penguin Books, 1981.

De Hass, Wills. *History of the Early Settlement and Indian Wars of West Virginia.* Wheeling: H. Hoblitzell, 1851.

Derounian-Stodola, Kathryn Zabelle, and James Arthur Levernier. *The Indian Captivity Narrative, 1550–1900.* New York: Maxwell Macmillan, International, 1997.

Doddridge, Joseph. *Notes on the Settlement and Indians of the Western Parts of Virginia and Pennsylvania.* Pittsburgh: John S. Ritenour and William T. Lindsey, 1912.

Downes, Randolph C. *Council Fires on the Upper Ohio.* Pittsburgh: University of Pittsburgh Press, 1940.

Doyle, James T. *The Organization and Operational Administration of the Ohio Militia in the War of 1812.* Columbus: Anthony Wayne Parkway Board and The Ohio State Museum, 1958.

Ebersole, Gary L. *Captured by Texts: Puritan to Postmodern Images of Indian Captivity.* Charlottesville: University Press of Virginia, 1995.

Edmunds, R. David. *The Shawnee Prophet.* Lincoln and London: University of Nebraska Press, 1983.

———. *Tecumseh and the Quest for Indian Leadership.* New York: Harper Collins, 1984.

———. "'A Watchful Safeguard to Our Habitations': Black Hoof and the Loyal Shawnees." In Frederick E. Hoxie, Ronald Hoffman, and Peter J. Albert, eds., *Native Americans and the Early Republic.* Charlottesville and London: University Press of Virginia, 1999.

———. "Forgotten Allies: The Loyal Shawnees and the War of 1812." In David Curtis Skaggs and Larry L. Nelson, eds., *The Sixty Years' War for the Great Lakes, 1754–1814.* East Lansing: Michigan State University Press, 2001.

Faragher, John Mack. *Daniel Boone: The Life and Legend of an American Pioneer.* New York: Henry Holt and Company, 1992.

Feest, Johanna E., and Christian F. Feest. "Ottawa." In Bruce G. Trigger, ed., *Handbook of North American Indians,* vol. 15, *Northeast.* Washington, D.C.: Smithsonian Institution, 1978.

Fenton, William N. "Structure, Continuity, and Change in the Process of Iroquois Treaty Making." In Francis Jennings, ed., *The History and Culture of Iroquois Diplomacy: An Interdisciplinary Guide to the Treaties of the Six Nations and Their League.* Syracuse: Syracuse University Press, 1985.

Filson, John. *The Discovery, Settlement, and Present State of Kentucke. . . .* Wilmington, Delaware: James Adams, 1784.

Finley, James B. *History of the Wyandott Mission at Upper Sandusky, Ohio Under the Direction of the Methodist Episcopal Church.* Cincinnati: J. F. Wright and L. Swormstedt, 1840.

————. *Autobiography of Rev. James B. Finley or Pioneer Life in the West.* Edited by W. P. Strickland. Cincinnati: Cranston and Curts, 1853.

————. *Life Among the Indians; or, Personal Reminiscences and Historical Incidents Illustrative of Indian Life and Character.* Cincinnati: Cranston and Curts: 1857.

Fischer, David Hackett, and James C. Kelly. *Bound and Away: Virginia and the Westward Movement.* Charlottesville and London: University Press of Virginia, 2000.

Fithian, Philip Vickers. *Journal, 1775–1776: Written on the Virginia-Pennsylvania Frontier and in the Army around New York.* Edited by Robert Greenhalgh Albion and Leonidas Dodson. Princeton: Princeton University Press, 1934.

Fitting, James E. "Prehistory—Introduction." In Bruce G. Trigger, ed., *Handbook of North American Indians,* vol. 15, *Northeast.* Washington, D. C.: Smithsonian Institution, 1978.

Flint, Timothy. *Recollections of the Last Ten Years in the Valley of the Mississippi.* Carbondale: Southern Illinois University Press, 1968.

Foster, Emily, ed. *The Ohio Frontier: An Anthology of Early Writings.* Lexington: University Press of Kentucky, 1996.

Foster, Steven, and Roger A. Caras, eds. *A Field Guide to Venomous Animals and Poisonous Plants: North America North of Mexico.* Boston and New York: Houghton Mifflin Company, 1994.

Funk, Robert E. "Post-Pleistocene Adaptation." In Bruce G. Trigger, ed., *Handbook of North American Indians,* vol. 15, *Northeast.* Washington: Smithsonian Institution, 1978.

Galloway, William Albert. *Old Chillicothe: Shawnee and Pioneer History.* Xenia, Ohio: Buckeye Press, 1934.

Garber, D. W. *Waterwheels and Millstones: A History of Ohio Gristmills and Milling.* Columbus: Ohio Historical Society, 1970.

Genheimer, Robert A., ed. *Cultures Before Contact: The Late Prehistory of Ohio and Surrounding Regions.* Columbus: Ohio Archaeological Council, 2000.

Grant, Roger. *Ohio on the Move: Transportation in the Buckeye State.* Athens: Ohio University Press, 2000.

Gray, Andrew. *The Experienced Millwright: Or, A Treatise on the Construction of Some of the Most Useful Machines, with the Latest Improvements. . . .* Edinburgh: Brown and Constable, 1804.

Griffin, James B. "Late Prehistory of the Ohio Valley." In Bruce G. Trigger, ed., *Handbook of North American Indians,* vol. 15, *Northeast.* Washington, D. C.: Smithsonian Institute, 1978.

Hansen, M. C. "The Scioto Saline: Ohio's Early Salt Industry." *Ohio Geology* 6 (1995): 1–4.

Harper, Josephine L. *Guide to the Draper Manuscripts.* Madison: State Historical Society of Wisconsin, 1983.

Hartman, David. "Leaping Buck: The Story of Samuel Davis." Typescript, Ohio Historical Society, 1976.

Heckewelder, John. *History, Manners, and Customs of the Indian Nations Who Once Inhabited*

Pennsylvania and the Neighbouring States. Philadelphia: Historical Society of Pennsylvania, 1876.

Henderson, A. Gwynn. "The Lower Shawnee Town on Ohio: Sustaining Native Autonomy in an Indian Republic." In Craig Thompson Friend, ed., *The Buzzel About Kentucky: Settling the Promised Land*. Lexington: University of Kentucky Press, 1999.

Hildreth, S. P. *Pioneer History: Being an Account of the First Examinations of the Ohio Valley and the Early Settlement of the Northwest Territory. . . .* Cincinnati: H. W. Derby and Co., 1848.

Hinderaker, Eric. *Elusive Empires: Constructing Colonialism in the Ohio Valley, 1673–1800*. Cambridge and New York: Cambridge University Press, 1997.

Horsman, Reginald. *Matthew Elliott: British Indian Agent*. Detroit: Wayne State University Press, 1964.

Howard, James H. *Shawnee! The Ceremonialism of a Native American Tribe and Its Cultural Background*. Athens: Ohio University Press, 1981.

Howe, Henry. *Historical Collections of Ohio: Containing a Collection of the Most Interesting Facts, Traditions, Biographical Sketches, Anecdotes, etc. . . .* Cincinnati: Bradley and Anthony, 1847.

——. *Historical Collections of Ohio in Three Volumes: An Encyclopedia of the State. . . .* Columbus: Henry Howe and Son, 1891.

Hulbert, Archer Butler, and William Nathaniel Schwarze, eds. "David Zeisberger's History of the Northern American Indians." *Ohio Archaeological and Historical Society Publications* 19 (1910): 1–189.

Hunt, George T. *The Wars of the Iroquois: A Study in Inter-tribal Relations*. Madison: University of Wisconsin Press, 1940.

Hunter, William A. "History of the Ohio Valley." In Bruce G. Trigger, ed., *Handbook of North American Indians*, vol. 15, *Northeast*. Washington, D. C.: Smithsonian Institution, 1978.

Hurt, Douglas. *The Ohio Frontier: Crucible of the Old Northwest, 1720–1830*. Bloomington and Indianapolis: Indiana University Press, 1996.

Jefferson, Thomas. *Notes on the State of Virginia*. Chapel Hill and London: Institute of Early American History and Culture at Williamsburg, Virginia, 1982.

Jennings, Francis, ed. *The History and Culture of Iroquois Diplomacy: An Interdisciplinary Guide to the Treaties of the Six Nations and Their League*. Syracuse: Syracuse University Press, 1985.

Johnson, Bruce E., and Donald A. Grinde, Jr., eds. *The Encyclopedia of Native American Biography*. New York: Henry Holt and Co., 1997.

Jones, David. *A Journal of Two Visits Made to Some Nations of Indians on the West Side of the River Ohio, in the Years 1772 and 1773*. Burlington: Isaac Collins, 1774.

Kappler, Charles J., ed. *Indian Treaties: 1778–1883*. New York: Interland Publishing, 1972.

Kauffman, Henry J. *The Pennsylvania-Kentucky Rifle*. Harrisburg: Stockpole Company, 1960.

Kennedy, Robert P. *The Historical Review of Logan County, Ohio. . . .* Chicago: S. G. Clarke Publishing Co., 1903.

Kennedy, Roger G. *Hidden Cities: The Discovery and Loss of Ancient North American Civilization.* New York: Free Press, 1994.

Kent, Donald H., and Merle Deardorff, eds. "John Adlum on the Allegheny: Memoirs for the Year 1794." *Pennsylvania Magazine of History and Biography* 84 (1960): pp. 265–324 and 435–80.

Kenton, Edna. *Simon Kenton: His Life and Period, 1755–1836.* Garden City, N. J.: Country Life Press, 1930.

Kinietz, W. Vernon. *The Indians of the Western Great Lakes, 1615–1760.* Ann Arbor: University of Michigan Press, 1940.

Klett, Guy Soulliard, ed. *Journals of Charles Beatty, 1762–1769.* University Park: Pennsylvania State University Press, 1962.

Klinck, Carl. F., and James J. Talman, eds. *The Journals of Major John Norton, 1816.* Toronto: Champlain Society, 1970.

Klopfenstein, Carl Grover. "The Removal of the Indians from Ohio, 1820–1843." Ph.D. diss., Western Reserve University, 1955.

Knight, Dr. [John], and John Slover. *Indian Atrocities: Narratives of the Perils and Sufferings of Dr. Knight and John Slover Among the Indians. . . .* Cincinnati: U. P. James, 1867.

Larkin, Jack. *The Reshaping of Everyday Life, 1790–1840.* New York: Harper and Row, 1988.

Lentz, Andrea, ed. *A Guide to The Manuscripts at the Ohio Historical Society.* Columbus: Ohio Historical Society, 1972.

Lewis, Richard T. "The Development of the Economic Landscape." In Leonard Peacefull, ed., *A Geography of Ohio.* Kent, Ohio and London: Kent State University Press, 1996.

"Logan, The Mingo Chief, 1710–1780." *Ohio Archaeological and Historical Society Publications* 20 (1911): 137–75.

McConnell, Michael N. *A Country Between: The Upper Ohio Valley and Its Peoples, 1724–1774.* Lincoln: University of Nebraska Press, 1992.

McDonald, John. *Biographical Sketches of General Nathaniel Massie, General Duncan McArthur, Captain William Wells, and General Simon Kenton. . . .* Dayton: D. Osborn and Son, 1852.

McKenney, Thomas L., and James Hall. *History of the Indian Tribes of North America.* 2 vols. Kent: Volair, 1978.

Malone, Miles Sturdivant. "The Distribution of Population on the Virginia Frontier in 1775." Ph.D. diss., Princeton University, 1935.

Martin, William. *History of Franklin County: A Collection of Reminiscences of the Early Settlement of the County. . . .* Columbus: Follett, Foster, and Co., 1858.

Medert, Patricia Fife. *Raw Recruits and Bullish Prisoners: Ohio's Capital in the War of 1812.* Chillicothe, Ohio: Ross County Historical Society, 1992.

Miller, James M. *The Genesis of Western Culture: The Upper Ohio Valley, 1800–1825.* Columbus: Ohio State Archaeological and Historical Society, 1938.

Mitchell, Robert D. *Commercialism and Frontier: Perspectives on the Early Shenandoah Valley.* Charlottesville: University Press of Virginia, 1977.

Nabokov, Peter, and Robert Easton. *Native American Architecture.* New York and Oxford: Oxford University Press, 1989.

Namias, June. *White Captives: Gender and Ethnicity on the American Frontier.* Chapel Hill: University of North Carolina Press, 1993.

Nelson, Larry L. "'Never Have They Done So Little': The Battle of Fort Recovery and the Collapse of the Miami Confederacy." *Northwest Ohio Quarterly* 64 (1992): 43–55.

———. *A Man of Distinction Among Them: Alexander McKee and the Ohio Frontier, 1754–1799.* Kent and London: Kent State University Press, 1999.

Nelson, Larry L., and David C. Skaggs. "Introduction." In David C. Skaggs and Larry L. Nelson, eds., *The Sixty Years' War for the Great Lakes: 1754–1814.* Lansing: Michigan State University Press, 2000.

O'Donnell, James H., III. "Logan's Oration: A Case Study in Ethnographic Authentication." *Quarterly Journal of Speech* 65 (1979): 150–56.

O'Malley, Nancy. *"Stockading Up": A Study of Pioneer Stations in the Inner Bluegrass Region of Kentucky.* Frankfort: Kentucky Heritage Council, 1987.

Pacheco, Paul J., ed. *A View from the Core: A Synthesis of Ohio Hopewell Archaeology.* Columbus: Ohio Archaeological Council, 1996.

Peacefull, Leonard, ed. *A Geography of Ohio.* Kent, Ohio, and London: Kent State University Press, 1996.

Potter, Martha A. *Ohio's Prehistoric Peoples.* Columbus: Ohio Historical Society, 1968.

Pratt, G. Michael. "The Battle of Fallen Timbers: An Eyewitness Perspective." *Northwest Ohio Quarterly* 67 (1995): 4–34.

Quaife, Milo M., ed. *The John Askin Papers.* 2 vols. Detroit: Detroit Library Commission, 1928–31.

Raitz, Karl, ed. *The National Road.* Baltimore: Johns Hopkins University Press, 1996.

Reames, O. K. *History of Zanesfield and Sketches of the Interesting and Historical Places of Logan County, Ohio.* Zanesfield, Ohio: O. K. Reames, 1929.

"Removal of Indians from Ohio: Dunhue Correspondence of 1832." *Indiana Magazine of History* 35 (1939): 408–26.

Ridout, Thomas. "An Account of My Capture by the Shawanese Indians." *Western Pennsylvania Historical Magazine* 12 (1929): 3–31.

Rowlandson, Mary. *The Soveraignty and Goodness of God.* Cambridge, 1682.

Romain, William F. *Mysteries of the Hopewell: Astronomers, Geometers, and Magicians of the Eastern Woodlands.* Akron, Ohio: University of Akron Press, 2000.

Rouse, Parke, Jr. *The Great Wagon Road from Philadelphia to the South.* New York: McGraw-Hill Book Co., 1973.

Sandefur, Ray H. "Logan's Oration—How Authentic?" *Quarterly Journal of Speech* 46 (1960): 289–96.

Sayre, Gordon M. *Les Sauvages Americains: Representations of Native Americans in French and English Colonial Literature.* Chapel Hill and London: University of North Carolina Press, 1997.

Scamyhorn, Richard, and John Steinle. *Stockades in the Wilderness: The Frontier Defenses and Settlements of Southwestern Ohio, 1788–1795.* Dayton, Ohio: Landfall Press, 1987.

Scheiber, Harry N. *Ohio Canal Era: A Case Study of Government and the Economy, 1820–1861.* Athens: Ohio University Press, 1987.

Shriver, Phillip R. "The Beaver Wars and the Destruction of the Erie Nation." *Timeline Magazine* I (1984/1985): 29–41.

Silverberg, Robert. *The Mound Builders.* Athens: Ohio University Press, 1970.

Simpson, John Warfield. *Visions of Paradise: Glimpses of Our Landscape's Legacy.* Berkley, Los Angeles, London: University of California Press, 1999.

Skaggs, David C. "The Sixty Years' War for the Great Lakes, 1754–1814: An Overview." In David C. Skaggs and Larry L. Nelson, eds., *The Sixty Years' War for the Great Lakes, 1754–1814.* Lansing: Michigan State University Press, 2001.

Skaggs, David C., ed. *The Old Northwest in the American Revolution: An Anthology.* Madison: State Historical Society of Wisconsin, 1976.

Skaggs, David C. and Larry L. Nelson, eds. *The Sixty Years' War for the Great Lakes, 1754–1814.* Lansing: Michigan State University Press, 2001.

Smith, Dwight L. "Wayne's Peace with the Indians of the Old Northwest, 1795." *Ohio State Archaeological and Historical Quarterly* 59 (1950): 239–55.

Smith, James. *An Account of the Remarkable Occurrences in the Life and Travels of Col. James Smith. . . .* Lexington: John Bradford, 1799.

Smith, William. *An Historical Account of the Expedition Against the Ohio Indians, in the Year 1764, Under the Command of Henry Bouquet, Esq. . . .* Philadelphia: William Bradford, 1764.

Sosin, Jack M. *The Revolutionary Frontier, 1763–1783.* Albuquerque: University of New Mexico Press, 1967.

Speed, Thomas. *The Wilderness Road: A Description of the Routes of Travel by which the Pioneers and Early Settlers First Came to Kentucky.* New York: Burt Franklin, 1886.

Spencer, O. M. *Indian Captivity: A True Narrative of the Capture of the Rev. O. M. Spencer by the Indians in the Neighborhood of Cincinnati.* New York: Waugh and Mason, 1835.

Sugden, John. *Tecumseh: A Life.* New York: Henry Holt and Company, 1997.

———. *Blue Jacket: Warrior of the Shawnees.* Lincoln and London: University of Nebraska Press, 2000.

Sword, Wiley. *President Washington's Indian War: The Struggle for the Old Northwest, 1790–1795.* Norman: University of Oklahoma Press, 1985.

Tanner, Helen Hornbeck. "The Glaize in 1792: A Composite Indian Community." *Ethnohistory* 25 (1978): 15–39.

Tanner, Helen Hornbeck, ed. *Atlas of Great Lakes Indian History.* Norman and London: University of Oklahoma Press, 1987.

Tanner, Helen Hornbeck, and Erminie Wheeler-Voegelin. *Indians of Ohio and Indiana Prior to 1795.* 2 vols. New York and London: Garland Publishing, 1974.

Tanner, John. *The Falcon: A Narrative of the Captivity and Adventures of John Tanner During Thirty Years' Residence Among the Indians in the Interior of North America.* With an introduction by Louise Erdrich. New York: Penguin Books, 1994.

Thatcher, Joseph M., Jr. *Infantry Small Arms, 1795–1815.* Columbus: Anthony Wayne Parkway Board and The Ohio State Museum, 1962.

Thwaites, Reuben Gold, ed. *Early Western Travels, 1748–1846. . . .* 32 vols. Cleveland: A. H. Clark Co., 1904–1907.

———. *The Jesuit Relations and Allied Documents: Travels and Explorations of the Jesuit Missionaries in New France, 1610–1791.* 73 vols. New York: Pageant Book Co., 1959.

Thwaites, Reuben Gold, and Louise Phelps Kellogg, eds. *Documentary History of Dunmore's War, 1774*. Madison: Wisconsin Historical Society, 1905.

Trigger, Bruce G., ed. *Handbook of North American Indians*, vol. 15, *Northeast*. Washington, D.C.: Smithsonian Institution, 1978.

Tooker, Elisabeth. "Wyandot." In Bruce G. Trigger, ed., *Handbook of North American Indians*, vol. 15, *Northeast*. Washington, D.C.: Smithsonian Institution, 1978.

Utter, William T. *The Frontier State, 1803–1825*. Columbus: Ohio Historical Society, 1942.

VanDerBeets, Richard. *The Indian Captivity Narrative: An American Genre*. Lanham, Md.: University Press of America, 1984.

Venable, W. H. *Beginnings of Literary Culture in the Ohio Valley*. Cincinnati: R. Clarke and Co., 1891.

Volney, C[onstantin]. F[rançois]. *A View of the Soil and Climate of the United States of America: With Supplementary Remarks upon Florida; on the French Colonies on the Mississippi; and Ohio, and in Canada; and on the Aboriginal Tribes of America*. Philadelphia: Conrad and Co., 1804.

Wallace, Anthony F. C. *The Death and Rebirth of the Seneca*. New York: Vintage Books, 1972.

Walley, Walter High. "The Saga of the Movable Alder Cabin." Typescript, Ohio Historical Society, 1989.

Washburn, Wilcomb E., gen. ed. *The Garland Library of Narratives of North American Indian Captivities*. 111 vols. New York and London: Garland Publishing, 1975–77.

Weisenburger, Francis P. *The Passing of the Frontier, 1825–1850*. Columbus: Ohio Historical Society, 1941.

Weld, Isaac. *Travels Through the States of North America and the Provinces of Upper and Lower Canada During the Years 1795, 1796, and 1797*. 2 vols. London: J. Stockdale, 1799.

Weslager, C. A. *The Delaware Indians: A History*. New Brunswick: Rutgers University Press, 1972.

Wheeler, Robert A., ed. *Visions of the Western Reserve: Public and Private Documents of Northeastern Ohio, 1750–1860*. Columbus: Ohio State University Press, 2000.

Wheeler-Voegelin, Erminie. *Indians of Northern Ohio and Southeastern Michigan: An Ethnological Report*. New York: Garland Publishing, 1974.

———. *Indians of Northwest Ohio: An Ethnohistorical Report on the Wyandot, Potawatomi, Ottawa, and Chippewa of Northwest Ohio*. New York and London: Garland Publishing, 1974.

White, Richard. *The Middle Ground: Indians, Empires, and Republics in the Great Lakes Region, 1650–1815*. Cambridge: Cambridge University Press, 1991.

Wilhelm, Hubert G. H., and Allen G. Noble. "Ohio's Settlement Landscape." In Leonard Peacefull, ed. *A Geography of Ohio*. Kent, Ohio and London: Kent State University Press, 1996.

Withers, Alexander Scott. *Chronicles of Border Warfare. . . .* Edited and annotated by Reuben Gold Thwaites. Cincinnati: Robert Clarke and Co., 1895.

Index

St. Clair, Arthur, 108
stagger wood, 30, 186n. 38
station settlements, 203n. 140
Staunton, Virginia, 3, 4
Stoner, Michael, 169
Story, John, 119
Strobirdige, Caleb, 163
Succohanes, 45–46, 50, 56–60, 61–62, 66–68, 85, 87, 100, 102
Sullivant, Lucas, 134, 140
Swank, 94–95
Sycamore Creek. *See* Little Darby Creek

Tanner, John, 197n. 102
Tarhe, 190n. 60
Taylor, Daniel, 120
Taylor, John, 119, 131, 165
Taylor, Richard, 119, 136
Tecumseh, 13, 88, 151, 152, 202n. 138
Tecumseh's Town, 152–53
Tenskwatawa, 13, 151, 202n. 138
Three Mile Run, 140
Timmons, Thomas, 107
Tippecanoe, Indiana, 152
Tippecanoe River, 152
tomahawk claim, 175, 204n. 164
Treaty of Fort McIntosh (1785), 192n. 70
Treaty of Ghent, 13
Treaty of Greenville (1795), 13–14, 16, 20, 85–87, 115–17, 151, 200n. 121
Treaty of Paris (1783), 12
Treaty Signed at the Foot of the Rapids of the Miami of Lake Erie (1817), 200n. 121
Trotter, James, 195n. 85
Tuscarawas River, 8
Tymochetee, 191n. 62

Union County Ohio, 81, 103
Upper Sandusky, Ohio, 15, 40, 97, 102–4, 113, 118, 121, 127, 139, 152, 154–55, 173–74
Urbana, Ohio, 175

Veach, William, 203n. 149
Veck, 168, 169, 175
Vincennes, Indiana, 202n. 139
Virginia Military District, 201n. 128

Volney, Constantin Francois, 201n. 125

Wabash River, 7, 174
Wachovia, 4
Wapakoneta, 195n. 83
Wapatomaka, 172
War of 1812, 154–60, 202n. 133
Ware, 130
Washington County, Virginia, 3
Watson, David, 155, 158–59
Wayne, Anthony, 13, 16, 80, 92, 109, 111, 113–17
Weld, Isaac, 196n. 97, 200n. 120
Wells, William, 196n. 97
Western Reserve, 17
West Liberty, Ohio, 204n. 158
Wheeling, West Virginia, 16–17, 173
Whinecheoh, 45–48, 57–60, 62–63, 65–67, 77, 85, 87
Whingway Pooshies. *See* Big Cat
Whitney, Sarah, 161–63
Wilderness Road, 5
Williams, Thomas, 168–69
Williamson, David, 190n. 61
Wilson, Alex, 153
Winchester, Virginia, 3–4
Wisconsin Ice Age, 6
witchcraft, 147–48
wolves, 94–95, 106–7, 144; superstition regarding, 95
Wood, Jonah, 124
Worthington, Hanna. *See* Hanna Alder
Worthington, Ohio, 163
Wythe County, Virginia, 3, 29, 135, 139, 187n. 42

Xenia, Ohio, 50

York, Pennsylvania, 4

Zane, Ebenezer, 190n. 60
Zane, Isaac, 46, 69, 188n. 52
Zanesfield, Ohio, 78. 168, 172, 175
Zanes Town, 188n. 52
Zane's Trace, 16
Zanesville, Ohio, 16, 124
Zeisberger, David, 16, 195n. 86, 195n. 88